AMERICA IN 2040:
STILL A SUPERPOWER?
A PATHWAY TO SUCCESS

DAVID M. WALKER
FORMER U.S. COMPTROLLER GENERAL
WITH
ADMIRAL BILL OWENS AND JOHN KNUBEL

authorHOUSE®

AuthorHouse™
1663 Liberty Drive
Bloomington, IN 47403
www.authorhouse.com
Phone: 833-262-8899

Published by AuthorHouse 09/25/2020

ISBN: 978-1-6655-0084-5 (sc)
ISBN: 978-1-6655-0082-1 (hc)
ISBN: 978-1-6655-0083-8 (e)

Library of Congress Control Number: 2020918579

Print information available on the last page.

Dedication

I am dedicating this book to my parents, wife, children, and grandchildren. My dad and mom, Dave and Dot Walker, raised me, paid for my college education, and instilled solid values in me. May they both Rest in Peace. My wife, Mary, has been my trusted and loyal partner for over 49 years. She has been understanding and supportive during my many years of public service and during the weeks I spent writing this book. My two children, Carol and Andy, and three grandchildren, Christi, Grace, and Danny, will be much more affected by the decisions that we make or fail to make, as outlined in this book. They represent our future.

CONTENTS

FOREWORD

I am honored to provide a Foreword for this important book. As our country searches for answers to new and serious social, health, and safety issues, including police reform, racial discrimination and now the coronavirus, there is a tendency to forget the *most* significant economic and fiscal challenges facing our country that are addressed in this book.

As the impact of an ever-increasing federal deficit as well as debt levels measured as a percentage of our gross domestic product (GDP) start to have an irreversible adverse impact on private-sector economic growth and job creation, we are likely to see other unprecedented changes in our economy, in our way of life, and in the American Dream. We have seen historically what this can mean in the example of the demise of the German Mark in the early 1900s. Rarely do we have someone as well-versed as Dave Walker to help us look at what the future will bring with respect to these issues.

Importantly, as America emphasizes "staying strong" over the decades ahead while maintaining a world-class economy and military, we rarely think about the need to have a sound and trusted dollar upon which to build both the American and the global economy. This book examines these and other interrelationships. Inevitably, as the U.S. debt continues its excessive growth, interest expense to the federal government will become even larger and will compete with and detract from the discretionary budget that previously has been largely devoted to our United States military. The nation will receive no current value for those growing future interest payments, which will balloon even further when interest rates return from today's historically low levels! This book is among the first to address the longer-term consequences of the Federal Reserve's new experiment in expansionist policies, including direct purchasing of federal debt seemingly without limit.

Still, in the face of this serious financial challenge, the reality is the United States must "stay strong" to face a myriad of changing security threats that are arguably greater than any we have faced since World War II. For example, while I am sympathetic to America accommodating its foreign policy to a rising China for the sake of the Chinese people and world peace, we must also understand that China is an authoritarian regime capable of aggressive action if not accommodated and/or deterred. It will, therefore, be very important for our country to maintain a strong military to ensure the preservation of our agenda of freedom, human rights, democratic principles, free and fair trade, and the protection of the other values and interests of the American people.

We will also continue to see threats emerge from the hubris of other countries. For example, there is Russia, as Putin flexes his muscles in an attempt to restore Russian global influence. In addition, challenges include North Korea and Iran with their unpredictable leadership and a desire to embarrass and demean the United States at every opportunity. We will also see new stress from the threat of strategic cyberattacks, from many sources of terrorism, and other disruptions in an ever-increasing multipolar world. Unlike the end of the Cold War when the United States had an opportunity to downsize our military and establish new global norms in a world that presented very few significant military challenges, the world today and looking forward is significantly different. It is filled with substantial and important new threats requiring significant funding for our military. In 1995, I was in a position to be directly involved with, and drive dramatic cuts in, the military budget while restructuring around new technology. Today the situation is very different. We need to preserve a stronger military and international alliances despite the budgetary threats outlined in this important book.

But as this book specifies so clearly, our country needs real reform of the Defense Department if it is to continue to maintain readiness and support our foreign policy despite the increased resource competition. Specifically, changes should include downsizing the Pentagon bureaucracy, reforming the requirements and procurement processes, and the pursuit of true jointness of the military services. These must be implemented to give us the best possible capability for the defense dollar, especially with the likely weakness of a declining dollar, along with increased interest payments and entitlement spending, which will combine to make less money available for defense.

Without prudent new solutions, many of which are mentioned in this book, the money will simply not be there for these critical national security purposes!

Importantly as this book emphasizes clearly, unless action is taken to reform America's fiscal irresponsibility, the loss of respect for the United States dollar as the primary global reserve and trading currency is likely. As this book discusses, this may be combined with radical inflation in the United States resulting in a struggle to maintain our economy, and importantly, our ability to continue being the beacon to the world for freedom, human rights, democracy, and a way of life not experienced anywhere else. To continue being the "exceptional" nation we have always claimed to be and a refuge for the oppressed and downtrodden of the world, we must take meaningful action *now*!

Thinking 20 years ahead is very difficult work, and is *rare* in our federal government. It takes wisdom, courage, and a deep knowledge of the subjects to suggest the possible solutions enumerated in this book. Only someone like Dave Walker, who has experienced our system at the highest level and has the depth and breadth of knowledge to understand all of its workings and interrelationships, is capable of writing a comprehensive book like this. I encourage the reader to pay careful attention to the thesis of this book, its careful description of the issues, and especially the very difficult solution sets that *must* be put into place to address the most pressing issues we face. Those challenges will also impact the future well-being of our children, grandchildren, and future generations of Americans.

Traditional budget controls designed to limit the growth of debt as a percentage of GDP have not worked. As a result, it is time to adopt a fiscal responsibility constitutional amendment focused on stabilizing public debt/GDP at a reasonable and sustainable level. Without such an action, U.S. economic growth, job creation, our national security, and even our domestic tranquility will continue to decline. Indeed, I believe that our growing debt burden represents our greatest national security threat.

My personal thanks to Dave Walker for his time and dedication in writing this important and timely book.

Admiral Bill Owens, United States Navy (retired), former Vice Chairman of the Joint Chiefs of Staff

PREFACE

America is at a critical crossroads. The international scene has changed dramatically since World War II and continues to change. The world is much more interconnected and interdependent today from an economic as well as a security perspective. The United States' (U.S.) global market share of gross domestic product (GDP) has declined dramatically and continues to decline as China, India, and other nations grow. The Union of Soviet Socialist Republics (USSR) is gone, and the Cold War was won. However, new and growing threats exist today that include China but go far beyond that nation. The demographic situation today is very different from how it was at the end of World War II, and it continues to change. Contrary to the post-World War II period from 1946 to 1980, the U.S. has lost control of its finances, especially since 2003. The U.S. is spending more on consumption and less on investment as debt burdens are projected to increase to record levels in 2021 and continue to rise thereafter. The COVID-19 experience should be a "wake-up call" from many perspectives. The plain and simple truth is that America's future is "at risk." The greatest threat to our collective future does not come from beyond our borders, but from within them. Current international and domestic policy paths need to be reviewed and revised. The good news is that we can control our own destiny. This book is designed to show us a way forward to create a better life for current and future generations of Americans.

WHEN?

I began writing this book on Jekyll Island, GA, the birthplace of the Federal Reserve, in May 2020 during the COVID-19 public health "crisis." COVID-19 had significant public/personal health, economic, individual liberty, governance, and national security dimensions. It demonstrated the lack of adequate planning and preparation in the U.S. for pandemics and many other issues. It also illustrated the difficulties associated with addressing major national challenges given the separation of powers at the federal, state, and local levels under our federalist system. The actions and activities associated with COVID-19 exacerbated the economic, social, fiscal, and national security challenges facing our country. Most importantly, the government actions related to COVID-19 also demonstrated how far our country has strayed from the basic principles and values on which our country was founded and that helped to make us exceptional. Actions related to COVID-19 also illustrate the potential for a future constitutional crisis in connection with fiscal, governance, and individual liberty matters. This book addresses all of these issues and many more.

WHAT?

This book is a professional, objective, nonpartisan, nonideological, and nonpersonal look at a number of critical issues facing America and Americans. It has been written for educational purposes with the hope that it will help to promote needed transformational changes within government. I am a political independent who is very concerned about our nation's future. At the same time, I am an optimist by nature and believe we will eventually make the tough choices and course corrections needed to create a better future. The real question is when and under what circumstances?

This book is a much-expanded sequel to my former best-selling book entitled *Comeback America: Turning the Country Around and Restoring Fiscal Responsibility* (Random House, 2010). It is timely given the economic, health, security, social, and governance challenges relating to the nation's response to COVID-19, the significant deterioration of the federal government's finances, the new "free lunch fallacy" (i.e., Modern Monetary Theory) being promulgated by some liberal economists, changing security threats, including evolving U.S./China relations, shifting strategic alliances, and a range of global challenges that cross geopolitical boundaries (e.g., pandemics, migration, climate change, terrorism, nuclear proliferation).

During the 2016 presidential election cycle, one candidate had "Make America Great Again (MAGA)" as the theme of his campaign. While it was successful in helping him connect with millions of dissatisfied Americans and helped him win the presidency, I and many others did not feel it was accurate. I believe that America was great then and still is.

After all, the United States is currently a global superpower and remains a beacon of hope, freedom, diversity, innovation, and opportunity around the world. There are, however, many factors currently at play that threaten our collective future, including changing security threats, our nation's fiscal irresponsibility, and growing gaps between the "haves" and "have nots." Therefore, consistent with the "Keeping America Great" theme of the Comeback America Initiative (CAI) that I founded in 2010 and led, the real question should be, "How do we Keep America Great for current and future generations?" This book provides a range of concrete answers to that very important question.

This book is divided into four sections. Section 1 includes two chapters that are "wake-up calls." Chapter 1 begins with a potential scenario for 2040 that is negative, both domestically and internationally, and plausible if the U.S. does not change course. Importantly, the scenario is illustrative rather than predictive in nature and can be avoided if appropriate actions are taken by key policymakers. Chapter 2 introduces discussion about COVID-19 and the lessons we should learn from it.

Section 2 includes six chapters that review key lessons from history, some timeless principles and values that were important at the founding of our country, and a number of recent events and trends that have contributed to putting America "at risk." Section 3 includes four chapters that discuss the biggest risks threatening America's future. Section 4 includes nine chapters that outline a number of specific and sensible solutions to a range of economic, fiscal, social, security, political, and other issues that can and should be taken to Keep America Great not just until 2040 but well beyond. The approach that I took in writing this book is consistent with my personal philosophy of "learning from the past and others while preparing for the future."

WHY NOW?

The United States has been the world's major superpower since the end of World War II. By "superpower," I mean a widely respected country that has global economic, military, and diplomatic power, as well as cultural influence around the world. In fact, based on these four dimensions, the

U.S. has been the only legitimate superpower during the entire period since World War II. While the Soviet Union was a global military and diplomatic power, it was never a global economic and cultural power. No other country has met these four criteria since World War II. However, looking forward, America's sole superpower status is being challenged by a new peer competitor — a rising China. It is also being threatened by growing societal gaps, changing security threats, evolving international alliances, and the deteriorating financial condition and fiscal outlook for the United States.

From a domestic perspective, Congress had already lost control of the U.S. budget before the COVID-19 "crisis." The response to that virus resulted in a rapid rise in U.S. debt held by the public/GDP to a level approaching the ratio needed to win World War II, and that level will be exceeded in 2021. It also served to highlight the income, wealth, education, and opportunity gaps that exist in our country. Anti-Chinese rhetoric was already on the rise before COVID-19 and has increased as a result of the virus that originated in Wuhan, China. Furthermore, the stark differences in policy choices that have already been outlined as part of the 2020 election cycle also accentuate the importance and timeliness of this book.

From an international perspective, this book presumes that China will be a legitimate superpower well before 2040 and that the U.S. will be much less powerful in 2040 than today. It also presumes that both China and India will have larger economies than the U.S. in 2040. In fact, China has already passed the U.S. in GDP based on purchasing power parity (PPP), and the gap is growing. These future outcomes are highly likely but by no means guaranteed.

The 2020 presidential and congressional elections demonstrate the great political and ideological divides that currently exist in the United States. These divides have increased over the years and have been a real obstacle to making the type of tough choices necessary to effectively address our current and emerging challenges. Time is running out for our key policymakers to recognize reality and act before others lose confidence in us and we lose confidence in ourselves to do what is right for current and future generations of Americans. If that confidence is lost, America and the world will never be the same, and the future will not be as bright as the past. We must not let that happen.

WHY ME?

My background and experience make me well-qualified to address the topics in this book. As the immediate former Comptroller General of the United States and former CEO of the U.S. Government Accountability Office (GAO), the Peter G. Peterson Foundation, and the CAI, and as a former board member of AARP and the Committee for a Responsible Federal Budget, I have significant experience pertaining to our nation's finances, fiscal outlook, and related policy choices, including significant public education and engagement experience connected with our fiscal challenges and possible solutions. As the former Chairman of the Strategic Planning Task Force and a member of the board for the International Association of Supreme Audit Institutions (INTOSAI), and a former Chairman of the Independent Audit Advisory Committee (IAAC) for the United Nations (UN), who has been fortunate to travel to every continent and more than 100 countries, I have significant international experience and perspective. As the current Distinguished Visiting Professor and the William J. Crowe Chair at the United States Naval Academy, a member of the Defense Business Board, and a graduate of the Capstone Program for Flag Officers at the National Defense University, I understand the intersection of economics and national security. As a person who has held substantive meetings with two Chinese premiers and who was a contributor, along with John Knubel, to Admiral and former Vice Chairman of the Joint Chiefs of Staff Bill Owens' recent book entitled *China–U.S. 2039: The Endgame? Building Trust Over Future Decades*, I have an informed perspective on U.S.–China issues. This will arguably be the most important bilateral relationship for the U.S. between now and 2040 — and beyond. Finally, as a member of the Sons of the American Revolution (SAR), a father, and a grandfather, I care deeply about our country and the need to discharge our stewardship responsibilities to both younger and future generations of Americans.

CONCLUSION

I believe you will find this book to be timely, informative, thought-provoking, and motivational. Make no mistake, the morning sky is "red" and our Ship of State, the USS United States, is taking on water. We must make tough choices and change course to steer her safely back to port. In the final analysis, it is "We the People" who must become informed and involved in order to ensure the vitality and sustainability of our republic. We are responsible for what our elected officials do, or fail to do, to save our ship. In that regard, I will continue to fight to encourage our elected officials to take the actions necessary to discharge their stewardship responsibility in order to ensure that our collective future is better than our past. I hope you will do your part as well. Working together, we can Keep America Great!

ACKNOWLEDGMENTS

I would like to thank Admiral Bill Owens for contributing the Foreword to this book. Hon. John Knubel worked diligently with me to help conduct research, provide input, and make comments on my drafts. Admiral Tom Hayward and Professors Kurtis Swope and Marvin Zonis provided comments on portions of the book. My brother Steve read portions of my draft book and provided comments, and my brother Rick created the cover concept for the book. Judy Wilson worked diligently to edit the book and made sure it was consistent with Chicago style. Admiral Mike Mullen, Hon. John Hamre, Nancy Jacobson, Maya MacGuineas and Ernie Almonte provided back cover quotes for the book. Thanks to all involved in making this book a reality.

CHAPTER 1

AMERICA AT RISK

INTRODUCTION

This chapter provides a plausible — not predictive, and certainly not preferred — forecast of what America could look like in 2040. There are certain economic, social, fiscal, monetary, and national security challenges that need to be addressed in a timely and constructive manner for the United States (U.S.) to remain a superpower in 2040 and beyond. By "superpower," I mean a country that is widely respected with global economic, diplomatic, military power, and cultural influence. These issues, as well as related potential solutions, are outlined in this book.

Reasonable people can and will differ with the assumptions underlying the following scenario and its potential implications. The author and those who contributed to this book are experienced and nonpartisan professionals with significant top-level civilian and military experience at the federal level. In addition, the following scenario was presented to a range of people for comment. Their consensus view is that this scenario is plausible, but they hope it will never come to pass. I agree.

You, the reader, must make up your own mind regarding the plausibility of this scenario. If you believe it is possible, regardless of your political party affiliation, if any, you should let your views be known and encourage others to read this book. Even if you have doubts about certain aspects of this scenario, you should read on to better understand the serious challenges we face and possible ways to address them. In either case, you need to vote in every election! The bottom line is that this is a bipartisan problem requiring a transpartisan solution.

HISTORICAL CONTEXT

It is September 1, 2040. One hundred and one years ago today, German tanks and troops crossed the Polish border. As a result, World War II (WWII) started. The United States did not formally enter the war until a little over two years later when the Japanese attacked the U.S. Pacific fleet at Pearl Harbor. In the interim, the U.S. provided billions of dollars in aid to its eventual allies, with most of the assistance going to Britain (the United Kingdom) and the Soviet Union (Russia).

WWII was a global conflict that lasted almost six years. The U.S. suffered more than 400,000 military and civilian deaths during WWII. In contrast, the Soviet Union (now Russia) and China (now the People's Republic of China, or PRC) each suffered more than 20 million military and civilian deaths during the war. At the end of WWII, the U.S. was the only major country to avoid significant damage and casualties in its homeland. U.S. critical infrastructure was undamaged, and its industrial capacity was poised to quickly shift from wartime to peacetime operations. Most of Europe and the combat zones in Asia were in ruins.

At the end of WWII, the debt held by the public/GDP ratio in the U.S. climbed to 106%, the highest in history. Unlike today, that debt was borne by Americans who demonstrated their patriotism and used their savings to buy war bonds because they wanted to do their part and were confident that they would be repaid in full when America won the war. That is very different from the attitude and actions of Americans today.

The U.S. achieved a great deal in exchange for the debt it incurred to win WWII; it defeated the Axis powers, saved the free world, avoided attacks on its homeland, and was poised for greatness. At the end of WWII, the U.S. represented about 50% of global nominal GDP. The U.S. had the most powerful military on earth, demographics were working in its favor, and the dollar was as "good as gold." Due to the belief that it would maintain its value, the dollar became the primary reserve currency for the world, replacing the British pound, which had played that role for about 200 years up until WWII.

Importantly, policymakers and the American people as a whole recognized the need to reduce the debt burden (i.e., debt held by the public/GDP ratio) after WWII. As a result, the U.S. dramatically reduced the size of the military, cut spending significantly, and restored fiscal responsibility after the war. America also invested in the rebuilding of Europe and Asia, including the defeated Axis powers through the Marshall Plan, invested in human capital (e.g., the GI Bill), and invested in infrastructure (e.g., interstate highway system). The Marshall Plan was also designed to help prevent the further spread of communism in Europe since the Communist Party ruled Eastern Europe and had gained a strong foothold in several Western European nations (e.g., Greece, France, and Italy).

The U.S. joined with the United Kingdom and other countries to form a number of international institutions after WWII (e.g., UN, World Bank, IMF, and the General Agreement on Tariffs and Trade [GATT], which later resulted in the creation of the World Trade Organization [WTO]). These institutions were designed to promote peace and prosperity through increased trade, the protection of human rights, and promotion of the rule of law around the globe.

The above actions combined with the birth of the "baby boom" generation and the promotion of free trade resulted in dramatic increases in economic growth and dramatic decreases in debt held by the public/GDP ratio. By 1980 that ratio had declined to about 35%, which was within the range of where it had been for most of the time from the founding of the Republic in 1789 until WWII. This reduction was accomplished without reducing the total debt. Rather, while the debt did increase somewhat, the economy grew much faster than the debt. With some help from inflation during the 34-year period, the debt held by the public/GDP ratio declined dramatically. This ratio is the key metric that should be focused on in the future to help achieve fiscal sustainability.

The debt held by the public/GDP ratio increased during the Reagan/Bush administration, primarily because of a defense buildup. Meanwhile, the Soviet Union collapsed when Chairman Gorbachev and Soviet leaders realized they could not compete with U.S. economic strength. Chairman Gorbachev introduced "Glasnost and Perestroika," and the slow process of democratization and economic reopening resulted in the USSR splitting into 15 countries. World War III was avoided and defense spending was reduced significantly.

The debt held by the public/GDP ratio soared in 2020 as a result of COVID-19 when federal spending increased dramatically while the economy contracted. In April 2020, the nonpartisan Congressional Budget Office (CBO) projected that debt held by the public/GDP ratio would increase to about 108% by the end of Fiscal 2021, the highest in history. CBO also projected that annual deficits would exceed $1.5 trillion each year even after the economy recovered from COVID-19. As a result, a number of government and nongovernment organizations were calling for the federal government to take steps to put the nation on a more prudent and sustainable fiscal path once the virus was defeated.

Contrary to the assertion of some "liberal economists," even John Maynard Keynes never believed in running deficits when the economy was growing, the country was at peace, at full employment and with no other national emergencies. In fact, he believed in "balancing the budget" over an economic cycle.

If the past misrepresentation of Keynesian economics was not bad enough, in 2020 some misguided economists were advocating a new macroeconomic concept they called "The Modern Monetary Theory." This theory would probably cause Keynes to roll over in his grave. As a result, they also referred to it as a post-Keynesian theory. You can read more on this new, unproven, and dangerous macroeconomic theory in Chapter 10.

THE U.S. IN 2040

The international and domestic scene is significantly different on September 1, 2040. Economically, the U.S. has declined from 50% of global nominal GDP at the end of WWII, and about 24% of global nominal GDP in 2019, to less than 18% of global nominal GDP and declining in 2040. The People's Republic of China (PRC, or China) and India have both passed the U.S. in nominal GDP and have far surpassed the U.S. in GDP based on purchasing power parity (PPP).

While the U.S. still has a higher GDP per capita than China and India, the gap continues to shrink. China's huge investments in infrastructure and research have served to greatly expand the size of their middle class. As a result, China now buys most of its own products.

From an overall population perspective, India and China have the largest, with Nigeria likely to climb past the U.S. for the number-three position by 2050. Demographics within the U.S. are very different. The total of U.S. minority populations is poised to surpass Caucasians (Whites) within the next several years. Hispanics remain the largest minority, and their share of the population has increased since 2020. Asians represent a larger share of the population than in 2020. Blacks still represent the second-largest minority, but their percentage has decreased since 2020.

There are increasing tensions between Hispanics and Blacks, which is contributing to a greater domestic tranquility concern. The Muslim Brotherhood's attempt to recruit in the U.S. has had limited success, but it is still a potential threat.

U.S. demographics are no longer working in favor of strong economic growth. The U.S. birth rate has remained at less than two per female and has been declining for more than two decades. The number of workers to retirees has declined from about 16:1 at the end of WWII to less than 2:1. The only reason the U.S. population is still growing is due to immigration. The annual legal immigration rate has declined due to weak economic growth, higher unemployment, continuing disparities in incomes, wealth, and a relative decline in U.S. standing in the world.

On a more positive note, the face of political leadership in the U.S. has changed significantly and is more diverse. Minorities hold a much larger and growing percentage of political positions, especially at the local and state levels. The U.S. has finally broken through another "glass ceiling" by electing its first female president.

Unfortunately, needed political reforms have not been achieved. As a result, partisanship has often "trumped" (no pun intended) the broader public interest and the ideological divide has increased.

The Supreme Court now has a "liberal" majority that has facilitated an expansion in the size and role of the federal government. Capitalism continues to be under attack by younger generations of Americans. As a result, the U.S. has become more of a social welfare state and the role of the private sector has declined. This has served to reduce American innovation and the country's relative competitive posture internationally. Environmentalist opposition to fracking has resulted in the U.S. having to import oil from the unstable Middle East once again.

China is growing at 4% annually and India at a slightly faster rate versus the U.S. at an anemic 1 to 1.25%. The European Union (EU) is growing at about 1.5% and even Japan is growing at almost 1.5% after reducing its national debt/GDP ratio to 165% and declining. That is under the U.S. ratio of debt held by the public/GDP in 2040, and the U.S. debt burden is rising. At the same time, economic growth is low, job creation is weak, and disparities continue to exist. Some believe this "economic decline loop," represented by higher debt burdens and lower economic growth rates, may be a new reality.

The three primary factors that serve to fuel economic growth (i.e., human capital/working age population, financial capital/investment, and innovation/productivity) have declined over the years; therefore, annual economic growth has slowed dramatically. As noted above, these factors have resulted in a continuous decline in the relative economic position of the U.S. globally. China and the EU have passed the U.S. in nominal GDP, and India is set to pass both China and the EU by 2050.

The ratio of U.S. debt held by the public compared to the GDP has exploded from 35% in 1980 to 170% in 2040 and climbing. This has happened despite several significant tax increases, major reductions in defense spending, and constrained investments to counter growth of interest on the debt and mandatory spending programs like Social Security, Medicare, and Medicaid. The defense cuts disproportionally fell on reductions in the active duty forces and cuts in platforms (e.g., ships, airplanes, and tanks). This is because the Defense Department failed to take adequate steps to dramatically reduce overhead, rationalize the cost of the all-volunteer force, right-size its footprint, and move to more unmanned vehicles. The U.S. continued to rely too much on mega manned weapons systems (e.g., nuclear aircraft carrier task forces) that were increasingly vulnerable to new Chinese and Russian standoff systems.

Due to higher debt levels and interest rates, interest costs have passed defense spending and the gap is growing. Interest continues to represent the fastest-growing cost in the federal budget and has become a huge economic burden. And what do you get for interest? Nothing! As a result, more and more Americans are protesting calls to raise taxes just to pay for rising interest costs. Health care costs continue to be the largest program-related cost and the greatest fiscal challenge at all levels of government.

History shows that increases in interest costs can come at very inopportune times. The failure to control interest costs and restore fiscal sanity has resulted in a flight from the dollar with the Chinese Yuan (or RMB) being the biggest winner. As a result of this trend and the loss of exchange controls, currency-based sanctions and other forms of economic "soft power" are no longer as viable a lever for the U.S. At the same time, China has used sanctions effectively to retaliate for U.S. actions relating to Iran and other Chinese allies. They also used them to coerce South Korea and other U.S. allies in Asia.

Increasing inflation has become a problem again in 2040. Enough so that even the Modern Monetary Theorists ("free lunch advocates") of the 2020 era are concerned and feel that something now must be done to reduce the debt burdens. But is it too late?

The combination of higher inflation, lower savings, and weak economic growth has brought back the days of "Stagflation" from the 1970s. However, Paul Volcker, who passed in 2019, is no longer around to fight it.

The international alignment has also changed dramatically since America turned more inward to deal with its domestic challenges. China, Russia, Iran, and North Korea formed an alliance in the early 2020s to counter the U.S. from an economic, diplomatic, monetary, and military perspective. This effort was a much more aggressive supplement to the former BRICS initiative that involved Brazil, Russia, India, China, and South Africa.

China's Belt and Road Initiative (BRI) had the intended impact of increasing China's economic, diplomatic, and military might far beyond its region. China passed the U.S. in the number of global diplomatic missions before 2020. China also significantly increased its diplomatic influence in a range of international organizations as a result of investments made through its strategic BRI. China's increased funding for various international institutions (e.g., United Nations, including the World Health Organization, or WHO) was intended to offset a reduction in related funding by the U.S.

China has become the global leader in promoting multilateral trade relationships in order to fill the vacuum created when the U.S. moved to bilateral trade negotiations. The Chinese multilateral trade negotiations were designed to increase its global influence and help fuel Chinese exports to the disadvantage of the U.S., the EU, and India. India has also become more active internationally, given its increasing population, GDP, and per capita GDP. At the same time, total global trade is declining due to slow global economic growth and a trend toward increased nationalism, including within the U.S.

China passed the U.S. in total military capabilities in 2030. China's PPP advantage and employment of conscription to address their military services has caused them to pass the U.S. in total military purchasing power in 2020. The gap has grown considerably since then. Another matter of major concern is the growing gap in the military industrial base between China and the U.S. This gap has resulted in China increasing its export of weapons systems and a reduction in U.S. market share. China's superior industrial capacity has also had implications in commercial markets, with China providing a growing percentage of commercial aircraft and ships.

China's economic growth, diplomatic efforts, and military capabilities have caused many historical U.S. alliance partners to change their alignment (e.g., Philippines and Thailand). Many other major countries have chosen neutral status (e.g., India and South Korea), and others, including Japan, are considering neutral status due to China's increased strength and influence. South Korea and Japan's alignment considerations changed considerably in the mid-2020s when China strengthened its bases in the strategic South China Sea, took control of Taiwan, and the U.S. decided not to intervene. The related U.S. decision was largely influenced by the country's domestic challenges, a desire to avoid a potential nuclear confrontation with China, and a decision to focus more on maintaining vital free trade routes rather than defending individual countries where no formal mutual defense treaty existed. Some groups in the U.S. had previously tried to support independence for Hong Kong when China imposed its national security legislation on that province. This effort was unsuccessful, and Hong Kong and Taiwan have gradually become more integrated with China over time.

Due to the rise of China, the above actions, the inability to denuclearize North Korea, and changing alliances, many U.S. forces have been withdrawn from South Korea and Japan. Both Chinese increased strength and U.S. fiscal pressures are building to remove the rest of U.S. forces from the region.

Tensions in the Middle East have increased considerably since 2020. China has strengthened its alliance with Iran since it made a major investment in Iran's oil infrastructure and deployed troops to protect its investment. Both Iran and Saudi Arabia have obtained nuclear weapons. Israel continues to have its own nuclear weapons to protect itself. Various terrorist groups and nonstate actors are aggressively seeking to gain access to tactical nuclear and other weapons of mass destruction (WMD) for their own purposes both in the region and around the world.

NATO's role has continued to diminish. The alliance suffered a major blow in the mid-2020s when a resurgent Turkey exited the alliance and strengthened its ties with Russia. Russia still has the largest nuclear stockpile and a relatively large but less threatening military. The global consensus is that China is the most powerful nation with greater global ambitions. NATO's military capabilities continue to be limited and have declined, primarily due to a reduction in the relative global conventional military capabilities of the U.S. As a result, the threat of military conflict has increased since 2020 because the U.S. and Western nations are significantly weaker from a conventional military capabilities perspective. The possession of nuclear weapons by several Western nations (e.g., U.S., France, and the UK) is the primary deterrent to a major war involving Russia and/or China.

The dollar has weakened considerably since 2020, and its global reserve currency market share has declined from about 60% in 2020 to about 40%. The Chinese Yuan (or RMB) gained the most from the decline in U.S. market share. The decline in U.S. market share was a result of a loss of confidence in the ability of the U.S. to put its financial house in order and the Federal Reserve's periodic massive interventions to promote economic growth in ways that resulted in increased inflation and higher interest rates over time. The advocates of the Modern Monetary Theory caused the Congress to become even more fiscally irresponsible and the Federal Reserve to intervene aggressively in ways that laid the groundwork for increased bouts with excess inflation.

For years the U.S. benefited from having the dominant reserve currency. Once investors began to lose confidence in the U.S. combined with the rise of China and broader acceptance of the Chinese version of the U.S. SWIFT system for processing international financial transactions, the alignment changed. In addition, China, Russia, Iran, and other countries declined to use dollars in connection with international transactions, and other countries (e.g., oil-exporting nations) converted to a basket of various currencies that included the dollar and several others (e.g., Chinese yuan/RMB, Euro, Japanese yen, British pound, and Swiss franc). The percentage relating to the dollar has continued to decline. China has also mandated the use of the Yuan/RMB in their trade agreements.

The federal government has grown from 2% of the U.S. economy in 1912 to about 21% in 2019 to more than 28% and growing in 2040. When you add state and local spending, government has grown to more than 40% of the U.S. economy, and the nonprofit sector has also grown significantly in 2040. As a result, the private sector, which tends to be the primary driver of economic growth and innovation, has declined considerably as a percentage of the economy. The federal government also pursued a more active regulatory policy after the Trump administration left office. These and other factors combined with the increasing debt burden served to further reduce recurring economic growth.

While the U.S. took specific steps to reduce reliance on China and other countries for selected items (e.g., prescription drugs and rare earth materials) in the aftermath of COVID-19, unlike energy, the U.S. has not achieved independence with these and other items. While many U.S. politicians seek to promote U.S. jobs and sourcing strategies, many corporations are global and have a duty of loyalty to shareholders rather than to a country no matter where they may be headquartered.

From a domestic perspective, as noted above, annual recurring economic growth is only 1 to 1.25%. While meaningful progress has been made on policing and judicial reforms to prevent discrimination and abuse of power, the disparity gaps in income, wealth, and education between the "haves" and "have nots" has increased since 2020. For example, the concentration of wealth and income among the top 1% has increased, and the education attainment gap has not been reduced.

Of particular concern is that about 50% of graduates from public elementary schools lack basic language, math, and technology skills. These are needed to effectively compete in an increasingly competitive and knowledge-based economy. This gap in basic skills, which is even more pronounced among Hispanics and Blacks, combined with the continuing educational attainment gap has served to decrease economic growth, individual opportunity, and America's competitive posture. It has also resulted in increased domestic tranquility concerns. As a result, "liberal" politicians are calling for higher taxes, increased welfare spending, and more redistribution of wealth.

Additional technological innovations plus the move to a knowledge-based economy has resulted in higher base unemployment levels. This is particularly true for the less educated segment of the workforce and those with fewer skills. Conversely, there are a significant number of highly skilled and technical positions that remain unfilled, while unemployment and underemployment rates are still higher in the Black and Hispanic communities.

The highest poverty rate continues to be among children, who represent our future. The poverty rate has increased among seniors due to the changes that were made to Social Security and Medicare just before the related "Trust Funds" were set to run dry in the mid-2020s (i.e., Medicare HI) and early 2030s (i.e., combined Social Security program), respectively. For example, while payroll taxes and premiums were increased, eligibility ages were raised and benefit levels were reduced. A cap was also imposed on federal health care spending, which served to reduce some services and shifted costs. Like the United Kingdom, the U.S. is seeing more health care being delivered outside the national health care system to avoid long wait times.

All these factors have served to increase protests that are threatening domestic tranquility at home. These caused the U.S. to focus more internally and withdraw further from its historical international leadership role. This helped to promote economic growth, free trade, the rule of law, freedom, and resulting peace and prosperity in many countries for decades after WWII.

Within the U.S., there has been an acceleration of migration from northern to southern and western states. Several states declared bankruptcy in the 2020s after the federal bankruptcy code was amended to allow it, and their relative tax burdens and unfunded pension and retiree health care obligations became too much for them to handle. This helped to reduce the outflow from their states but did not stop it. As has been the case since the founding of the Republic in 1789, most Americans will move within the states but not outside the states. Unfortunately, a growing number of middle-upper-income individuals, especially the very wealthy, are now considering that possibility, with Canada likely to be the biggest beneficiary.

In summary, America's position in the world and at home has declined significantly since 2020, and the country is not well positioned for the future. As a result, the relative global peace and prosperity that existed in the world from 1946 until the mid-2020s, and during the "Pax Americana" era, is over. Sadly, for the first time in U.S. history, the quality of life for future generations of Americans may not be better than the past.

Importantly, this is an illustrative and not a predictive scenario. The U.S. can avoid this adverse scenario if policymakers make tough choices. This book includes a number of sensible solutions designed to create a better future and discharge our stewardship responsibility to younger and future generations of Americans.

CHAPTER 2

THE PANDEMIC: COVID-19

INTRODUCTION

This chapter focuses on the 2020 coronavirus (COVID-19) pandemic. It is included in the early part of this book because COVID-19 brought to light a number of serious challenges that our country has been in denial about for too long. COVID-19 is a serious public health challenge that needs to be taken seriously. It has had serious adverse impacts on public/private health, the economy, national security, and personal liberty. It will also have lasting implications in these and other areas (e.g., office space, workplaces, travel, telecommuting, online conferences/learning, and housing preferences) over time. Hopefully, it will accentuate and accelerate actions by public officials to begin addressing a range of preexisting fiscal and other public policy challenges that were made worse by the virus. These challenges need to be addressed once the virus has been defeated. Importantly, the comments and opinions that I express in this chapter have been consistent with my views and statements throughout the pandemic. There is no armchair quarterbacking or hindsight involved.

DISCUSSION

In December of 2019, a new coronavirus appeared in the city of Wuhan, China. This new virus was eventually named COVID-19. Most people probably never heard of Wuhan, but it is a modern Chinese city with historical significance and a population of more than 11 million people in central China. Some have referred to Wuhan as the Chicago of China. The Three Gorges Dam, the largest power station in the world, is located nearby. Wuhan is a major manufacturing center with significant automobile and iron/steel production facilities. It also has a number of important emerging industries, including pharmaceuticals, biological engineering, new materials, and environmental protection. What most people do not know is that Wuhan is also the center for China's biological weapons research.

The virus started in Wuhan and its origin has still not been verified. What is clear is that when the virus outbreak occurred in Wuhan, the Chinese central government took aggressive steps to contain it to Wuhan. They mandated "stay-at-home" orders that were strictly enforced, conducted testing, and engaged in contact tracing. China ramped up production of personal protective equipment (PPE) and forbid travel out of Wuhan into other parts of China.

Importantly, China did not prohibit international travel from Wuhan. Given its importance and the significant amount of foreign investment in Wuhan, there were many direct flights from Wuhan to Europe, the United States, Southeast Asia, and the Middle East. Given the amount and ease of global travel today, this failure to limit international travel resulted in a spread of the virus to other parts of the world. In contrast, when it was evident that the virus was more serious than originally thought and was being spread through international travel, President Trump banned flights from China effective February 2, 2020, from most of Europe effective March 13, 2020, and from Brazil effective May 29, 2020 as that country's cases rose rapidly when it entered its late fall season. However, even when international travel was banned, U.S. residents were allowed to return but were supposed to "self-quarantine." However, there was no enforcement of the self-quarantine requirement. To put things into perspective, as of March 12, there had only been 1,135 confirmed cases and 38 deaths attributed to COVID-19 in the U.S. and the highest numbers of cases and deaths at that time were in China, Italy, and Spain.

There are significant differences between the Chinese and U.S. governance and economic systems. For example, China has a strong central government that can direct provinces regarding what to do and what not to do. Second, China has many state-owned enterprises that it controls and can direct, and significant influence over private-sector enterprises. Finally, and most importantly, China does not have a constitutional Bill of Rights that protects the personal liberty of its citizens. In contrast, the U.S. has a federalist system that provides a separation of powers between the federal and state governments. Most enterprises in the U.S. are privately owned and the government has little to no direct control over their activities. The government does, however, regulate and provide certain tax preferences and grants to private-sector enterprises in order to promote economic growth and protect the public interest. Most importantly, the U.S. Constitution contains a Bill of Rights that is designed to provide significant protections for individual rights and protect against an overly intrusive or abusive government. These differences are huge and have a direct impact on how the governments in China and the U.S. can and should address pandemics.

There are different accounts regarding how transparent the Chinese were in the early stages of the virus and the nature and extent of the actions of the World Health Organization (WHO) in assessing the threat, as well as their effectiveness in communicating that threat to various public health organizations around the world. Questions still remain regarding the degree of transparency and accuracy regarding China's infection and mortality statistics and actions in connection with the virus. In addition, an independent investigation is ongoing regarding the WHO's actions. As a former Chair of the UN's Independent Audit Advisory Committee (IAAC), I can attest that the WHO, like other UN agencies, is a politically headed organization with a public interest mission. Although the WHO is involved in public health, politics also plays a role.

What is clear is that while China took steps to control the virus within the country's borders, it did not take adequate steps to prevent the spread beyond China's borders. According to the Global Health Security Index, the U.S. was rated as the number-one country in the world in connection with its preparedness for a pandemic in 2019. The United Kingdom, Netherlands, Australia, Canada, Thailand, Sweden, Denmark, South Korea, and Finland were rated numbers two through 10, respectively. Clearly, despite the ranking, the U.S. was not adequately prepared and did not have a sufficient national stockpile of PPE or an adequate number of respirators to draw upon once the virus spread in the U.S.

Interestingly, most of the world's PPE and pharmaceuticals are manufactured in China. Therefore, there was little question that China had the ability to control production and distribution in a manner that protected its own interests. This supply chain issue has prompted the U.S. and other countries to reconsider their reliance on China for certain materials (e.g., PPE, pharmaceuticals, and rare earth minerals).

While the initial outbreaks outside of China were concentrated in Europe, most notably Italy and Spain, the virus eventually spread to more than 200 countries and territories around the world, with significant variances regarding the degree of infection and the mortality rates. According to Statistica, as of August 13, 2020, there were about 20.8 million cases and 747,327 deaths attributed to COVID-19 around the world.

The first case of COVID-19 in the U.S. was not discovered until January 2020. The initial outbreak was in a nursing home facility in the state of Washington. Eventually the virus spread to all 50 states with significant variances regarding the degree of infection and mortality rates. According to Statistica, as of August 13, 2020, there were about 5.3 million cases and 165,716 deaths attributed to COVID-19 in the U.S. As of August 13, 2020, the U.S. had the most accumulated cases in the world but was ranked number eight in death rate. While all deaths are tragic, the death rate is a better metric for benchmarking purposes.

While the virus was initially concentrated in the Northeast, it spread around the country and increased rapidly in some southern and western states starting in the summer, in large part due to crowds of younger people on beaches and in bars. While the death rate among younger persons is very low, those persons should be more concerned about others and exhibit it by wearing masks and maintaining social distancing. As a result of the increase in cases, some pulling back from actual and planned phased reopening policies was appropriate and occurred. It also resulted in many schools choosing to use distance learning in the fall and some colleges cancelling or postponing fall sports.

As an internationally recognized leader in the accountability community and a professor of economics and national security at the U.S. Naval Academy, I am very disappointed in how the media is handling COVID-19 reporting. Most reports are designed to stoke fear and lack contextual sophistication. In some cases, the statistics presented are unreliable, and in other cases, they are misleading. In addition, the media typically fails to put the statistics into context (as compared to past pandemics and diseases). The media seems to overly focus on the public health dimension while failing to adequately address the economic, personal health, and individual liberty dimensions of the government's response to the "crisis." Finally, the media did not adequately report on the division of responsibilities and authorities between the federal and state governments. The following are some examples.

Everything in the world is relative and some statistics are more relevant than others. For example, in 1918 the U.S. and the world were hit with the "Spanish flu." It was a coronavirus and resulted in about 50,000,000 deaths worldwide and about 600,000 deaths in the U.S. Given the increase in the size of the global and U.S. populations, that would be the equivalent of 217,000,000 deaths globally and 2,000,000 deaths in the U.S. today. Compare these numbers to the total global and U.S. deaths as of August 13, 2020 (i.e., 747,327 globally and 165,716 in the U.S). Did you ever hear the media discuss these benchmarks?

The U.S. typically has about 35,000 to 60,000 deaths from the flu every year, more than 600,000 deaths from cancer every year, and about 200,000 deaths from drug/alcohol abuse and suicides every year. According to the Centers for Disease Control and Prevention (CDC), the U.S. had more than 600,000 reported abortions in 2016, down from more than 1.4 million in 1990. Did you ever hear any of these other numbers discussed to put the COVID-19 numbers into context? In addition, while the related studies have yet to be completed, there is little questioning that "stay-at-home" orders and the adverse personal economic impact relating to COVID-19 increased some of these non-COVID-19 death numbers. Why? Because people delayed various medical screenings and treatments, and depression and financial stress levels increased dramatically during that period of time when people were staying home. Did you hear much about these factors from the media or the politicians?

As of August 13, 2020, the states with the highest death rates were New Jersey, New York, Massachusetts, and Connecticut, while the states with the most total cases were California, Florida, Texas, and New York. Obviously these statistics change over time. The key is that they should be presented fairly, with contextual sophistication, and in a nonpartisan fashion.

The media also tried to make a big deal about the rising infection rates, especially in connection with states that had Republican governors (e.g., Florida, Texas, and Arizona). However, they failed to note that while their infection rates were rising, the death rates in these states were a small fraction of those rates in New Jersey, New York, and Connecticut, all of which had Democrat governors. Candidly, reporting on things like

COVID-19 should be fact-based and uninfluenced by partisan politics, but that is not today's America. According to Statistica, New Jersey and New York had the highest death rates as of August 13, 2020. In contrast, the death rate in New Jersey, which had the highest death rate, was 5.4 times greater than Texas and 4.4 times greater than Florida. Did the media mention this? I wonder why?

What about relevancy and reliability? Many media outlets would report daily on the accumulated total of COVID-19 cases, hospitalizations, and deaths in the country and for their area. They would typically use line graphs to show their data. While their data may have come from authoritative sources, the resulting presentations were technically accurate but very misleading. Why? Because such a graphic presentation meant that the line graphs would go up forever until no one else was infected, hospitalized, or died from the virus. And they would never go down! A more honest representation would have been to report the number of new cases, hospitalizations, and deaths by day, with a disclosure of accumulated totals. That type of graphic presentation would have been very different because it would more clearly show when the relevant statistics were trending down and therefore signaling that the tide had turned. Governor Cuomo (D, NY) started using this approach in his daily briefings and eventually a number of media outlets started doing the same, especially when states started to move away from one-size-fits-all "stay-at-home" orders and needed this type of data to help make decisions regarding whether, when, and how to ease the related restrictions. Supplementing these daily statistics with seven- or 14-day moving averages is also appropriate given the reopening criteria recommended by the CDC and in order to not overly emphasize the statistics for an individual day.

Even the number of deaths attributed to COVID-19 is questionable. Why? Because the federal government provided financial incentives of between $11,000 and $38,000 per person for any hospitalization and use of a ventilator attributed to COVID-19, whether or not the person was actually tested for COVID-19 or the death was directly attributable to the virus. Just another example of perverse incentives that can result in skewed statistics and excess payments. I hope and expect that various investigations and congressional oversight efforts will help to determine the extent of fraud, waste, and abuse that occurred due to this financial incentive.

In reality, absent universal testing and the elimination of financial incentives to report hospitalizations and deaths as being related to COVID-19, the only metric that is somewhat reasonable and can be used for benchmarking is the number of confirmed deaths related to COVID-19 as a percentage of the total population. On this basis, the death rate from COVID-19 was a small fraction of the Spanish flu of 1918. In addition, the CDC has stated that it estimates the actual number of COVID-19 infections are about 10 times the reported numbers. If that is the case, the death rate is one-tenth of what is being reported. It is simple math.

COVID-19 death rates in the U.S. varied greatly based on various demographic and geographic factors. For example, while younger people could get the virus, the death rate was extremely low. On the other hand, seniors with underlying chronic health conditions had a much higher death rate than other segments of the population.

The COVID-19 experience also demonstrated the lack of adequate planning and preparation at the federal, state, and local levels in connection with a pandemic. Unlike China, the U.S. is not very good at long-range planning. This must change! As noted previously, national PPE stockpiles were inadequate and the U.S. was overly reliant on China to provide PPE when needed. In addition, the separation of powers between the federal government and the states under the U.S. Constitution meant that while the president could and should recommend appropriate actions to deal with the pandemic and use the presidential "bully pulpit" to "lead by example" and encourage all Americans to take appropriate measures (e.g., wearing masks, practicing social distancing, washing hands or using hand sanitizer), the governors were ultimately responsible and accountable for making the decisions regarding what to do in their respective states and enforcing any related orders. In this regard, some governors took the public health crisis more seriously than others, and for a significant period of time President Trump did not take it as seriously as he should have and did not lead by example in connection with wearing a mask and other matters. The division of responsibilities in the U.S. also meant that states had to compete with each other and the federal government in trying to acquire PPE and other equipment, thereby driving up prices and the cost to the taxpayers. Furthermore, in the absence of adequate planning and effective early and consistent execution, the adverse economic and personal impact of COVID-19 was much, much worse than the 1918 Spanish flu, even though the death rate was much lower.

As time progressed it became clear that a majority of deaths from COVID-19 occurred in nursing homes, assisted living facilities, and prisons. In addition, the death rates in urban areas and among certain minority communities were also higher than average. Most of these variances can be attributed to the fact that the population density and the degree of underlying health conditions are greater among these populations. As a result, it is prudent to take specific and more aggressive actions within these communities. The same actions may not be necessary or appropriate in other geographic areas, communities, and demographic populations. Again, as with many things, government should employ a "risk-based" approach that considers geographic, demographic, and other appropriate factors in trying to achieve a reasonable balance between public health, economic, private health, and individual liberty considerations. While many governors, including Governor Cuomo, started to consider these factors when they were contemplating "opening up the economy" in their states, most should have employed a risk-based approach much earlier. In this regard, government should also impose civil sanctions on persons, businesses, and other organizations that violate mask, social distancing, and maximum gathering orders. In summary, more flexibility should be coupled with increased transparency and accountability. Hopefully the government will do a much better job the next time we face a pandemic. There will be a next time, we just do not know when.

What about the economic impact of COVID-19? While the death rate for COVID-19 is much lower than the 1918 Spanish flu, the adverse economic impact has been much, much worse. As noted above, the early actions by most governors, who were the elected officials with the most power to act regarding what to do in their states, did not adequately consider employing a "risk-based approach" in their decision-making. All too many imposed "one-size-fits-all" "stay-at-home" orders within their entire states rather than differentiating between the areas and populations within their states that were at highest and lowest risk. In addition to encouraging telecommuting, social distancing, personal hygiene, and mask-wearing practices, they also forced the closure of most "nonessential" businesses and other organizations (e.g., churches and other houses of worship, museums, and sports and entertainment venues), although the definition of "nonessential" varied by state. In many cases, these actions had a disproportionate adverse impact on small businesses and lower-income workers. The result of the above actions was national unemployment levels of almost 14% (from a 50-year low of 3.5% before the virus), a massive contraction of the economy (from a record period of sustained economic growth before the virus), and a huge decline in the stock market (from an all-time high in early 2020). The stock market started to rebound at the end of March from a 37% decline from the record level set in January 2020. By June, while the Dow and S&P 500 were still down considerably from the January record high, the NASDAQ had set a new record high. While the Dow was still down, the S&P had almost fully recovered and was approaching an all-time high on August 13, 2020.

The initial months of the COVID-19 experience were particularly devastating from an economic perspective. U.S. GDP growth declined by 5% in the first quarter of 2020. The decline in GDP during the second quarter of 2020 was about 33% on an annualized basis. This was the highest single quarterly decline in history. At the same time, a partial rebound was expected in the second half of the year.

Shockingly, due to the rise in debt and the decline in the economy attributable to COVID-19, debt held by the public as of June 30, 2020 was 106% of GDP, and total federal debt was 136% of GDP!

The governors' decisions to close "nonessential" businesses and organizations and issue "stay-at-home" orders across a vast majority of the country resulted in more than 40 million Americans filing for unemployment between late March and the end of May. This was a record that far exceeded numbers even during the Great Depression. The closure of nonessential businesses was particularly challenging for small stores, bars/restaurants, and individuals in the personal services industry, many of which were driven out of business. Ironically, state and privately owned liquor stores were deemed to be essential, while churches and places of worship were not? The result was record liquor sales and fewer in-person faith-based activities to help people cope with the stress and depression associated with the governments' actions.

In order to put things into context, it is important to know that about 50% of Americans do not have significant savings and live paycheck-to-paycheck. In addition, about 50% of all jobs in America are in the small business sector (i.e., employers with fewer than 500 employees). In most cases, the individuals in these categories do not have jobs whereby they can telecommute. As a result, they are affected the most by "stay-at-home" orders and closing of "nonessential" businesses. The owners of such businesses are also disproportionally affected. As a result, having compassion means also considering the adverse impact that unduly restrictive "stay-at-home" and "business closure" orders have on these persons, which total in the tens of millions.

In response to the above circumstances, the Congress passed several pieces of legislation designed to help individuals, businesses, and governments deal with these adverse economic impacts. These bills had an approximate $3 trillion price tag and represented the biggest economic rescue/stimulus package in the history of the country. The legislation included paying every person who filed a tax return up to $1,250, or $2,500 for couples who filed jointly. Mary and I received a card worth about $1,100 for both of us. We did not need it, since I was teaching remotely and our income did not decline. Just another example of poor targeting of assistance and the use of taxpayer dollars.

In June 2020, the U.S. Government Accountability Office (GAO) determined that at least $1.4 billion of the above-referenced payments had been made to dead persons. Shockingly, the federal government did not cross-reference the planned payment files to its death record files. This is an example of the poor internal controls that exist in the federal government.

The legislation also included paying an additional $600 per week until July 31, 2020 to individuals who were receiving unemployment. Ironically, that meant that some low-income workers could make more by staying unemployed than working. Not a good idea. In fact, I heard from several small business owners directly that some of their workers did not want to return to work since they were making more money sitting at home and doing nothing!

There were hundreds of billions of dollars in loans and grants to small businesses to help them and encourage them to keep their workers on staff through September 30, 2020. That was known as the "Paycheck Protection Program" (PPP) since 75% of the funds had to be used to pay workers in order for the loan to be converted to a grant. Congress later reduced that percentage to 60%. The initial amount of $349 billion was claimed within 13 days, including by some major employers who tried to exploit a loophole in the legislation. Namely, they had many locations nationwide with total employees far in excess of the small business definition but given the structure of their businesses (e.g., separate corporations by location); they filed for many locations that had fewer than 500 employees. Many of these companies returned the money when this information became public and the Treasury put pressure on them. Since the first $349 billion went so quickly, Congress acted and added another $250 billion. A significant amount of the $250 billion PPP appropriation remained as of June 30, 2020. Realistically, a vast majority of the PPP loans will either be forgiven because the conditions for conversion to a grant will be met or "written off" because the borrower goes out of business. As a result, the taxpayers will pick up the tab and assume the related debt burden.

Congress allocated about $150 billion to help the states, municipalities, and tribal governments deal with the extra costs associated with COVID-19. However, the governors felt that was not enough and sought another $500 billion+ to help deal with the loss of revenue resulting from their closure of "nonessential" businesses and stay-at-home orders. In response, the House passed the Health and Economic Recovery Omnibus Emergency Solutions Act (HEROES Act), in May. The HEROES Act proposed to spend another $3.4 trillion and included almost $1 trillion in funding for state and local governments, as well as funds for businesses and individuals. It also included a number of items that had nothing to do with COVID-19. It was a real overreach and, as a result, it was not taken up by the Senate.

In late July 2020 the Senate offered to spend about $1 trillion, and its proposal included some non-COVID-19 provisions too, primarily items related to defense spending. Due to a breakdown in negotiations, President Trump issued several controversial executive orders in early August designed to help the unemployed, prevent foreclosures and evictions, and delay student loan payments. Ultimately, I expect that Congress will pass a new round of legislation that will cost $1 trillion to $2 trillion and address the issues that were the subject of President Trump's executive orders. It will likely provide additional aid for businesses and governments (e.g., schools), with restrictions on how the funds can be used, additional payments to individuals, adjustments to unemployment benefit amounts, and some liability protections for businesses, schools, and others. Hopefully, Congress will not provide funds to "bail out" state pension funds. In my view, this would be both inappropriate and irresponsible. One thing is clear, whatever the final cost ends up being, it will just add to our deficits and debt burdens.

I and many other people felt that state and local governments should only receive federal assistance for any direct and incremental costs they incurred that were clearly attributable to COVID-19. After all, the governors and municipal leaders were the persons who made the decisions regarding the closure of "nonessential" entities and "stay-at-home" orders, and many states had serious budget and financial problems long before COVID-19. In many cases these preexisting state and local budget challenges were attributable to huge unfunded pension and retiree health care obligations for state and local workers and retirees. You can read more about this issue in Chapter 8.

The legislation also included hundreds of billions in loan and grant authority to help large corporations and encourage them to keep workers on staff through September 30, 2020. These programs were to be administered by the Treasury and Federal Reserve. The Treasury was allocated $500 billion, which was to be targeted to industries that were especially hard hit by COVID-19 (e.g., airlines) and $454 billion to the Federal Reserve. Given the structure of the Federal Reserve, it had the ability to leverage its $454 billion allocation to more than $4 trillion! These provisions were the most controversial parts of the legislation.

Given the size of the spending in the legislation, Congress included several new oversight mechanisms, including a special inspector general, a special government-wide inspectors general coordinating entry, and a new congressional commission along with funding for all these entities and additional funding for the GAO and selected department inspectors general. Shockingly, while the Congress talks a good game about transparency, oversight, and accountability, often its actions do not match its words. For example, as of August 13, 2020, Speaker Nancy Pelosi and Senate Majority Leader Mitch McConnell had still not been able to agree on a chair for the congressional commission who would take the job! This is hardly "leading by example." Clearly, Congress does not care about accountability as much as they claim. In my view, it is outrageous that

Congress has failed to fill this position to help oversee their past spending authorizations when they are contemplating spending even more.

While some action was clearly called for, the above spending actions served to further exacerbate the federal government's mounting public debt/GDP challenge. Hopefully, they will serve as an incentive to accelerate needed actions to defuse the nation's ticking debt bomb after the crisis passes. In fact, according to the April 2020 Congressional Budget Office (CBO) forecast, as a result of additional spending and the contracting economy, federal debt held by the public/GDP is projected to increase to about 108% by the end of Fiscal 2021, up from 79% at the end of Fiscal 2019! That is in excess of the previous record of 106% set at the end of World War II. At that time, our debt held by the public/GDP ratio was going down and demographics were working in our favor. The opposite is the case today.

The Federal Reserve also took a range of unprecedented actions to help promote economic growth and provide a financial backstop to corporations as well as state and local governments. These actions amounted to trillions of dollars and went far beyond their historical role of being the lender of last resort for financial institutions. The unprecedented fiscal and monetary actions related to COVID-19 serve to underscore the unsustainability of recent fiscal and monetary policies.

COVID-19 also had an impact on the financial condition of the Social Security and Medicare programs. The economic and public health impacts from the virus resulted in reduced revenues and increased expenses for the combined Social Security, and Medicare programs. As a result, in June 2020 the CBO estimated that the dates of exhaustion for the combined Social Security (Retirement Insurance and Disability Insurance) and Medicare Part A (Hospital Insurance) Trust Funds would be accelerated by three years from the 2035 and 2026 dates prior to the virus, to 2032 and 2023, respectively. Importantly, when the related Trust Funds are exhausted, these programs will not be able to pay full benefits in a timely manner. As a result, legislation that either reduces benefit payments and/ or increases revenue will be necessary to restore the financial sustainability of these important social insurance programs.

What about the impact on education? COVID-19 resulted in the closure of most public and private schools and universities in the spring.

From a personal perspective, as a professor at the U.S. Naval Academy (USNA), I was directly affected. For the first time in history the USNA went to distance learning. While the transition was successfully achieved, the resulting educational experience was not as effective or satisfying for either the professors or the students as in-person learning. I also have three grandchildren who converted from in-person to online learning. They also felt that the online experience was not as effective or satisfying as in-person learning. This conversion also had a disproportionally adverse impact on homes with single parents and those homes where the parents did not have a high level of educational attainment. Fortunately, the USNA is planning to return to primarily in-person studies for the fall semester of 2020 with appropriate safeguards. This is driven in part because 89% of the midshipmen said they preferred in-person learning and because the Academy can create a semi-bubble environment since it is a military base. However, many universities and schools have decided to stay with virtual learning, and their decisions will have significant implications not just for the students but also their parents and siblings.

While many are aware of the above factors, most Americans may not realize the current and future national security implications of COVID-19. During the public health crisis the USS Theodore Roosevelt (CVN-71) was put out of action and had to port for several weeks in Guam as a result of about 1,000 members of the crew testing positive for COVID-19, although only one sailor died of the virus. The TR, otherwise known as the "Big Stick," was the lead ship in a carrier task force that was forward deployed to help protect U.S. interests in the Pacific, especially in connection with freedom of navigation issues in the strategically important and contested South China Sea. This serves to demonstrate the adverse implications of biological threats on readiness and the need to move to more unmanned air, sea, and ground platforms. In addition, the huge increase in debt held by the public/GDP resulting from COVID-19 will clearly have adverse implications for future defense budgets, thereby further complicating our future national security interests.

To put things into perspective, while both the U.S. and China experienced a decline in GDP as a result of COVID-19, China's Chairman and President Xi Jinping announced increased defense spending due to heightened security threats while the U.S. leaders were openly talking about defense cuts.

In summary, several COVID-19 related lessons learned seem clear to me. First, President Trump did not lead by example from the outset in connection with recommended public health strategies. Second, the government at all levels in the U.S. did not engage in adequate planning, preparation, and execution. In particular, state governments did not achieve a reasonable balance between public health, economics, personal health, and individual liberty considerations. Third, national stockpiles of PPE and critical medical equipment were inadequate and the U.S. was far too reliant on China for PPE, critical medical equipment (e.g., ventilators), and prescription drugs. Fourth, the media overly hyped the public health aspects of COVID-19, which resulted in excessive fear among the overall population given the relative risks. While COVID-19 is a serious public health matter and any loss of life is unfortunate, the media has a responsibility to provide a fair and balanced view of the relevant data and to ensure the contextual sophistication of their related reporting. They clearly failed in this regard during the first several months of the crisis, and they still have a long way to go. Fifth, as is all too frequently the case, the Congress acted in a "crisis management" fashion and took a range of very costly steps in an effort to help individuals, companies, and state and local governments deal with the adverse economic effects of COVID-19. Many of these steps may have been necessary but were not well designed. They also served to increase our mounting debt held by the public/GDP challenge and accelerate the need to address our nation's ticking debt bomb. Sixth, the Federal Reserve engaged in a range of unprecedented actions in an attempt to prop up the economy and backstop both private- and public-sector entities. Many of these steps raise real questions regarding the appropriate role of the Treasury and the Fed in connection with the private sector. They also serve to reinforce the fact that the nation's current fiscal path and monetary policies are unsustainable. Seventh, the domestic and overseas disruptions caused by COVID-19 serve to emphasize the need to view biological threats as new economic and national security challenges that must be addressed. Eighth, Congress is not leading by example in connection with COVID-19 oversight and accountability issues. Finally, given the current partisan and ideological divides in the U.S., even a major public health and economic crisis can be politicized. It became clear during the pandemic that certain partisan political forces and media outlets wanted to primarily emphasize the public health aspects of COVID-19 and downplay the adverse economic, individual liberty, and private health aspects (e.g., delayed screenings and treatments, hypertension, depression, and the additional deaths that undoubtedly resulted) of the coronavirus, especially in connection with the segments of the population that were most adversely affected by the governors' orders. As a political independent, I would hope that it was not a conscious effort to stoke fear and impede the economic recovery for partisan or personal reasons, but I fear that, in some cases, it was. This is just one of many reasons why the public's opinion of the media is so low.

From an economic perspective, the U.S. free enterprise system is the engine of economic growth, job creation, and innovation. This process is aptly called by economists the process of "creative destruction." It involves risk, reward, success, and sometimes entrepreneurial failure. The federal government has intervened with increasing aggressiveness in the private sector as a result of the 2008–2009 financial crisis and the 2020 COVID-19 crisis. While some intervention was appropriate in the short term, care needs to be taken to ensure that such intervention does not result in a situation where if it is heads the private investor wins and if it is tails the public sector loses. Stated differently, a system where gains are privatized and losses are socialized. The market rather than the government should ultimately pick the winners and losers. Any economic system that does not incorporate these principles will not be successful at achieving high levels of sustainable economic growth, innovation, and job creation over time. Regardless of what the results of the 2020 elections may be, we need to learn from the past and others and take steps to create a better future. COVID-19 should serve as a wake-up call and impetus to act sooner versus later.

CHAPTER 3
LEARNING FROM PAST MAJOR POWERS

Today, the U.S. is clearly a global superpower with worldwide economic, diplomatic, and military power, as well as cultural influence. These are the four factors that should be used to ascertain whether a country should be called a superpower today. The U.S. is the only country that has met all four of these criteria since WWII. While the former Soviet Union clearly met the diplomatic and military power criteria, they did not meet the economic and cultural criteria. China will soon clearly meet all four of these criteria. The Chinese government and some others would assert that China has already met these four criteria. It is debatable but only a timing difference in any event.

History clearly shows that the most important factor in achieving and maintaining great power or superpower status is economic power. Economic strength brings diplomatic influence and enables military power. Therefore, it is critically important that the U.S. maintain a strong economy if we want to remain a superpower in the future.

While history includes a number of past great powers, none has stood the test of time and, as discussed in Chapter 1, the U.S. is at risk of losing its superpower status in the future. This chapter is intended to help us learn from the past and from others before we turn and focus on the future.

There have been a number of empires, most of which came into being before the establishment of countries, which have existed over time. While there are too many empires to cover, this chapter will focus on four of them: the Roman Empire, the Ottoman Empire, China, and the British Empire.

ROMAN EMPIRE

Rome was the first republic, which is a representative form of government. The Roman Republic lasted for about 500 years but fell when Caesar Augustus became Emperor of Rome in 27 BC. The Roman

Empire lasted much longer but ultimately fell for several reasons. These included the following:

- Decline in moral values
- Decay of political civility
- Overextended military
- Inability to control/protect its borders
- Fiscal irresponsibility

Do the above factors sound familiar? Sadly, the answer is "yes." There is little question that moral values have declined in the U.S. during the past several decades. Although the public has not resorted to being entertained by gladiators who fight to the death, there are other moral concerns. For example, abortions exceed 600,000 per year and divorces have increased dramatically, while church attendance has declined significantly since the 1970s. References to God in public schools and buildings have been all but eliminated, and the mere mention of God in public often results in the person being questioned or ridiculed.

Political civility in the U.S. has also declined dramatically. While it has been many years since a member of Congress has attacked another member physically on the floor of the House or Senate, verbal attacks in public have increased at an alarming rate. Although reasonable people can and do differ, especially in connection with important public policy issues, they do not need to be confrontational, vitriolic, or overly emotional in doing so. The sad truth is that the two major political parties have tried to divide us, rather than unite us. From the perspective of the two political parties, you are either for the Blue Team (Democrats) or the Red Team (Republicans). While unaffiliated/independent voters represent the largest percentage of registered voters, they are mostly unrepresented in Congress, state legislatures, and on government boards and commissions. They are also typically ignored until it comes to general election time. Serious and substantive debate has also declined dramatically in what was previously known as the world's "greatest deliberative body" — the U.S. Senate.

The U.S. military has bases in about 35 countries around the world. All too frequently the U.S. is the country that must take the lead in deterring or responding to aggression or oppression around the world.

Unlike Rome and most other past great powers, the U.S. has generally not sought to acquire additional land as a result of foreign wars. To paraphrase former Secretary of State and General Colin Powell, the U.S. has generally only sought enough land after foreign wars to bury its dead.

Most major democracies, especially in Europe, have let their militaries decline after the fall of the Soviet Union. Even the U.S. has reduced its total active duty force structure from about 3.5 million in 1968 and 2.1 million in 1988 to about 1.3 million today. On the other hand, several authoritarian countries (e.g., China, Russia, Iran, and North Korea) have increased their military capabilities irrespective of the size of their active duty forces.

Regarding geography, the U.S. only shares land borders with two nations — Canada and Mexico. Fortunately, we have friendly relations and major trade activity with those two countries, and they do not pose any military threat to the U.S. At the same time, given instability in parts of Central and South America and the relative stability, individual liberty, and opportunity in the U.S., large numbers of people try to cross our borders illegally, primarily our southern border with Mexico, each year. In addition, even in situations where people legally enter the U.S. by land, sea, or air, many are overstaying their visas, thereby being in the country illegally.

As has been mentioned already in this book, the U.S. has lost control of its finances and is on an unsustainable fiscal path. This represents a direct threat to the future economic strength of the U.S. We will discuss this topic in-depth later in this book.

The U.S. is the second-largest democracy on earth, surpassed only by India. While the U.S. is currently the longest-standing republic, it has only existed as a republic for about 230 years, whereas the Roman Republic lasted about 500 years. In total, Rome dominated most of the known Western world for almost 1,000 years, and it continued to dominate much of the known Eastern world in the form of the Byzantine Empire for about 1,000 years more before falling to the Ottoman Empire (modern-day Turkey). It is important that we learn lessons from Rome and do our best to set a new record for the longest-lasting republic in the history of mankind.

OTTOMAN EMPIRE

The Ottoman Empire lasted for about 600 years and fell in 1922 after WWI. At its peak in the 1500s it was a major economic and military power that controlled Asia Minor, most of the Middle East, Northern Africa, and Southeastern Europe.

There are a number of reasons why the Ottoman Empire fell. First, it was too agrarian and did not have an adequate domestic industrial base to compete with Britain, France, Russia, and others over time. Second, it was not as integrated as it needed to be due to its very diverse ethnicity, languages, economics, and geography. Third, its population was undereducated and only 5% to 10% of its population was literate. Fourth, other competing empires encouraged rebellions within the Ottoman Empire (e.g., Russia, Austria, United Kingdom, and France), which faced a particularly bitter rivalry with Russia. Finally, it picked the wrong side to ally with in WWI. It was allied with Germany, Austria-Hungary, and Bulgaria, and they were defeated by the U.S., United Kingdom, France, and other allied powers.

CHINA

China has been a great regional power in some form for much of its history, except for its "period of humiliation" (1859–1949). The territory that is now China was comprised of many different tribes for centuries. China became a unified and centralized empire for the first time during the Han Dynasty, which lasted about 425 years until 220 AD. At that time, China was the eastern end of the Silk Road and its trade and economy flourished. Unlike Rome, the Han Dynasty was not defeated by nomadic tribes. Rather, it experienced internal conflict and the country was ultimately split into three separate kingdoms.

During the fifteenth century the Chinese had the most powerful Navy in the world. China was engaging in a significant amount of trade both in Asia and other parts of the world. As recently as the latter part of the nineteenth century, China had the largest economy in the world. The U.S. then overtook China around 1900 and now China is rising again. Before

COVID-19, China was expected to surpass the U.S. based on nominal GDP in about 10 years. However, China had already passed the U.S. in purchasing power parity (PPP)-based GDP in 2014 and the gap has grown since then. Importantly, the jury is still out on what the long-term impact of COVID-19 will be on the economic growth, trade, and other relations within and between China and the U.S.

Historically, China has been more of a regional military power with a strong economy and significant trade that spanned much of the world. China's Chairman and President Xi Jinping is clearly seeking to be a major global player when it comes to economic, diplomatic, military, and cultural matters. In fact, China has already achieved some of these and will most assuredly achieve superpower status in the near future, if they have not already done so. The only real questions are when, and for what purpose?

BRITISH EMPIRE

The British Empire is the most recent one to rise and fall. Although the Empire fell, the United Kingdom is still a major nation and the British Commonwealth (an association of sovereign states that are former British colonies, including such countries as Australia, Canada, India, New Zealand, Nigeria, Pakistan, South Africa, the United Kingdom, and a number of other smaller countries) still spans the globe. As a result, while the sun used to never set on the British Empire, it still never sets on the British Commonwealth.

The British Empire lasted for more than 400 years, and its peak was arguably around 1914. At its peak, it comprised almost 25% of both the world's population and land mass.

There are numerous reasons why the British Empire declined and ultimately fell. First, the British military was overstretched trying to maintain control over a large and globally dispersed empire. Second, the native populations within the various colonies sought self-rule and then independence over time. Third, other countries rose in both economic and military power (e.g., U.S., Germany, Soviet Union, France, and Japan). Fourth, the economic and human cost of WWI and WWII took a major toll on the United Kingdom. Fifth, Britain's debt burden increased dramatically and its finances deteriorated significantly, which resulted in less investment and less economic growth, thereby causing other countries to pass it and for it to have less global capability, flexibility, and influence.

Many people view the Suez Crisis in 1957 as being the confirmation of the decline of the British Empire. At that time, both Britain and France sought to challenge Egypt's claim of sovereignty over the strategic Suez Canal. Heavy political pressure from both the U.S. and the USSR led both Britain and France to withdraw. Many believe that President Eisenhower's threat to sell British Pound Sterling bonds held by the U.S. Government, which would have caused a financial crisis in the UK, was the straw that broke Britain's back. This served to demonstrate that too much debt, especially if that debt is held by foreign governments, is a risky endeavor both from an economic and national security perspective.

Most people view the return of Hong Kong to China (PRC) in 1997 after the British 99-year lease expired as the end of the British Empire. While the Empire is surely gone, the Commonwealth remains. And while the United Kingdom is still an important country and a strong ally of the U.S., it is a mere shadow of its former self.

The above covers four former major powers. There are many others, including the Greek/Macedonian Empire (modern-day Greece and Macedonia) and the Persian Empire (modern-day Iran). These empires ruled much of the known world in their time. However, today, Greece has a weak economy and is in very poor financial condition. In addition, Iran has a weak economy and a totalitarian government.

The above examples of past great powers serve to reinforce the fact that we must learn from the past and others, and prepare for the future. It is tough to become a great power or superpower. It is even tougher to stay one! We must take steps to make sure that the U.S. will stand the test of time, not for ourselves, but for future generations of Americans.

CHAPTER 4

THE GREATEST POLITICAL DOCUMENT IN HISTORY

The U.S. governance system is based on what I believe is the greatest political document in the history of man — The U.S. Constitution. That document was forged as a result of conflict (i.e., The Revolutionary War) and compromise (e.g., the Federalists vs. Anti-Federalists debates). While the Constitution has been amended 27 times over the years, it is based on a number of timeless principles and values that have helped to make America exceptional.

The U.S. Constitution was not the first governing document for the new nation that was created when the 13 colonies defeated their mother country, England, to gain independence. The initial governing document in the U.S. was called the Articles of Confederation. That document was written in 1777 but not adopted until 1781. A central concept of the Articles of Confederation was the recognition of the power and sovereignty of the states. As a result, the powers vested in the central government were limited and proved to be inadequate over time.

The lack of adequate central power was made particularly evident in connection with Shays' Rebellion of August 1786 to June 1787, which involved an armed rebellion in western Massachusetts. Shays' Rebellion was stoked by a debt crisis when the state of Massachusetts tried to raise taxes on individuals and trades to fund the debt arising from the Revolutionary War. Shays' Rebellion provided fuel to Alexander Hamilton and other Federalists who sought a stronger federal government. It also caused General George Washington to come out of retirement and to participate in the Constitutional Convention in Philadelphia. That convention lasted from May to September 1787.

After extensive discussion and debate, the U.S. Constitution was approved by a Constitutional Convention on September 17, 1787 (Constitution Day) and sent to the 13 states for ratification. The Constitution was ratified by the requisite number of states on June 21, 1788 and became effective on March 4, 1789. The contents of the Constitution were the subject of significant discussion and debate, in particular with regard to the proposed powers that would be granted to the new federal government. There were strong points of disagreement between the Federalists (e.g., Alexander Hamilton, John Jay, James Madison, and John Marshall), who supported a strong central government, and the Anti-Federalists (e.g., Patrick Henry, Thomas Jefferson, James Monroe, and George Mason), who advocated for a more limited central government with certain rights being retained by the states. The Anti-Federalists also protested the lack of an express enumeration of specific rights to protect individual liberties in the original Constitution. These differences were the subject of various writings (e.g., The Federalist Papers) and heated debate in the Constitutional Convention, as well as in each of the state legislatures as part of the ratification process. In the end, the Federalists' position prevailed in adopting the initial Constitution. However, additional individual liberty protections (Amendments 1-9) and states' rights were preserved (10th Amendment) when the Bill of Rights (the first 10 amendments to the Constitution) was incorporated into the Constitution.

The Bill of Rights was largely drawn from George Mason's (an anti-Federalist) Virginia Declaration of Rights. James Madison (a Federalist) wrote the amendments in 1789 when they were approved by Congress and sent to the states for ratification. Ultimately, 10 of the originally proposed 12 amendments that were sent to the states for consideration were ratified on December 15, 1791. The two that were not ratified related to a formula for determining the size of the House of Representatives based on the population of the states, and the basis for determining when Congress can change its pay. The second item ultimately became the basis for the 27th Amendment that was ratified in 1992.

While the Constitution was born out of conflict, it included many compromises. Six key compromises stand out with regard to the original Constitution. First, the creation of a republic (which is a representative form of democracy rather than a direct democracy). Second, adoption of three branches of government in order to achieve important "checks and balances" and avoid an excessive concentration of power. Third, the creation of a bicameral legislature (i.e., the Senate and House of Representatives) to balance the interests of the large and small states. Fourth, the selection of what is now Washington, DC as the capital, which at that time was centrally located among the 13 states. Fifth, assumption of all state debts at the federal level to create a financial "level playing field" among the states at the beginning of the republic. Sixth, a decision to allow slavery and to count each slave as three-fifths of a person for purposes of determining the number of members of the House to be allocated to each state.

I believe that the first five of the above compromises were wise and have largely stood the test of time. I also believe that, while the sixth may have been necessary at the time in order to keep the states together and achieve ratification of the Constitution, it was morally wrong. As we know, slavery was the primary issue that resulted in the Civil War in 1861, and it was ultimately banned via the 13th Amendment that was adopted in 1865. The 14th and 15th amendments, which related to post-Civil War issues and voting rights, were adopted in 1868 and 1870, respectively, and provided additional protections. However, it took many more years before additional civil rights were adopted via legislation (e.g., Civil Rights Acts of 1870, 1871, 1875, 1957, 1960, 1964, 1968, 1987, and 1991; Voting Rights Acts of 1965, 1970, 1975, 1982, and 2006; and the Fair Housing Act of 1988).

Interestingly, two key concepts and words did not appear in the Constitution. The word "God" and words "political parties" are not included. While God is referenced in the Declaration of Independence, that word is not contained in the Constitution. Arguably, the reason was because the Declaration of Independence used the inalienable rights conferred by God as a basis to justify separation from oppressive rule by the King of England, while the Constitution was designed to be a secular governing document. Although God is not expressly referenced, most founders believed in God, and they also believed in the "separation of church and state." As a result, they included in Article VI of the Constitution a provision noting that "no religious test shall ever be required as a qualification to any office of public trust under the United States."

With regard to political parties, the Founding Fathers did not originally intend for politics to be partisan although there were significant ideological differences among the founders. Our first president, George Washington, refused to belong to a political party, which he referred to as factions. In fact, one of the four warnings in his Farewell Address related to factions.

One important item that did not receive much attention during the Constitutional Convention was the rights of women. While women were counted as citizens and for representation purposes, they were not accorded the right to vote. This was not rectified until adoption of the 19th Amendment in 1920. Additional protections for women were incorporated into the Civil Rights Act of 1964. While there was an attempt to adopt a women's Equal Rights Amendment beginning in the 1970s, not enough states ratified it within the prescribed time frame. There has recently been discussion about reviving that effort.

In 1789, married women did not have the right to own property in their own names. Interestingly, this provision served to discourage marriage if a woman was independently wealthy and/or self-supporting. This limitation did not begin to change until 1839 when Mississippi, and eventually other states, adopted various Married Women's Property Acts. From a personal perspective, until recently my wife, Mary, and I jointly owned a historical townhome in Old Town Alexandria, VA that was built in 1800. Interestingly, we discovered through research that the first owner of the townhome was a free Black single woman who owned a laundry business. My wife and I found this to be both unusual and fascinating and, as a result, we donated the related research material to the Black History Museum in Alexandria when we sold the townhome in 2019. They were very happy to have it.

I recently discovered a very troubling example from my direct Walker line's past when conducting genealogical research. Specifically, in the mid-1800s my great-great-great-grandfather, John W. Walker, a poor farmer who married well, inherited a plantation and 24 slaves from his father-in-law in Tuscaloosa, Alabama. He was married to Elizabeth Pate, whose father was very wealthy. Since she was married, her father left his "property" to John Walker. This was a sad shock to me. After all, I believe that slavery was morally wrong. Interestingly, I discovered that up to 50 free Blacks worked on the plantation after the Civil War and until it was abandoned in the early 1890s.

From an education attainment perspective, I am only the second Walker in my direct line to graduate from college. My father, David S. Walker, Jr., was the first. All of my direct Walker line American ancestors prior to my father were of very modest means and were farmers, ministers, or miners by occupation. The ownership of this plantation, which was worked by slaves, did not last long, and the slaves were freed by the end of the Civil War. Many stayed to work and others joined them as free persons after the war.

Returning to the Constitution, it is also important to reflect on the Preamble of the Constitution. While the Preamble was not actually voted on by the Constitutional Convention, it was drafted and inserted after the vote to help reflect the intent of the founders. The Preamble reads as follows:

> "**WE THE PEOPLE** OF THE UNITED STATES, in order to form a more perfect union, **establish** justice, **insure** domestic tranquility, **provide** for the common defence, **promote** the general welfare, and **secure** the blessings of liberty to ourselves and our **posterity**, do ordain and establish this Constitution for the United States of America."

Importantly, the bolded words noted above have different meanings that arguably were intended to convey a different degree of responsibility and authority to the federal government by the founders. For example, the words "establish," "insure," "provide," and "secure" seem to convey more responsibility and authority to the federal government. On the other hand, the word "promote" would seem to be designed to ensure that the federal government encouraged related actions short of the federal government actually providing certain benefits or services directly. Finally, the use of the word "posterity" clearly noted the founders' desire to consider the implications of acts that were taken, or failed to be taken, on future generations of Americans.

In considering the meaning of these key words in the Preamble, it is also important to remember that power was not only separated between three branches at the federal level (i.e., legislative, executive, and judicial) but also between levels of government (i.e., federal and states). In this regard, it is also important to remember the words of the 10th Amendment:

"The powers not delegated to the United States by the Constitution, nor prohibited by it to the States, are reserved to the States respectively, or to the people."

The above language seems to be consistent with the idea that the states are sovereign entities that are closer to the people. As a result, they should have more ability to decide what types of "general welfare" related actions should be taken within their respective states provided that such actions do not otherwise violate the Constitution, including any adopted amendments to the original document.

As we look at the federal government and the actions of the federal government today, it is clear that it has expanded far beyond what our founders would have envisioned. It is also clear that states' rights have largely been eviscerated. Sadly, it is also evident that our country has strayed from many of the key principles and values on which it was founded and that made it exceptional.

Beyond the express words in the Preamble and the document itself, it is important to remember that the Constitution was based on a number of principles and values that were designed to stand the test of time. These included such principles and values as:

- Limited but effective government
- Individual liberty and opportunity
- Personal responsibility and accountability
- Rule of law and equal justice under the law (with the initial exception of slaves and women!)
- Fiscal responsibility and intergenerational equity

The above principles and values are generally consistent with an important psychological theory: Maslow's Hierarchy of Needs. In 1943, Abraham Maslow published a paper entitled "The Theory of Human Motivation." That paper outlined a hierarchy of human needs. I learned this in college psychology class, and it has always stuck with me. As I was taught, the most fundamental human need is "self-preservation" and the ultimate desire is "self-actualization."

The U.S. is a land of unparalleled freedom and opportunity. This is generally consistent with the concepts of "self-actualization" and securing the blessings of liberty to ourselves and our posterity. In my view, a person with a good education, positive attitude, strong work ethic, and solid moral and ethical values has virtually unlimited potential.

With regard to self-preservation, the government has an affirmative responsibility to establish justice, provide for the common defense, and insure domestic tranquility. Establishing justice includes a responsibility to prevent discrimination and help ensure equal opportunity. At the same time, the government cannot ensure equal results. Those results are dependent in large part on the willingness and ability of the individual and their family to capitalize on the opportunities presented in the country and our society. We must remember that America is far from perfect, and it never will be perfect. However, we must strive for continuous improvement in order to "create a more perfect union." I have written more on this subject in Chapter 9.

There is another key element that is worth considering from the early days of our republic. When George Washington declined to run for a third term, he gave a famous farewell speech. In that speech, he outlined four important warnings. In today's language they are:

- Avoid foreign wars
- Avoid excessive debt
- Avoid regionalism
- Avoid factionalism

As we look back, it is clear that we have not listened very well. We have engaged in a number of foreign wars over the years even though they were not always the result of a declaration of war by the Congress under the Constitution. Some of these wars were the result of us being attacked (e.g., the Spanish–American War, WWI, WWII, the Global "War" on Terrorism [GWOT], and second Gulf "War"), and some were designed to protect freedom of the seas (e.g., the War of 1812, the Barbary Pirates "War"). Some were designed to help defend others (e.g., the Korean "War," the Vietnam "War," the First Gulf "War"), and one was a major internal conflict (the Civil War).

While some of these "wars" were clearly justified, others were not. All of these cost American lives and treasure to varying degrees. In my view, other than a temporary and limited action to protect American interests, the U.S. should never invade another country or its territory and seek to topple its government unless Congress officially declares war. In addition, any such declared war should be financed, to the extent possible, by a temporary tax in order to ensure that the American public has a direct stake in the conflict, to prevent extended and costly actions with no clear end (e.g., the Vietnam "War," and the GWOT, including our actions in Iraq and Afghanistan), and to prevent the further mortgaging of our country and protect the future of our children, grandchildren, and future generations of Americans.

While the U.S. avoided excessive levels of debt until WWII, the assumption of high levels of debt as a result of that war was justified and later rectified when debt held by the public/GDP declined from 106% in 1945 to about 35% in 1980. In fact, to defeat the most powerful military on earth and to achieve adoption of the U.S. Constitution, which included assumption of all states' debt at the time, total federal debt held by the public/GDP was only about 35%. In addition, until WWII, this ratio rarely exceeded 40%, even during WWI and during the Great Depression. However, the U.S. will soon have a ratio of debt held by the public/GDP in excess of the levels of debt at the end of WWII, and much of that debt is not justified. It seems that America has become addicted to debt.

The U.S. used to run deficits and accumulate debt during times of war, serious recessions, and during national emergencies. However, today the U.S. regularly runs deficits and accumulates debt during peacetime, when the economy is growing, and when we do not have any national emergency. This approach is irresponsible, unethical, and immoral. It must stop, and much of this book includes specific ideas about how we can do so.

What about regionalism? The primary failure in this regard was the inability to resolve the slavery issue and the resulting Civil War. However, in recent years, regionalism is starting to spring up again, especially in connection with the increasing flight from northern states to southern and western states due to climate considerations, state tax/financial challenges, and other issues. At times, some states talk about seceding (e.g., California) and forming their own country. Importantly, we already fought a bloody and costly Civil War over secession and we surely do not want to fight another one. However, while no state has the right to secede, Texas retains the right to divide into up to five states as part of its admission to the union. And why might Texas ever want to do that? With five states they would get 10 versus two U.S. Senators. The five new states should also receive the same total number of members in the House of Representatives since House members are determined by population.

Finally, let's talk about factionalism. When Washington spoke of that, he was referring to political parties. Importantly, while Washington was a Federalist philosophically, he refused to belong to a political party. In fact, Washington and other founders were concerned that one day, duty of loyalty to a political party might trump (no pun intended) duty of loyalty to our country. Can you imagine that?! Today, it looks more and more like Washington was right, which is one reason that a growing plurality of voters, including my wife and me, are political independents.

Since a lot of this book addresses the financial and fiscal challenges facing the United States and how to address them, it is appropriate to review some of the key related provisions in the Constitution. Some of the most important ones in plain English are as follows:

- Under Article I of the Constitution, Congress has the "power of the purse" and control over "fiscal policy" (i.e., taxes and spending). While the president proposes a budget, Congress disposes and enacts all related spending/appropriations bills. Under the Constitution, no public funds may be spent that are not authorized and appropriated by law.
- Under Article I, all tax bills must begin in the House of Representatives, whose members are elected every two years versus every six years in the Senate.
- Under Article I, a regular state of account of receipts and expenditures of all public money shall be published from time to time. Interestingly, the first consolidated financial statements of the U.S. Government were not published until the 1990s.

- Under Section 4 of the 14th Amendment, the only two financial items that are guaranteed by the U.S. Constitution are U.S. public debt, including interest thereon, and Union Civil War pensions.
- Importantly, there are two fiscal-related matters that you will not find in the U.S. Constitution: There is no "balanced budget" requirement, as is the case for all but one state (Vermont), and there is no credit card limit.

The above provisions are important and will be discussed further later in this book.

While our Declaration of Independence is somewhat akin to a birth statement for the nation, our Constitution is somewhat akin to a marriage contract between states and the federal government. A contract that outlines the rights of the federal and state governments as well as the people. Like a marriage contract and related pledge, failure to abide by it can result in separation or irreparable harm. We must not let that happen.

In summary, while our country's current governance model was founded based on the greatest political document in history, we have strayed from the founders' original intent, and the principles and values on which our nation was founded and that made America exceptional. It is important that we return to those timeless principles and values so our future can be better than our past. This book includes a number of specific ideas of how we can and should do so.

CHAPTER 5
THE EVOLUTION OF AMERICA SINCE 1789

The United States has grown steadily in size, scope, power, and influence over time. At the founding of the American republic in 1789, the new country was comprised of 12 states with a population of about less than 4 million. Rhode Island did not become the 13th state until 1790. In 1789, all U.S. territory was east of the Mississippi River. The Spanish controlled Florida, the French and Spanish held much of the territory west of the Mississippi, and Russia controlled Alaska. At that time, the British controlled Canada and the Spanish controlled Mexico.

Over the years the U.S. moved west and acquired significant additional land, which later became states, through either purchase (e.g., Louisiana Purchase from France in 1801, Florida purchase from Spain in 1821, Gadsden purchase from Mexico in 1854, and Alaska purchase from Russia in 1867), through war reparations (e.g., Treaty of Guadalupe Hidalgo with Mexico in 1848), or annexation (e.g., the Republic of Texas in 1845 and Hawaii in 1898). The U.S. did acquire additional territory as a result of past wars (e.g., Cuba, Philippines, Puerto Rico, and Guam after the end of the Spanish–American War in 1898). However, unlike many great powers in the past, the U.S. has not fought wars with the express desire to involuntarily and permanently incorporate these territories into the U.S.

Given the above, the total number of states has grown from 12 in 1789 to 50 today, and the total U.S. population has grown from less than 4 million to more than 330 million in 2019. The U.S. is now the third largest country in land area on the globe, exceeded only by Russia and Canada, and has the third largest population, exceeded only by China and India.

From an economic perspective, the U.S. grew from fledgling nation with a largely agricultural-based economy and an estimated $189 million (or about $5.1 billion in 2019 dollars) of gross domestic product (GDP) in 1790 to a highly diversified economy with a GDP of about $21.4 trillion in 2019. The U.S. had the largest economy in the world based on nominal (not inflation adjusted) GDP in 2019 but ranked second behind China in purchasing power parity (PPP)-based GDP in 2019. The use of PPP in comparing the U.S. and China is more relevant than typically is the case, since the U.S. economy is market-based and dominated by private-sector enterprises, whereas China has many state-owned enterprises (SOEs) and can exert much more control over companies than the U.S. can. This is an especially important issue when comparing defense spending and pandemic responses.

U.S. per capita GDP in 2019 was number seven in the world at $65,111 versus the global average of $11,355. China and India still lag far behind the U.S., but they have made major gains in the last 20 years and are continuing to make gains.

From a diplomatic perspective, in 1789 the United States was largely focused on internal affairs and only had formal diplomatic relations with four countries (i.e., Britain, France, Spain, and the Netherlands). The U.S. did not engage in significant international/multilateral activities until the early 1900s. U.S. entry into WWI in 1917 was a major factor in assuring an allied victory over the Central Powers (i.e., Germany, Austria/Hungary, Ottoman Empire, and Bulgaria).

At the end of WWI, President Woodrow Wilson was a strong advocate for the League of Nations, but the U.S. Senate declined to ratify the related international agreement. U.S. international engagement declined between WWI and WWII, especially during the Great Depression years (1929–1939). The U.S. was thrust back onto the international scene with the outset of WWII in 1939. The U.S. formal entry into the war in 1941 was decisive in helping to achieve an allied victory over the Axis powers (i.e., Germany, Japan, and Italy).

At the end of WWII, the U.S. was the only major nation that was not subject to serious devastation as a result of the war, and its industrial base was intact. The U.S. represented about 50% of global GDP and possessed the most powerful military with the Soviet Union being the only other major military power. Given the U.S.'s economic position, the dollar became the world's dominant reserve currency as a result of the Bretton Woods Agreement in 1944. In addition, the U.S. supported the creation of the United Nations (UN) in 1945. The U.S. became the host country for the UN with 51 initial member countries. The U.S. also became one of the UN's Permanent Security Council Members along with the United Kingdom, France, the Soviet Union (now Russia), and China (now the PRC). Over time UN membership has expanded to over 190 nations and the UN has created a number of affiliated organizations (e.g., the World Health Organization, Food and Agricultural Organization, United Nations Education, Scientific and Cultural Organization, World Bank, International Court of Justice, and International Monetary Fund). These UN-related institutions have been supplemented by a range of other international institutions designed to promote peace, prosperity, democracy, global trade, rule of law, and a range of other elements associated with the so-called "liberal order." But, as noted in the Chapter 1, things started to change in the twenty-first century and, as a result, the future could be very different.

In 2019, the U.S. had diplomatic relations with more than 190 countries around the globe (number two behind China). In addition, the U.S. had a leadership position and played a key role in virtually every major international organization in the world (e.g., United Nations and its affiliated organizations). The U.S. also had free trade agreements with 20 countries and military alliance agreements with a number of countries (e.g., ANZUS [Australia and New Zealand], Japan, NATO [most European countries and Canada], New Zealand, Philippines (being reconsidered), and the Rio Treaty [most Central and South American countries], and South Korea). Interestingly, the Southeast Asia Treaty Organization [SEATO] that involved Australia, France, New Zealand, Pakistan, the Philippines, Thailand, the United Kingdom, and the U.S., was dissolved in 1997.

From a military perspective, the U.S. had less than 1,000 active duty military personnel in 1789 and they were all located in the U.S. The states had various militias that were designed to supplement the standing Army, as necessary. In 1789 the Navy was very small and the Marine Corps was suspended between 1783 and 1798. A separate Navy Department was reauthorized and organized in 1798 with an estimated strength of about 1,850 active duty personnel. The Marine Corps was reauthorized and organized in 1798 with less than 100 active duty personnel. By 1798, the Army had risen to about 4,000 active duty personnel.

The all-time high for total active duty U.S. military personnel was about 12 million in 1945 split between the Army, including the Army

Air Corps (est. 8.3 million), the Navy (est. 3.3 million), and the Marines Corps (est. 470,000). In 2019, the U.S. military had more than 1.3 million total active duty personnel (est. Army: 470,000; Navy: 325,000; Air Force: 325,000; and Marine Corps: 185,000) and about 800,000 total Guard and Reserve personnel (est. Army Guard/Reserve: 525,000; Navy: 58,000; Air Force Guard/Reserve: 175,000; and Marine Corps: 38,000). The Coast Guard, which is under the Department of Homeland Security during peacetime, had about 42,000 active duty personnel and about 6,000 reserve members in 2019. In 2019, the U.S. military was generally viewed as the most capable and experienced fighting force in the world, and the U.S. had military bases in 35 countries around the globe.

From a cultural perspective, the U.S. was largely viewed as a minor and backwater nation with little to no international influence in 1789. Over the years, international awareness of the U.S. and the influence of American culture grew immensely. Today, no nation rivals the U.S. in global cultural influence (e.g., individual liberties, movies, music, food, and clothing). Other countries have significant influence in some dimensions, but not nearly as many as the U.S.

There are a number of major reasons why the U.S. has done so well since its founding. America has benefited from both geographic and demographic comparative advantages. From a geographic perspective, most U.S. territory is inhabitable and in a temperate region that facilities agricultural activities and allows the U.S. to be self-sufficient pertaining to energy, water, and food supplies. The U.S. is also blessed with an abundance of land and many natural resources for expansion and development.

From a security perspective, the U.S. is only bordered by two nations (Canada and Mexico) with which it has had positive relations for more than 170 years. In contrast, China is bordered by 14 nations, including Russia. The U.S. also benefits from having three large bodies of water that separate it from most nations (Atlantic Ocean, Pacific Ocean, and Gulf of Mexico).

From a demographic perspective, the U.S. has been a magnet for individuals who seek both freedom and opportunity since its inception. Until recent years, the U.S. has had an above-average birth rate for an industrialized nation. The U.S. is the most diverse country on earth and is comprised of people of many races, religions, ethnicities, national origins, and other factors. This represents a significant comparative advantage to the U.S. in international affairs and helping to build bridges between other countries and cultures.

With regard to economics, the three primary factors that drive economic growth are human capital (number of hours worked, which is heavily influenced by the nature and size of the working age population), financial capital, and innovation that drives productivity improvements. All three of these factors worked in favor of the U.S. for many years. However, demographic trends are changing, huge government deficits reduce capital available for private investment, and the U.S. now has much more international competition in connection with technological and other innovations, especially from China.

The U.S. political system is stable, although dysfunctional at times, and the U.S. Constitution, supplemented with the rule of law, governs all private and public activities. In particular, the Bill of Rights within the U.S. Constitution is designed to protect individual liberty while safeguarding against an overly intrusive government.

From a broader global perspective, during the post-WWII or so-called Pax Americana era when the U.S. was the only true superpower, the world has benefited greatly. For example, a number of global organizations have been formed (e.g., United Nations), the "Cold War" ended, the world has avoided another global conflict, and no nuclear weapons have been used. Deaths from military conflicts have plummeted from about 100 per 100,000 persons to less than .5 per 100,000 persons. Death from famine has plummeted from about 395 per 100,000 persons to about 3 per 100,000 persons. Polio has been virtually eliminated, and great progress has been made on a number of other infectious diseases. Infant mortality has declined, life spans have increased significantly, and there has been a dramatic reduction in global poverty rates. Literacy rates have improved and technology is expanding and enabling the availability of information and education rapidly. Finally, democracies have expanded in the aftermath of the colonial era. In summary, much progress has been made, and yet much remains to be done.

Finally, there are some key philosophical issues that will affect our future. In the early days of writing this book, my wife, Mary, brought an opinion piece to my attention that I found to be very disturbing and thought-provoking. It was written by Garret Geer and was entitled "Are We Playing Right Into Their Plan?" At first glance one might think that it was referring to China or some other country. However, it was referring to the huge and growing ideological divide in the U.S. The piece focused on the writings of Saul Alinsky, and the following is a direct excerpt from his opinion piece.

"There are eight levels of control that must be obtained before you are able to create a social state. The first is the most important.

1. **Healthcare:** Control healthcare and you control the people.
2. **Poverty:** Increase the Poverty level as high as possible; poor people are easier to control and will not fight back if you are providing everything for them to live.
3. **Debt:** Increase the debt to an unsustainable level. That way you are able to raise taxes, and this will produce more poverty.
4. **Gun Control:** Remove the ability to defend themselves from the government. That way you are able to create a police state.
5. **Welfare:** Take control of every aspect of their lives (Food, Housing and Income).
6. **Education:** Take control of what people read and listen to - take control of what children learn in school.
7. **Religion:** Remove the belief in the God from the government and schools.
8. **Class Warfare:** Divide the people into the wealthy and the poor. This will cause more discontent, and it will be easier to take (tax) the wealthy with the support of the poor."

Do the above points sound familiar? Are they consistent with the principles and values on which our nation was founded and that made America exceptional? The truth is, how America resolves this huge philosophical difference will have a major impact on whether our future will be better than our past. Many elements of this fundamental philosophical difference were also evident during the 2020 election cycle. More on the 2020 election cycle in Chapter 20.

Importantly, Alinsky referred to himself as a socialist. However, socialism can be compatible with individual liberty and a democracy. The fact that Alinsky refers to the creation of a "police state" makes it pretty clear that his philosophy was more akin to the practices employed by communist and fascist states.

In summary, the U.S. has grown from a minor nation in 1789 to a global superpower in 2020 with unparalleled economic, diplomatic, military, and cultural influence around the globe. However, the U.S. faces a range of serious security, fiscal, philosophical, and other challenges that serve to threaten its future and that must be addressed. This book will cover many of them and will also offer a range of sensible solutions.

CHAPTER 6

TWO PIVOTAL YEARS

As noted earlier in this book, COVID-19 has had significant health, economic, fiscal, national security, and other impacts on our nation. It will also have significant long-term implications. Prior to the actions taken in connection with COVID-19 in 2020, there were two years of particular significance in connection with expanding the size and scope of federal government, undercutting states' rights, and demonstrating that federal policymakers had lost fiscal sanity. Those two years are 1913 and 2003, and the related actions are described below.

1913

In 1912, the U.S. federal government spending was only 2% of the economy (GDP). In that year, Congress also controlled (appropriated) 97% of all federal spending. The only "mandatory spending" item was interest on the federal debt. The other types of statutory and formula-driven (i.e., mandatory spending) programs that exist today (e.g., Social Security, Medicare, and agricultural subsidies) had yet to be enacted into law.

Three things happened in 1913 that served to expand the size and scope of the federal government and undercut states' rights. They were as follows:

- Adoption of the 16th Amendment, which allowed for the adoption of a national income tax.
- Passage of the Federal Reserve Act, which created the U.S. Federal Reserve System (the Fed).
- Adoption of 17th Amendment that provided for the direct election of U.S. Senators rather than them being appointed by state legislatures.

Prior to the adoption of the federal income tax as a result of the 16th Amendment, the federal government raised most of its revenue from duties and tariffs. The one exception was during the Civil War. However, the adoption of the 16th Amendment meant that the federal government had a new source of steady revenue that could be adjusted from time to time. This new and adjustable source of revenue resulted in increases in federal spending over time.

The adoption of the Federal Reserve Act and creation of the Federal Reserve in 1913 was designed to create an independent entity that could provide a safer, more flexible, and stable monetary and financial system that hopefully would be beyond partisan politics. The Act was a result of a banking crisis that caused many bank failures and the depositors losing their savings. The resulting political compromise set up a decentralized central banking system that was designed to help balance the interests of private banks and the general public. For many years, the Federal Reserve limited its actions to basic monetary policy (e.g., setting lending rates to banks) and overseeing the financial integrity of the banking system. The Federal Reserve's initial primary goals were to help maximize employment and keep inflation levels low.

In more recent years, the Federal Reserve has engaged in a number of actions designed to serve as the lender of last resort for banks, including for non-U.S.-based financial institutions (e.g., Deutsche Bank, Royal Bank of Scotland) as a result of financial crisis and the Great Recession in 2008–2009. More recently, the Federal Reserve has engaged in a range of additional and unprecedented actions as a result of COVID-19 that includes purchasing both corporate and municipal bonds for the first time. In addition, the Federal Reserve has purchased trillions of dollars in federal Treasury securities during the past 10 to 15 years in an effort to hold down interest rates. In my view, this is troubling since, in effect, it represents self-dealing. By that I mean the Fed buying Treasury debt rather than relying on the market to set rates based on the supply and demand and bids by unrelated parties.

Through holding down interest rates, the immediate pain associated with increased federal debt has been moderated. This has caused policymakers, the press, and the public to be less concerned with rising debt levels since total interest costs as a percentage of the budget have not increased significantly since the 1980s due to a decline in interest rates to historically low levels. This reduced concern about deficits and debt has served to fuel additional federal spending and periodic tax cuts. It has also served to increase the risk of a loss of confidence by investors that would cause significant inflation and/or another fiscal or dollar devaluation crisis over time. Given the interconnectivity and interdependence in today's world, such a crisis would not be confined to the U.S.

The direct election of U.S. Senators was a result of a populist movement in the early 1900s. In fact, a number of states passed resolutions calling for this change and got within one state of the number required for a state-led Constitutional Convention under Article V of the U.S. Constitution. However, Congress did not want to lose control of the process and preempted a state-led action by passing a related constitutional amendment that was sent to the states and was ratified.

While the direct election of Senators may have been a populist measure, in hindsight, it also served to help fuel growth in the size and scope of the federal government and undercut states' rights. Why? Because prior to the direct election of U.S. Senators they were appointed by state legislatures. While this was a less democratic process, it did result in much greater protection of states' rights. Why? Because if U.S. Senators did not respect states' views and protect their rights, they were not likely to be reappointed. Today, U.S. Senators do not have to worry about this factor. As a result, the federal government's role has expanded dramatically, despite the 10th Amendment to the U.S. Constitution.

2003

When I became Comptroller General of the United States and head of the GAO in 1998, the federal government was running a budget surplus. It may be difficult to believe, but the federal government actually ran a budget surplus for four straight Fiscal Years (i.e., 1998–2001). Those days are gone! I hope not forever.

We are all aware of the tragic events of September 11, 2001. If you were alive, you probably also remember where you were when you found out about the planes that flew into the Twin Towers of the World Trade Center in New York City. For me, I was at the GAO and actually saw the second plane hit the second tower live on television. We also know that a third plane hit the Pentagon and a fourth plane crashed in Pennsylvania when the passengers decided to fight back against the terrorists. By doing so, they sacrificed their lives but probably saved the U.S. Capitol from destruction.

As a result of the tragic events of September 11, 2001, the undeclared Global War on Terrorism (GWOT) began. The costs associated with that "war" coupled with slower economic growth and other factors resulted in deficits of varying magnitudes for Fiscal Years 2002 until today. While it is difficult to declare a formal war on a non-nation state, it should be done when invading a sovereign nation, especially when one of the purposes is to achieve a regime change. Failure to do so arguably violates the U.S. Constitution.

While deficits during times of "war" are understandable and possibly even necessary, running deficits when the economy is growing, the country is at peace, and there is no national emergency is irresponsible, especially if the size of the deficit exceeds the growth of the economy. Unfortunately, the federal government now runs deficits of varying magnitudes on a recurring basis and, based on reasonable assumptions, is expected to continue to do so for the indefinite future.

And how have the size of the federal government and the control of the federal budget changes been since 1912? Total federal spending as a percentage of GDP has grown from 2% in 1912 to 21% in 2019 and rising. In addition, the percentage of annual spending controlled by Congress through the annual appropriations process has declined from 97% in 1912 to 29% in 2019 and is continuing to decline.

Three things happened in 2003 that demonstrated federal policymakers had lost their fiscal bearings. These three things were as follows:

- A second round of tax cuts (the first round being in 2001) that were supposed to "pay for themselves" but fell far short of doing so.
- The U.S. invaded a sovereign nation (i.e., Iraq) without declaring war and without raising taxes to help finance it.
- Medicare was expanded to include prescription drugs that added about $8 trillion in new unfunded obligations when Medicare was already underfunded by about $19 trillion.

One of the biggest misrepresentations in fiscal policy is that "tax cuts pay for themselves." In reality, not all tax cuts are equal, and very few, if any, tax cuts actually pay for themselves. By that I mean that you generate more total revenue after the tax cut than you otherwise would have. Nonetheless, in early 2003 President Bush sought and Congress passed a tax cut designed to stimulate the economy in the short term. At the time of consideration, the nonpartisan Congressional Budget Office (CBO) estimated that the legislation would increase the federal deficit and debt by about $350 billion over 10 years. Given recent actions, that sounds like "chump change" today! The legislation had some positive short-term effect, but it was not accompanied by spending cuts and fell far short of paying for itself. As a result, it added to federal deficits and debt.

In October of 2003, the United States invaded Iraq, allegedly because Iraq had ties to Al Qaeda and was stockpiling non-nuclear weapons of mass destruction (WMD). Both of these claims proved to be false. At that time, Vice President Cheney also alleged we should not worry about the cost because the Iraq "war" would "pay for itself." Does this sound familiar?

Vice President Cheney was probably hoping that the oil-rich Gulf States in the Middle East would underwrite the cost as they had in the 1990–1991 first Gulf "war" (Operations Desert Shield and Desert Storm). However, that war was to counter Iraqi aggression (i.e., invasion of Kuwait and threatened invasion of Saudi Arabia) and was widely supported by most Gulf States. In contrast, the second Gulf War (the Iraq War) that started in 2003 involved an invasion of an Arab state that was not widely supported within the region. As a result, after many years of fighting, the Iraq war and subsequent occupation cost thousands of American lives and trillions of dollars, and the financial cost was just charged to the nation's credit card. And did we leave after we had defeated the Iraqi military and toppled the government? No, we stayed for many years and still have troops in the country.

While Saddam Hussein was clearly a bad person, the evidence shows that he did not sympathize with or harbor Al Qaeda, and he clearly hated the leadership in Iran. After all, Iraq and Iran fought a bloody war to a stalemate in the 1980s. Therefore, prior to the U.S. invasion, in which our son participated as a Marine Corps officer, Iraq actually provided a deterrent to Al Qaeda and a valuable check and balance against the greater ambitions of Iran. While we won that "war," the elimination of Saddam Hussein served to empower Iran and destabilize the region. Today, rather than Iraq being a check and balance against Iran, Iraq's government is largely under the influence of Iran. In addition, Syria is a mess.

Finally, in December of 2003, Congress passed and President Bush (43) signed legislation that added prescription drug coverage (Part D) to Medicare. While something needed to be done to address this large coverage gap in Medicare, in my view, it should have been done as part of a broader Medicare reform plan. After all, Medicare already had a $19 trillion unfunded obligation and the new benefit added an estimated $8 trillion dollars to that number. As a result, we dug our Medicare financial hole deeper.

While, unlike most government cost estimates, the initial cost of the prescription drug benefit was not as high as originally estimated, based on the 2020 Medicare Trustees Annual Report, the related unfunded obligations still amount to $8 trillion. Under current fiscal policies, these costs are being passed on to our children, grandchildren, and future generations.

And why did the prescription drug benefit pass in December 2003 as a standalone piece of legislation rather than as part of a broader Medicare reform plan that would have also addressed the existing unfunded obligations? The answer is simple. Politics and punting! Prescription drug benefits were expected to be a major issue in the 2004 elections and the Republicans wanted to "take it off the table" despite the price tag. In addition, most politicians, especially career politicians, do not want to make tough choices unless and until they have to. Why? Because they want to keep their job and they do not think that the American people can handle the truth or accept tough choices. As discussed in Chapter 13, they are wrong and COVID-19 should serve as an increased impetus for action.

Most politicians today have little problem making more promises, cutting taxes, and spending more today even though it may serve to mortgage our future and increase our longer-term risk. They also tend to punt on addressing tough choices that require additional taxes and/ or spending cuts for as long as possible. This reminds me of character Wimpy from the Popeye cartoon series who used to say, "I will gladly pay you Tuesday for a hamburger today." That sounds a lot like our current political system. In addition, many current politicians assume they will be out of office when Tuesday finally comes. But Tuesday will eventually come, and hopefully before a major crisis forces action.

Arguably, each of the above three actions was fiscally irresponsible, and collectively they were fiscally reprehensible. They also serve to demonstrate how short-sighted and cavalier our elected officials have become about our nation's finances and their stewardship obligation to future generations of Americans. This must change, and "We the People" need to make sure that it does!

CHAPTER 7

AN OPPORTUNITY SQUANDERED: THE SIMPSON–BOWLES COMMISSION

My previous best-selling book, *Comeback America: Turning the Country Around and Restoring Fiscal Responsibility* (Random House, 2010), was published in early January 2010. Among many things, that book recommended the creation of a transpartisan commission on fiscal responsibility and sustainability to help "set the table" for an up-or-down vote on needed tax and spending actions designed to restore fiscal sanity. Later in January, fiscal responsibility and sustainability-related legislation was debated in the Senate. That legislation would have created a statutory commission that would make a package of related recommendations that would have been subject to an up-or-down vote in Congress, without any amendments. In late January 2010, that bill failed in the U.S. Senate by a vote of 53-46 when six Republicans who had co-sponsored the legislation voted against it. As a result, they had a lot of explaining to do!

After the legislation failed in the Senate, President Barack Obama (D-IL) formed the National Commission on Fiscal Responsibility and Reform by executive order. Since the Commission was not formed by legislation, it could not include a requirement for a vote by Congress on its recommendations. However, then-Speaker Nancy Pelosi (D-CA) and then-Senate Majority Leader Harry Reid (D-NV) committed to bringing the Commission's recommendations for an up-or-down vote if they achieved the required supermajority voting requirement. Specifically, the Commission set up by President Obama required that three-quarters, or 14 of 18, of the Commission members had to vote for the package of recommendations in order for them to be adopted by the Commission. This very high threshold did two things. First, it required that any set of recommendations had to have significant bipartisan support, given the composition of the Commission. Second, it enabled a relatively small number of Commission members to scuttle any recommendations for whatever reason(s) they may have. The first of these concepts had merit. The second did not.

According to President Obama, the purpose of the Commission was to identify "policies to improve the fiscal situation in the medium term and to achieve fiscal sustainability over the long run." I was pleased to see this action by President Obama since I had noted the need to address our mounting debt burdens and the possible need for a Commission when President Obama called on me during a special White House Conference on fiscal sustainability in the spring of 2009. I was, however, disappointed when only one political independent was appointed to the Commission. The appointed independent was a good person but by no means an expert on fiscal issues.

The 18-member Commission was comprised of 12 Members of Congress (six from the House and six from the Senate) and six private citizens. It included nine Democrats, eight Republicans, and only one independent. This despite the fact that independents represented a plurality of registered voters at the time, a plurality that has grown since then. Former Clinton White House Chief of Staff Erskine Bowles (D-NC) and former Senator Alan Simpson (R-WY) were named as co-chairs. The other members were Dave Cote (R), Honeywell CEO, Ann Fudge (I), former Young & Rubicam CEO, Andy Stern (D), former president of the Service Employees International Union, Alice Rivlin (D), former Office of Management and Budget (OMB) and Congressional Budget Office (CBO) Director, and former Vice Chair of the Federal Reserve, Senator Richard Durbin (D-IL), Senator Max Baucus (D-MT), Senator Kent Conrad (D-ND), Senator Judd Gregg (R-NH), Senator Tom Coburn (R-OK), Senator Mike Crapo (R-ID), Rep. John Spratt (D-SC), Rep. Xavier Bacerra (D-CA), Rep. Jan Schakowsky (D-IL), Rep. Paul Ryan (R-WI), Rep. Jeb Henserling (R-TX), and Rep. Dave Camp (R-MI). Bruce Reed (D), Chief of Staff to Vice President Joe Biden, was named by President Obama as Executive Director for the Commission.

The Commission first met on April 27, 2010, and issued its final report on December 1, 2010. The report was issued after the updated paperback version of my book was published in October 2010. In total, the Commission held six public meetings, all of which were in Washington, DC. It took testimony from a number of parties, including the Chairman of the Federal Reserve, Director of OMB, Director of CBO, and three current or former GAO officials. While I was somewhat surprised that I was not asked to testify, my recently published book (which was sent to all Commission members), along with my numerous testimonies on the topic when I was Comptroller General of the United States, and my being prominently featured in the critically acclaimed documentary *I.O.U.S.A.* in 2008 were probably more than enough information regarding my views for them to digest. In addition, GAO's expressed views were based on policies developed during my tenure as Comptroller General of the United States and head of the GAO.

As time went on, the Commission came to be referred to as the Simpson–Bowles Commission, which were the names of the two co-chairs. Some people questioned why it was not referred to as the Bowles–Simpson since the Democrats controlled the White House and both Houses of Congress and Bowles was the Democratic co-chair. I was told that the reason was because a shorthand for Bowles–Simpson was BS and they did not want the Commission to be referred to as the BS Commission. I am sure you know what people would say that BS meant. Just one example of how words and acronyms matter.

On November 10, 2010, the co-chairs presented a package of recommendations for consideration by the full Commission. Those recommendations included a number of specific spending cuts and tax increases that were designed to reduce debt held by the public/GDP from a little over 60% at the outset to 60% by 2025 and declining to 40% by 2035 and declining thereafter. At the time, CBO projected that debt held by the public/GDP would rise to 80% by 2035 and continue to rise. And where are we today? CBO estimated in January 2020 that it could rise to 180% by 2050. And that was before COVID-19! As discussed previously, the impact of COVID-19 alone will cause debt held by the public/GDP to rise by at least 25 percentage points due to increased spending, reduced revenues, and a decline in GDP. CBO estimated in April 2020 that debt held by the public/GDP is likely to be about 108% by the end of 2021, and that was before what is likely to be another round of coronavirus-related legislation.

COMMISSION RECOMMENDATIONS

The co-chairs' package included a number of important and controversial recommendations that involved both raising taxes and cutting spending from current and projected levels. In total, the co-chairs' package reduced the projected deficit by nearly $4 trillion over 10 years as compared CBO projections. These reductions related to the below categories:

- Cutting projected discretionary spending by about $1.67 trillion over 10 years by imposing discretionary spending caps without providing details regarding how to accomplish that.
- Almost $1 trillion in additional revenue over 10 years through comprehensive tax reform that broadened the tax base and reduced marginal tax rates for both corporations and individuals, raising the gas tax, and changing the basis for calculating cost of living for indexing tax brackets.
- About $340 billion in health care savings over 10 years through a variety of actions while also proposing a goal of limiting the long-term health care growth rate to GDP growth+1% without enough specifics regarding how to achieve it.
- About $215 billion in mandatory savings over 10 years by changing the basis for calculating the Consumer Price Index (CPI) for federal benefit programs, reforming the military and civilian retirement systems, reducing farm subsidies, reducing student loans, and various other reforms.
- About $240 billion in Social Security savings by gradually increasing the early and normal retirement ages to 64 and 69, respectively, by 2075 and indexing the eligibility to life expectancy thereafter, increasing the payroll tax cap, changing CPI indexing, slowing the growth in benefits for medium- and high-income workers, and requiring that all state and local workers hired after 2020 be included in Social Security.
- Budget reforms that included caps in total federal spending at 21% of GDP and total federal revenues at 20% of GDP. At the time

federal spending was about 23% of GDP and federal revenues were about 14.6% of GDP.

- An estimated $675 billion in savings over 10 years due to reduced interest costs resulting from adopting the above reforms.

A number of the proposed changes were controversial among the Commission members and several special interest groups. It should be no surprise that Americans for Tax Reform opposed tax increases, even though the proposal included reductions in marginal income tax rates, or that AARP expressed concern about proposed changes to Social Security, Medicare, Medicaid, and several other social welfare programs, or that the military/industrial complex expressed concerns about reductions in defense spending. All of these items needed to be "on the table" in order to restore fiscal sustainability then, and even more so now. On the other hand, Tea Party supporters expressed concern that the proposed changes to social insurance programs were too little and not being phased in fast enough.

On December 1, 2010 the formal Commission proposal was unveiled and on December 3, 2010 the Commission members voted on the proposal. Unfortunately, only 11 of the 18 members voted for the proposed package. This represented a majority but it was three votes shy of the three-quarters requirement. Five Republicans and five Democrats, as well as the sole independent, voted for the proposal while four Democrats and three Republicans voted against it.

Importantly, President Obama did not support the Commission's proposals even though he created the Commission. His failure to use the "Bully Pulpit" that only a president has seriously harmed the ability to achieve the required number of votes on the Commission.

Members who voted "No" generally did so either because they opposed raising taxes or opposed the proposed changes to social insurance and safety net programs. This is no surprise but it is frustrating. Why? Because both must be done to varying degrees in order to come up with a politically feasible package that will achieve a reasonable and sustainable debt held by the public/GDP goal. That is even more the case in 2020, especially after the adverse impacts caused by COVID-19. Unfortunately, most Republicans do not want to raise taxes and most Democrats do not want to reduce spending, which leads to a stalemate. Even worse, all too frequently the political compromise is to cut taxes and increase both defense and nondefense spending without reforming mandatory spending programs (e.g., Social Security, Medicare, and Medicaid), which represent the biggest part of our spending problem.

Since the three-quarters vote requirement was not met, Congress did not consider the Commission's package of recommendations. However, in the spring of 2012, a House bill was introduced that was based largely on the Simpson–Bowles recommendations. It was overwhelmingly defeated by a vote of 382-38. This vote serves to demonstrate the degree of difficulty in achieving needed reforms. It also serves to reinforce the need for a fiscal responsibility amendment to the Constitution that will force action. This proposal will be discussed further in Chapter 14.

In July of 2012, the Committee For a Responsible Federal Budget (CRFB), of which I was a board member from 2008–2017, created the Fix The Debt (FTD) initiative at the urging of Senator Alan Simpson and Erskine Bowles. The FTD initiative was co-chaired by Senator Judd Gregg (R-NH), a former Commission member, and Governor Ed Rendell (D-PA). FTD raised more than $10 million, largely from major corporations, in an effort to try to influence the 2012 presidential and congressional elections. Their goal was to re-raise the Simpson–Bowles proposal and urge its consideration by the next president and the next Congress.

FTD engaged in a range of speaking and media engagements, advertising, and social media activities. While it was an important and worthwhile effort, it was not successful. One of the primary criticisms of the FTD effort was that it was funded largely by donations from major corporations and was advocating for a reform package that included tax cuts for large corporations. That charge was an overly simplistic and slanted view, but it was somewhat effective.

FTD partnered with the Concord Coalition during 2016 on a joint initiative entitled "First Budget." That initiative included holding a number of Town Hall-style forums in Iowa and New Hampshire to try to raise visibility on the fiscal issue. It also included a range of articles, op-eds, and radio interviews, as well as a publication that could be used by individual citizens to ask questions directly to the candidates.

CRFB published a number of fiscal analyses and a comparison of the presidential candidates' positions on major fiscal issues in 2010, 2016, and plans to do so for 2020. However, as of August 13, 2020, FTD was not planning to engage in any "on the ground," "outside the Beltway," or special media efforts in connection with the 2020 election cycle. Evidently, FTD is waiting for a time when both the president and Congress might be willing to address the fiscal issue in a meaningful manner. Among other things, that will require the creation of a new Commission with new players that hopefully is designed in a way that learns lessons from the Simpson–Bowles Commission effort. Some of those lessons and ways to address them are noted below.

The Simpson–Bowles Commission was an important and good faith effort. While a significant majority of their recommendations had merit and deserved serious consideration, there were a few co-missions and omissions that I expressed concern about once the report was released.

They included:

- The Commission recommended imposing a cap on federal revenues at 20% of GDP. While I fully agree there is a limit as to how much Americans and U.S. businesses should be taxed in order to encourage economic growth and assure that we are competitive internationally, the 20% cap did not seem realistic given known demographic trends, rising health care costs, tax levels at the time (i.e., 14.6% of GDP in 2010), and political feasibility considerations.
- The Commission recommended limiting total federal spending to 21% of GDP. While I fully agree that some caps on federal spending are appropriate, for the reasons noted above, and the fact that federal spending had already exceeded 23% of GDP at the time, I did not believe the proposed level was feasible. As discussed later in the book, you cannot cap interest expense and you can reform Social Security in a manner that you do not need a hard spending cap for that program. Other than those two items, there should an annual cap on all other spending. Importantly, as noted in Chapter 14, imposing overall and enforceable caps on total federal revenues and spending would likely require a constitutional amendment.
- The Commission did not have nearly enough recommendations in connection with how to control health care costs over the longer

term. Health care represents the fastest-growing program-related expense. Every other major industrialized country on earth, including Sweden, has a basic level of health care for all *and* caps annual health care spending by the government. No country should write a "blank check" for health care. This is an especially important point given the overall spending cap referenced above.

- In addition, given the importance of national defense and the fact that it cannot be delegated to lower levels of government or the private sector, we should provide a minimum of 3.25% of GDP for annual defense spending. Any additional funding could be provided in the event of a declared war or when there are clear and compelling national security reasons to do so. However, any additional funding decisions should be made on an annual basis.

There are a number of lessons to be learned from the Commission effort as well. The following are just a few:

COMMISSION STRUCTURE

- While a Commission will be needed to "set the table" for the tough tax and spending choices that Congress and the president must act on, the next Commission must be statutory in order to gain buy-in from both the Congress and the president up front.
- The Commission should be transpartisan in nature. That means it should have more political independents who are knowledgeable and respected in connection with fiscal matters and fewer elected officials. Rightly or wrongly, the reality is that elected officials who are affiliated with one of the major parties, of which all but three out of 535 are in 2020, will not be viewed as being objective by the general public. At the same time, in the end, Congress and the president must act and therefore some elected officials and potential Cabinet officials should be part of the process. For example, eight members of Congress, two from each side of the aisle in both houses of Congress, the Secretary of the Treasury, the

Director of OMB, and eight qualified members of the public, of which at least three should be political independents.

- Only two-thirds of the members of the Commission should be required to vote for the package of recommendations in order for them to be voted on by the Congress. If two-thirds is good enough to override a presidential veto it should be good enough for a set of Commission recommendations.

- Each House of Congress should be required to vote on any approved package of recommendations with limited amendments. Amendments should be required to achieve 60% support to be included in the final package, but the final package should only require a simple majority vote as is the case during the Budget Reconciliation process.

COMMISSION PROCESS

- Any Commission should conduct a significant amount of outreach, including conducting public hearings, outside of Washington as a supplement to public hearings held in Washington, DC. This outreach effort should be conducted to build public awareness and support for the need for reform and to help determine the proposed package of recommendations. Outreach efforts should also be conducted after a package of reforms is agreed to help the public and the press understand what was proposed and why it was proposed, and to counter interest groups with narrow agendas.

- The Commission should have a professional website and an active social and general media presence in order to inform the public and gather input from the public.

- The Commission should form an advisory group that would include representatives from a range of think tanks and special interest groups that cross the political and ideological spectrum. It is important for these groups to be heard and contribute. However, special interest groups should not have representatives on the Commission who might focus too narrowly on their key issues in a manner that might unduly undercut the ability to achieve the required two-thirds vote on a Commission package of recommendations.

- The Commission should never refer to itself using the name of any living person(s), including the sponsors of the legislation and the co-chairs. The related effort must rise above individuals and needs to be embraced by a wide range of individuals and groups, including elected officials, many of whom will want to claim credit. In this regard, it's important to remember one of President Reagan's famous sayings, "You can get a lot done if you don't care who gets the credit." We abided by that principle in connection with the 2012 $10 Million a Minute Tour, which will be covered in Chapter 13.

In summary, the Simpson–Bowles Commission did great work. It was very unfortunate that their recommendations did not receive the required supermajority vote and that, for the most part, they have not been adopted by Congress. I was also very disappointed when President Obama did not put the weight of his office behind the Commission's work and basically abandoned them after their appointment.

In my view, we will need another national fiscal responsibility and sustainability commission in the future. When such a commission is actually being considered, hopefully the above Commission structure and process-related recommendations will be both helpful and adopted.

CHAPTER 8
FEDERAL, STATE, AND LOCAL FISCAL FOIBLES

FEDERAL

As mentioned in Chapter 6, 2003 was a very bad year for federal fiscal policy. Three things happened then to demonstrate that Congress and the president had discarded concern over growing deficits and debt levels. While 2003 was a milestone year, 2019 was also a very bad year for fiscal policy. The following three things happened in that year as part of a "budget deal" that was included in the Bipartisan Budget Act of 2019:

- Increased spending and budget caps for both defense and nondefense discretionary expenditures for Fiscal Years 2020–2021.
- Extended the sequestration (automatic spending cuts) for certain mandatory spending programs through Fiscal Year 2029.
- Suspended the debt ceiling limit for two years through July 31, 2021.

The above was a bipartisan "compromise" between Republicans and Democrats. Like many recent compromises, it discarded fiscal prudence and involved giving both sides the spending increases they sought. The Republicans achieved an approximate $170 billion increase in spending caps for defense and about $140 billion in funding for Overseas Contingency Operations (OCO) for Fiscal Years 2020–2021. The Democrats achieved an increase in budget caps for nondefense discretionary spending of about $150 billion for Fiscal Years 2020–2021.

While Congress and the president had agreed to additional spending and increases in the defense and nondefense budget caps in the past, the increases in caps escalated dramatically for Fiscal Years 2018–2021. In fairness, the agreed-upon levels were below what President Obama's Fiscal 2012 budget request was for years 2018–2021.

The budget provisions calling for automatic cuts in selected mandatory spending programs that were scheduled to expire in Fiscal 2021 were extended until Fiscal 2029. Importantly, Social Security and Medicaid are exempt from these automatic spending cuts, and this type of approach has failed to achieve needed reforms in the related programs in the past. As a result, these sequester (automatic spending cuts) provisions are really more form than substance.

The debt limit was suspended through July 31, 2021. Stated differently, Congress and the president agreed to write a "blank check" until then. This was before the additional $3+ trillion in spending as a result of COVID-19. Candidly, the debt ceiling limit has not worked. The U.S. is the only major industrialized nation with such a limit. To demonstrate how badly it has failed, total debt has increased from $1 trillion in 1980 to more than $26 trillion as of the end of June 2020 and rising! The debt ceiling needs to be repealed and replaced with a public debt/GDP (gross domestic product) limit. More on this topic in Chapter 14.

STATE AND LOCAL

While this book is focused primarily on federal issues, it is important to understand that a number of state and local governments also face serious fiscal challenges. And as we all know, the law of gravity says that "bad news flows downhill." As a result, when the federal government eventually takes steps to restructure its finances, the resulting downdraft will adversely affect state and local governments to differing degrees. In fact, some recent tax reforms have already served to reduce the competitive posture of states that have very high state and local tax burdens. Specifically, the Tax Cuts and Jobs Act of 2017 limited the amount of deduction that individuals can take for state and local income, property, and sales taxes to $10,000 per year.

It is important to remember that states are sovereign entities under the U.S. Constitution. As a result, they are not currently covered by federal bankruptcy laws. There have been some recent debates regarding whether states can and should be covered, especially in the aftermath of economic and fiscal implications of COVID-19. In my view, providing an optional provision for states to use under the federal bankruptcy law would not seem to violate the Constitution. In the absence of such a provision, states have to figure out ways to put their finances in order and engage in financial restructuring, if necessary. In addition, contrary to the assertions of some, a state's decision to modify a state contract for its employees would not violate the Constitution. Because states are sovereign entities under the Constitution, the related contracts are between the states and public sector unions within the state.

While the federal government does not have a constitutional requirement to "balance its budget," 49 of the 50 states do have such a requirement, typically as part of their state constitution. The only state that does not have one is Vermont.

While you might think that such a requirement would ensure that states do not get into financial trouble, such is not the case. Why? Because of the way most states define a "balanced budget." Most define it according to a cash basis of accounting rather than an accrual basis. As a result, states just need to ensure they have enough cash to make required payments for the year.

So what would be the problem with the above? First, states can defer making payments, including pension contributions and aid to local governments and nonprofit groups. Second, they can draw from "rainy day funds," if any. Third, they can provide incentives to accelerate tax collections. Fourth, in some cases they even borrow (e.g., tax obligation bonds) in order to generate cash to make payments. Most importantly, they can make lucrative pension, retiree health care, and other promises to state workers and not fund them!

Unlike private sector employers that offer defined benefit pension plans, government employers (federal, state, and local) are exempt from the minimum funding requirements under the Employee Retirement Income Security Act (ERISA). They are also not covered by the pension insurance program operated by the Pension Benefit Guaranty Corporation (PBGC). I can speak to these issues with confidence since I have headed two of the three federal ERISA agencies. In addition, very few states provide state constitutional protections for pension benefits. The primary exceptions are Arizona, Illinois, Louisiana, Michigan, New Mexico, and New York. Most state and local pension and retiree health care benefits are provided and protected through contract law. As a result, they can be restructured in appropriate circumstances. All of these factors result in much greater benefit risk to employees and retirees that are covered by government pension plans in troubled states and localities.

Private sector retiree health care plans are not subject to minimum funding and anti-cutback provisions. Therefore, private sector employers have great flexibility in how they design, revise, or event terminate such plans. In addition, retiree health care plans are not insured. As a result, once private sector employers realized the economic cost of these benefits when the accounting for them changed in the late 1980s, they dramatically reduced or eliminated these benefits.

Given the above, due to the expense of retiree health care and the lack of funding requirements, unfunded retiree health care obligations can exceed unfunded pension obligations for many states and localities. While considerable attention has been focused on unfunded state and local pension benefits, not enough attention has focused on unfunded retiree health care benefits.

Based on many years of research and financial analysis, it is clear that the biggest financial and fiscal challenge facing the government at all levels is unfunded pension and retiree health care benefits. At all levels of government this includes employee-related pension and retiree health care, military, first responders, and other civilian personnel. At the federal level it also includes the two largest social insurance programs (i.e., Social Security and Medicare). In addition, at the federal and state levels it includes the portion of Medicaid that relates to long-term care for seniors.

A primary source for assessing the financial condition of the states is the work done by the Institute for Truth in Accounting (TIA), a nonprofit organization based in Chicago, IL. In the interest of full and fair disclosure, I am a member of TIA's Advisory Board.

I firmly believe it is impossible to adequately assess performance at any level (e.g., country, state, municipality, company, agency, nonprofit, team, or individual) unless you consider three elements. First, actual performance as compared to plan. Second, the trend in actual performance over time. Third, actual performance as compared to the relevant competitor or comparator (peer) group. This type of comparison needs to focus to the maximum extent possible on outcomes versus activities using common definitions and consistent methodologies.

The most recent TIA rankings of the states based on their accumulated surplus or (deficit/burden) per taxpayer are as follows:

1. Alaska: $74,200
2. North Dakota: $30,700
3. Wyoming: $20,800
4. Utah: $5,300
5. Idaho: $2,900
6. Tennessee: $2,800
7. South Dakota: $2,800
8. Nebraska: $2,000
9. Oregon: $1,600
10. Iowa: $700
11. Minnesota: $200
12. Virginia: ($1,200)
13. Oklahoma: ($1,200)
14. North Carolina: ($1,300)
15. Indiana: ($1,700)
16. Florida: ($1,800)
17. Montana: ($2,100)
18. Arkansas: ($2,300)
19. Arizona: ($2,500)
20. Nevada: ($3,100)
21. Wisconsin: ($3,200)
22. Georgia: ($3,500)
23. Missouri: ($4,300)
24. New Hampshire: ($5,000)
25. Ohio: ($6,600)
26. Kansas: ($7,000)
27. Colorado: ($7,200)
28. Washington: ($7,400)
29. Maine: ($7,400)
30. West Virginia: ($8,300)
31. Mississippi: ($10,000)
32. Alabama: ($12,000)
33. Texas: ($12,100)

34. New Mexico: ($13,300)
35. Rhode Island: ($13,900)
36. South Carolina: ($14,500)
37. Maryland: ($15,500)
38. Michigan: ($17,000)
39. Pennsylvania: ($17,100)
40. Louisiana: ($17,700)
41. Vermont: ($19,000)
42. New York: ($20,500)
43. California: ($21,800)
44. Kentucky: ($25,700)
45. Delaware: ($27,100)
46. Hawaii: ($31,200)
47. Massachusetts: ($31,200)
48. Connecticut: ($51,800)
49. Illinois: ($52,600)
50. New Jersey: ($65,100)

The above figures represent the surplus or (deficit/burden) of unrestricted assets as compared to current liabilities and unfunded promises based on the audited financial statements for the states for the year ended June 30, 2018. It is calculated on a per-taxpayer basis in order to facilitate comparison between states. It does not, however, consider the relative wealth (e.g., median household income) within each state, or the difference in assumptions used by various states in calculating unfunded pension obligations (e.g., discount rate based on assumed rate of return on pension investments).

Based on the latest TIA analysis of the states, 11 states have accumulated surpluses and 39 have accumulated deficits/burdens. There are some common denominators between many of the states that have accumulated surpluses per taxpayer. Many of them are states that are blessed with abundant natural resources, have smaller populations, and smaller state governments. Many of the states with huge accumulated deficits per taxpayer have large populations, larger state governments, and are not blessed with abundant natural resources. They also tend to be states with a much larger percentage of unionized workers with much more generous pension and health care benefits for public employees and retirees. Many of the states with the largest accumulated deficits also have higher tax and regulatory burdens, and costs of living. As a result, absent a significantly increased economic growth rate within the state and/or a rightsizing of government and restructuring of retirement and other employee compensation, their tax burdens are likely to increase further over time. This will make these states less competitive from an economic perspective over time.

As previously mentioned, the single largest financial challenge for most states, especially the most challenged states, is unfunded pension and retiree health care obligations. For example, New Jersey is rated last (number 50) in the latest TIA rankings, and $191 billion of their $235 billion in total liabilities and unfunded promises, or 81%, relate to unfunded pension and retiree health care obligations. In addition, total unfunded retiree health care obligations in New Jersey are close to the total amount of unfunded pension obligations. In some cases, total unfunded retiree health care benefits exceed total unfunded pension benefits (e.g., California) and for some states (e.g., New York) they far exceed them. If you want to find out more about your state, see www.truthinaccounting.org.

Other organizations also rate the financial position and fiscal health of the states using alternative methodologies. For example, George Mason University's latest (2018) bottom five ranked states are: Illinois (50), Connecticut (49), New Jersey (48), Massachusetts (47), and Kentucky (46).

During the time I served as a senior advisor to PricewaterhouseCoopers (PwC) Public Sector (now Guidehouse), we performed a separate analysis of the states that was more sophisticated for three reasons. First, it normalized the calculation of unfunded pension obligations by using a standard discount rate based on the rate that Moody's was using at the time (i.e., 5%). This made the unfunded pension obligations comparable. Second, we also considered the relative wealth of each state based on the median household income for each state. This resulted in somewhat different rankings of the states, but in all rankings, New Jersey, Illinois, Connecticut, and Kentucky were deemed to be among the most troubled states. Third, PwC also considered the relative competitive posture of the states based on several independent business surveys (i.e., CEO Magazine, Forbes, and CNBC). Those rankings placed states in one of five tiers, with Tier 1 being the best and Tier 5 being the worst. There was a general consensus among various rating organizations on the bottom four states. They and their competitiveness quintile rankings by tier were: New Jersey (5), Illinois (4), Connecticut (5), and Kentucky (4). Importantly, the competitiveness rankings were as of 2015 and have not been updated since I left PwC. It is, however, unlikely that they have changed very much since then.

Many municipalities also face serious financial challenges. TIA ranks large cities based on taxpayer burden, and their latest rankings include 75 cities, of which the following are the bottom five:

71. New Orleans: ($18,800)
72. Philadelphia: ($25,500)
73. Honolulu: ($26,400)
74. Chicago: ($37,100)
75. New York City: ($63,100)

Given the above, the financial burden for New York City alone would rank it as number 49 if it were a state, with only New Jersey being worse ($65,100). In addition, New York City residents need to consider the financial burden of the State of New York, which is ($20,500) for a total burden of ($83,600). And these numbers are before the effects of COVID-19, for which New York City was Ground Zero. These are two of many reasons why Mary and I did not live in New York City when I was based there.

CONNECTICUT: A RELEVANT CASE STUDY

The State of Connecticut is an example of what can happen when a government and its leaders lose their way. During the 1970s and most of the 1980s, Connecticut was viewed as an oasis in a very troubled region of the country. It was and remains a beautiful state, with a proud history, a wonderful location, and an excellent quality of life. It was fiscally responsible and very competitive, not just in its region but also within the entire country. Connecticut was home to the headquarters of many Fortune 100 companies. It did not have an income tax, did not overregulate, was investing in infrastructure, and was growing. In summary, things were good and the future was bright.

How do things look in 2020? Connecticut is consistently rated as one of the bottom three states in financial condition and in the bottom quintile in competitiveness. The state now has above-average income, estate and gift taxes, and high property taxes, much more significant regulatory burdens, a deteriorating infrastructure, and very high utility rates. As a result, many Fortune 500 companies have left the state and others are actively contemplating leaving. The state's population has been declining, and an increasing number of people have decided to vote with their feet, including my wife, Mary, and me in late 2018.

What happened? The state lost its way, and state leaders became complacent. They began to benchmark themselves against the surrounding states rather than the nation as a whole. Political leaders began to coddle to the public sector unions in order to gain and keep political office and maintain labor peace. In doing so, they agreed to unreasonable, unaffordable, unfunded, and unsustainable pension and retiree health care programs that seriously mortgaged the future of the state. In doing so, no one was at the "bargaining table" representing current and future taxpayers. The state dramatically expanded its social welfare programs, which included providing above-average benefits to illegals. In addition, when Puerto Rico was in crisis in the aftermath of Hurricane Maria in 2017, Connecticut actually advertised for Puerto Ricans to come to the state and touted its generous welfare benefits. Importantly, Puerto Ricans are American citizens and have the right to migrate anywhere in the U.S.

Given the above, due to declining revenues and growing mandatory spending, the state reduced or eliminated its pension plan contributions, tapped its "rainy day fund," and borrowed in order to "balance its budget." While this allowed the state to claim that it had met its constitutional requirement to balance the budget, the amount of debt and unfunded pension and retiree health care obligations skyrocketed. Importantly, these unfunded retirement obligations represent deferred taxes absent a significant resurgence of the state's economy and/or restructuring of its finances.

Connecticut is also a "land of disparities" where statewide averages are meaningless and misleading. The state has some of the wealthiest towns and poorest cities in the nation. It also has some of the best and worst school systems in the nation. It is one of only two states in the nation without county government. The other one is Rhode Island, which is the same size as a very large county in some states. As a result, cities and towns are largely on their own to deal with finances, schools, public safety, and other key needs. In fairness, the state does provide some funding to municipalities to help with education and other costs, and some small towns rely on the state police to protect and defend their citizens.

Unfortunately, some of the poorest cities in the state have followed the bad example of the state. Waterbury, Bridgeport, Hartford, and other cities have outrageous property tax rates and huge unfunded retirement obligations. As a result, they are uncompetitive and face a worse future absent a restructuring of their finances either through bankruptcy or otherwise. Enterprise zones targeted to these troubled cities can help, but they will not solve the problem. Tough choices are required to create a better future.

From a political perspective, one party has controlled the state legislature and the city councils of these troubled cities for more than 25 years, and that party is unduly reliant on public sector unions for political support. In addition, the state has not had a governor — of either major political party — who has been willing to take on the public sector unions and restructure the existing contractual arrangements in a manner that is fair and sustainable to all parties, including the taxpayers. The COVID-19 experience will only serve to make Connecticut's financial situation worse, and bad news at the state level will flow downhill to the troubled cities. However, as a result of COVID-19, there are some signs that wealthy New York City (NYC) residents may relocate to the wealthy towns in southwest Connecticut (e.g., Greenwich, Westport) near NYC. This will help but will not come close to making a real dent in Connecticut's structural financial challenge. Any such migration will also serve to increase disparities within the state.

Like the federal government, Connecticut is on an imprudent and unsustainable fiscal path. Unlike the federal government, it cannot print money or manipulate interest rates. It also cannot declare bankruptcy based on current federal law. As a result, without a change in the federal bankruptcy code, the governor needs to declare a "Fiscal State of Emergency" and move to restructure the state's finances in cooperation with the state legislature. This will include changing the current tax system, municipal aid formulas, and labor contracts, especially in connection with retirement plans. Unlike Illinois and certain other states, there are no state constitutional protections for the labor contracts that need to be restructured, and those who argue that the U.S. Constitution bars related actions are wrong. States are sovereign entities under the Constitution, and state contracts with private parties within the state are not covered by the "contracts clause" in the U.S. Constitution.

Restructuring the state's finances will require a governor who has the courage to do what is right for all citizens of Connecticut, for both today and tomorrow. It will also require a major public education and engagement effort along the lines of the $10 Million a Minute Tour, which is discussed in Chapter 13, to build the "burning platform" case and forge a consensus on a way forward. I hope that eventually comes to pass, for the sake of our many friends and others in Connecticut.

In summary, the federal government is not the only level of government that faces serious financial and fiscal challenges. These state and local level financial challenges are driven primarily by unfunded retirement obligations. It is time for policymakers at all levels of government to wake up and start making tough choices to put their finances in order. After all, most Americans have no desire to leave the U.S. However, most will leave a city or state unless they have family or a job that ties them there.

CHAPTER 9

RACIAL, ECONOMIC, AND POLITICAL DIVIDES

America is an exceptional nation comprised of people from all over the world who represent a broad range of races, religions, ethnicities, and personal preferences. The one thing that binds us together is the belief in freedom and opportunity. And the one thing that should guide us beyond each person's individual faith, if any, is the Constitution of the United States.

GROWING GAPS

Although America is a diverse country, there are growing gaps in our society that threaten to tear us apart over time. These gaps have various dimensions, including race, gender, income, wealth, and education.

As discussed previously, the adoption of the original U.S. Constitution was an exceptional and historic accomplishment. It did, however, require several political compromises in order to become a reality. Some of those made sense and others did not but were still necessary to achieve adoption of the Constitution based on the culture and conditions that existed at the time. In my view, the single most significant wrong was the lack of equal treatment of all races; that is, the continuation of slavery and the practice of counting each slave as three-fifths of a person. This was directly contrary to the words of the Declaration of Independence, which state "all men are created equal." It was also immoral. The second-biggest wrong was lack of equal treatment of both males and females; that is, not giving women the right to vote and not allowing married women to own property in their name.

The above wrongs were ultimately addressed either through constitutional amendments many years after the adoption of the Constitution and/or through both state and federal legislation over many decades. Slavery was abolished in 1865 as a result of the 13th Amendment to the Constitution. Unfortunately, it was only adopted after a bloody and costly Civil War. Women were given the right to vote in 1920 as a result of the 19th Amendment to the Constitution. As discussed previously, a number of civil rights pieces of legislation relating to minorities, women, and various personal preferences have been adopted both at the state and federal levels over the years. To date, the proposed Equal Rights Amendment (ERA) to the Constitution, which relates to women's rights, has not been adopted despite past attempts to do so.

Despite all of the above and the progress that has been made over the years, several societal tensions still exist. Arguably the largest remaining tension relates to racial discrimination against minorities, especially Blacks. While discrimination based on race, religion, gender, and other factors is illegal, there are differences between the law, ethics, and morality. In my view, the law is the floor of acceptable behavior. Ethical considerations represent a supplemental and higher calling than the law. Some professions, including mine as a CPA, have strong professional and ethical standards of conduct. From my perspective, the highest standard is a moral standard. I have always believed that all of us should reach for the ceiling and not crawl on the floor. Therefore, anyone who tells me that their proposed action is "not illegal" is not the kind of person I want to deal with.

I make the above points because even when something is deemed to be wrong by people with strong ethical and moral values, it may not be considered illegal in a court of law. As has been said many times, "You can't legislate morality." Or as James Madison said, "If men were angels no government would be necessary." In many cases, the U.S. has the right ideals, but some Americans do not live by those ideals.

A good example of this potential disconnect is what resulted in May 2020 when four Minneapolis policemen were involved in the arrest of George Floyd and his subsequent death due to asphyxiation. Importantly, all four officers were terminated from the force in a timely manner. However, no charges were filed by the district attorney until after a video of the incident appeared on social and mainstream media. The video made it clear that excessive force, as well as inappropriate and unapproved tactics, had been used by one officer and resulted in George Floyd's death. The video also made it clear that three other officers stood by and did little or nothing to stop the asphyxiation and subsequent death of George Floyd despite multiple pleas by George Floyd and from people who were on the scene and witnessing the incident. The video understandably resulted in outrage among a broad cross section of society, including my family. As a result of this broad-based public concern, the district attorney initially filed a Murder 3 charge against the officer who was responsible for George Floyd's death. This was subsequently changed to a Murder 2 charge, which, in my view, should have been the initial charge. Initially, no charges were filed against the three officers who stood by and did nothing. Subsequently, they were all charged with aiding and abetting in the murder.

The above event was just one of several prominent police incidents that have occurred in recent years involving the arrest of a nonwhite person that has resulted in the person's death. While the others received national media attention and resulted in some local protests, the deaths of George Floyd in Minneapolis in May and Rayshard Brooks in Atlanta in June resulted in more significant national media attention, as well as larger protests in a number of cities lasting many days. Most of the protests were appropriate and peaceful, although a vast majority of the protestors did not maintain social distancing and some did not wear masks as recommended by public health officials. Unfortunately, some participants engaged in violence and looting that, in some cases, may have been instigated and led by outside groups of anarchists (e.g., Antifa).

The above events presented challenges for politicians and law enforcement officials in balancing the constitutional rights of individuals to protest while enforcing the rule of law against those who were rioting and destroying property. Clearly, judicial reforms and changes in policing practices are needed in the aftermath of these deaths. It is also clear that racial tensions at home harm the image of the U.S. abroad, and our adversaries try to exploit this.

From a personal perspective, I strongly support the right of people to engage in peaceful protests, but I strongly oppose violence and the destruction of private or public property. Peaceful protestors should be protected, but those who engage in violence or destruction, no matter the reason, should be prosecuted to the fullest extent of the law.

With regard to racism, I think that Martin Luther King Jr. (MLK) had it right. People should be judged by the content of their character rather than the color of their skin. People who do not believe in this simple concept are probably racists, whether they know it or not, irrespective of the color of their skin.

While the above events are good examples of police abuse and the underlying racial tensions in America, there are several large and growing societal gaps that threaten our future economic growth, individual opportunity, and even domestic tranquility. They include our income, wealth, and education gaps.

A recent study by the Pew Research Center noted the following key points regarding income inequality:

- Over the past 50 years, the highest-earning 20% of U.S. households have steadily brought in a larger share of the country's total income.
- Income inequality in the U.S. is the highest of all G-7 nations (i.e., U.S., UK, Italy, Japan, Canada, Germany, and France) according to data from the Organization for Economic Cooperation and Development.
- The Black–White income gap in the U.S. has persisted over time.
- Overall, 61% of Americans say there is too much economic inequality in the country today, but views differ by political party and household income level.
- The wealth gap between America's richest and poorer families more than doubled from 1989 to 2016.
- Middle-class incomes have grown at a slower rate than upper-tier incomes over the past five decades.

Another recent Pew Research study on income and wealth noted that:

- Household incomes have grown only modestly in this century, and household wealth has not returned to its pre-recession level.
- Economic inequality, whether measured through the gaps in income or wealth between richer and poorer households, continues to widen.
- Household incomes have resumed growing (from a recent floor in 2011 with a significant acceleration in the past 3 to 4 years) following the Great Recession (of 2007–2008).

- The gaps in income between upper-income and middle- and lower-income households are rising, and the share held by middle-income households is falling.
- The overall wealth of U.S. families is yet to recover from the Great Recession.
- The richest families are the only group to have gained wealth since the Great Recession.

The above statistics do not consider the impact of transfer payments from various social welfare programs. As a result, the actual resources available to the poor and near-poor can be much greater than the statistics noted above. While these payments can significantly impact the amount of annual resources available to welfare recipients, they do not have any meaningful impact on the wealth gap.

Importantly, before COVID-19 hit, real wages were increasing and unemployment was at a 50-year low, including for Blacks and other minorities. Nonetheless, there are still significant income and wealth gaps in America. One prominent contributor to both of these gaps is the education gap in America.

According to a 2019 study by the Organization for Economic Cooperation and Development (OECD) on math and science achievement for 15-year-olds, China was rated number one in the world and the U.S. was rated number 25. East Asian countries held seven of the top 10 rankings. Canada tied with Taiwan for number eight. As is the case with other education rankings, Hispanics and Blacks in the U.S. did worse in these ratings than other races. As a result, these rankings are not good news for future U.S. competitiveness internationally and social equity domestically.

According to Statistica, about 90% of the eligible population had attained a high school degree in 2018. Asians and Pacific Islanders were at the highest level of attainment at 90.5% and Hispanics were at the lowest at 71.6%. As of 2018, about 35% of the eligible population had attained a college degree or greater. Again, Asians and Pacific Islanders were at the highest at 56.3% and Hispanics were at the lowest at 18.3%.

According to the Bureau of Labor Statistics, the degree of unemployment in 2019 bore a direct and inverse relationship to the level of educational attainment. Namely, the higher the level of education, the lower the unemployment rate. Specifically, the unemployment rates by level of education were as follows:

- Doctorate: 1.1%
- Master's: 2.0%
- Bachelor's: 2.2%
- Associate: 2.7%
- Some College: 3.3%
- High School: 3.7%
- Less than High School: 5.4%

A U.S. Census Bureau report noted that there is a strong degree of correlation between poverty and educational attainment. That report noted the following correlations in 2014:

Attainment Level	Poverty Rate
No High School Diploma	29%
High School Diploma	14%
Some College	10%
Bachelor's Degree or Higher	5%

These are all very revealing statistics. After all, we have moved from the agricultural age, to the industrial age, to the knowledge age in the United States. As a result, the amount and type of education one has is very important to obtaining a desirable job that can provide both an adequate amount of income and opportunity for advancement. At the same time, it is important to remember that not all colleges/universities and degrees are equal. In addition, education is a lifelong need, especially in a rapidly changing, highly competitive, and knowledge-based economy.

Another key factor relates to training and skills development outside the traditional education system. Germany does a very good job of assessing the interests and abilities of individuals and providing them with appropriate skills training to help them be successful and productive citizens in society.

In many cases this means obtaining training that prepares them for a trade, rather than obtaining a college education. It has worked well for Germany and its people. We need to learn from them and other countries to help us create a better future in America.

OUR DYSFUNCTIONAL DEMOCRACY

As noted previously, the U.S. is a republic that is a representative democracy rather than a direct democracy. As a result, we vote for people who are supposed to represent us and they vote on issues that are supposed to relate to the broader public interest. Direct democracies involve the people voting directly on issues, such as in the case of initiatives and referenda that are allowed in some states to resolve important public policy matters (e.g., term limits for state officials, property tax caps).

The U.S. currently has the longest-standing republic and is the second-largest democracy, exceeded only by India. At the same time, it is becoming more and more evident that the U.S. has become a republic that is neither representative of, nor responsive to, the general public. And why is that?

First, contrary to the wishes and of George Washington and many of the nation's Founders, many federal elected officials today are career politicians rather than public servants who leave their regular occupation for a temporary period of time to do public service and then return to their regular occupation. As a result, given the lack of congressional term limits and the power, privilege, and perks associated with federal elected office, many members of Congress want to keep their job for as long as they can.

Second, contrary to Washington's warning, factions (i.e., the two major political parties) have gained great power. As a result, all too often, the duty of loyalty to party trumps (no pun intended) the duty of loyalty to country. This despite the fact that the largest and growing plurality of voters do not belong to one of the two major political parties.

In the spring of 2020, Gallup polls estimated that 37% of registered voters nationally were unaffiliated (independent), 31% were registered Democrats, and 28% were registered Republicans, although there are major differences in party registration between states.

While it is unrealistic to expect that factions (e.g., political parties and special interest groups) will be eliminated, it is important to take steps to help ensure that private and partisan political interests do not prevail over the broader public interest. This can be accomplished through appropriate conflict-of-interest, transparency, campaign finance, and other reforms.

Third, technology has advanced to the degree that congressional and other districts can be drawn down to the block level in an effort to advantage one political party over another. This is referred to as gerrymandering. As a result, we now have situations where politicians pick their voters rather than voters picking their politicians. In addition, a vast majority of congressional seats are deemed to be "safe seats" whereby the elections are effectively resolved in closed-party primaries.

According to the Cook Political Report in the spring of 2020, only 73 of the 435 House seats were deemed to be in swing districts, meaning that a nominee of either party had a chance to win the seat in the general election. Therefore, 362 of the 435 seats were effectively decided in party primaries, where turnout is typically low.

According to Ballotpedia, 14 of 50 states had "closed" primaries for congressional races, meaning that only registered members of the applicable party could vote. Sixteen states had "semi-open" primaries, meaning that party members and unaffiliated/independent voters could vote in the primary. Twenty states had "open primaries," meaning that anyone could vote in a primary but a voter had to choose which party primary to vote in because they could only vote in one.

Closed-party primaries give a small minority of party activists, who tend to be more liberal or conservative than the overall voting population, a disproportionate influence on selecting the candidates that everyone gets to vote on in the general election. They can also result in two relatively unattractive choices being the only viable options from which to choose.

The gerrymandering of congressional districts is one of the primary reasons why there is such a huge split between what voters think of any one member of Congress versus Congress as a whole. In most elections, more than 90% of congresspersons who seek reelection win. At the same time, according to a May 2020 Gallup opinion poll, only about 31% of voters approve of Congress as a whole. The approval percentage of Congress dropped to 18% in late July 2020. Both of these public opinion figures are bad, but they are above the twenty-first century low of just 9% in November 2013.

The majority party in the Senate and House sets the agenda. In addition, party leaders make committee assignments and select committee leaders (i.e., chairs and ranking members). Furthermore, party members are expected to raise money for their reelection as well as for the party. Members who fail to tow the party line can be denied appointments on key committees and can lose the support of the party if they are challenged in a primary.

Fourth, there is too much money in politics. It costs way too much to run for federal office, and special interest group members who cannot vote have too much influence on elections (e.g., corporations, unions, selected nonprofit groups). In addition, elected members of the House typically spend 25% or more of their time raising money! As a result, many capable and caring people decide not to run for elected office.

Fifth, the 24/7 news cycle has caused many media outlets to hype issues and divide the people based on their personal political and ideological views irrespective of the facts, and without contextual sophistication. Today, there are too many "fact-free zones" in the media and few, if any, media anchors and commentators who are admired across a broad range of Americans. Stated differently, for those who are old enough to know, there are no Walter Cronkite's today. He was the nationally known and respected anchor for the CBS Evening News for many years. As President Lyndon B. Johnson once said, if he lost Walter Cronkite he had lost America! In addition, most media outlets lean to the "left" or "right" and gear their programs and coverage accordingly. And too many Americans select their preferred media source based on their own political or ideological perspective, which tends to harden their views and polarize the population along partisan and ideological lines.

As a result of the above and other factors, the country is very divided and Congress is stalled on too many issues unless a crisis forces them to act. This must change, and I will discuss some needed reforms later in this book.

CHAPTER 10

THE FEDERAL RESERVE, MONETARY POLICY, INFLATION, AND THE DOLLAR

THE FEDERAL RESERVE

At the beginning of the American republic, Alexander Hamilton and the Federalists won the debate with the anti-Federalists, led by Thomas Jefferson, regarding the need for a central bank. As a result, the First Bank of the United States was established in 1791. That bank ceased to exist in 1811 when its 20-year charter expired after an attempt to extend it failed. In 1816, a Second Bank of the United States was established, but it ceased to exist in 1836 when President Andrew Jackson declared the bank to be unconstitutional because he believed it gave the federal government excessive power and vetoed its recharter. This was one year after the only time in history that the United States had no national debt. That won't happen again!

The "free banking era" was when the federal government operated without a national bank, and covered the period between 1837 and 1863. During this period, thousands of state-chartered banks issued currency and provided credit without federal regulation. This was inadequate to finance the Civil War. Therefore, the National Banking Act was passed in 1863 and created a uniform national currency and mandated that only nationally chartered banks could issue currency. It did not, however, create today's central banking structure.

After the Civil War, runs on banks were fairly common. A "run" occurred when there were rumors that a bank did not have enough cash on hand to satisfy depositor withdrawal requests. If one bank failed and depositors lost money, a panic frequently occurred whereby more banks would fail and more depositors would lose money. As a result, there were a series of bank failures, especially during the period between 1873 and 1907.

In 1907, a major banking crisis happened. The crisis was stopped when J.P. Morgan, a very wealthy financier, used his private fortune to make emergency loans to banks and prevent their closure. This sparked the beginning of the banking reform movement.

In 1908, Senator Nelson Aldrich (R-RI) sponsored a bill with Representative Edward Vreeland (R-NY) that created the National Monetary Commission to study potential reforms to the financial system. In November 1910, six men held a secret meeting at the exclusive Jekyll Island Club in Georgia. The meeting was organized by Aldrich, Chairman of the Senate Finance Committee, and included A. Piatt Andrew, Henry Davison, Arthur Shelton, Frank Vanderlip, and Paul Warburg. J.P. Morgan was a member of the club and most likely arranged the meeting. At the time, the Jekyll Island Club was viewed as the most remote and exclusive club in the world. The meeting and its purpose were closely guarded secrets that were kept until the 1930s. But clearly, the issues raised by the National Monetary Commission were discussed. The National Monetary Commission report and the results of this meeting set the stage for adoption of the current Federal Reserve System.

The Federal Reserve System (Fed) was established by Congress in 1913 as a decentralized "central bank." It was created to provide the nation with a safer, more flexible, and stable monetary and financial system.

The Federal Reserve's 12 regions were set up in 1914. They are Boston, New York, Philadelphia, Cleveland, Chicago, Minneapolis, Richmond, Atlanta, Dallas, Kansas City, St. Louis, and San Francisco. Each regional bank monitors the condition of their local economy and the federal banking system in their region. Since the United States is such a large and diverse country, there are meaningful differences in economic growth, unemployment, and cost of living both between and within these 12 regions.

The Fed's role has evolved over time and most rapidly in recent years. Most change came from periods of economic instability such as what we are experiencing today. For example, the Great Depression of the 1930s resulted in passage of the Banking Act of 1935 that established the Federal Open Market Committee (FOMC), the Fed's monetary policymaking body. This act responded to resistance to the Fed taking much-needed actions to combat the Great Depression of the 1930s. Another example was in 1977 when Congress passed the Federal Reserve Reform Act during a period when the Fed was charged with being ineffective in dealing with inflation.

As a result, price stability was added as an express policy goal for the Fed. Without stable prices both people and businesses are hindered from making financial decisions by difficulty estimating future inflation rates and prices. Importantly, economies with stable prices are healthier in the long run.

On a personal note, the chairman of the Fed during the 1980s high-inflation period was Paul Volcker. He was a giant of a man in many ways, including his height, his courage, and his integrity. He made very tough choices to ensure a positive interest rate was earned on savings even after adjustments were made for inflation. That resulted in very high interest rates, but it also broke the back of inflation that began in the 1970s, which was fueled, in part, by a sharp increase in oil prices resulting from the oil crisis of 1973. Paul was also a fiscal responsibility advocate and encouraged me to take the position of chairman of the United Nations Independent Audit Advisory Committee. He passed in December of 2019 and will be remembered as a great public servant.

In 1978, Congress passed the Full Employment and Balanced Growth Act, which established the maintenance of full employment as a policy goal for the Fed. It also required the Fed to report to Congress on their current interest rate policy and goals twice a year. The last major piece of legislation was passed following the severe financial crisis of 2007–2008 when Congress passed the Dodd–Frank Wall Street Reform and Consumer Protection Act of 2010. More commonly known as the Dodd–Frank Act, this law affected the Fed in many ways. It changed the Fed's governance, made its operations more open to scrutiny, and expanded its supervisory responsibilities. It also increased bank capital requirements and necessitated drafting a dissolution plan called a "living will."

To summarize, the primary goals of the Fed today are to:

- **Promote economic growth:** This enhances individual opportunity, increases revenues, and helps the government to meet its constitutional responsibilities.
- **Promote full employment:** This enables individuals to "pursue happiness" and support themselves and their families while reducing unemployment and welfare costs to governments.
- **Promote stable prices:** This helps businesses and individuals plan without fear of losing significant purchasing power.

The Fed accomplishes the above three goals by performing the following four functions:

- Conducting the nation's monetary policy by influencing the supply and value of money while promoting favorable credit conditions and the pursuit of economic growth, full employment, and stable prices.
- Supervising and regulating banks and other important financial institutions to ensure the soundness of the nation's banking system while protecting the credit rights of consumers. This includes monitoring for systemic risk. This risk relates to factors that are associated with the movement of the market as a whole rather than a component of the market. An example is a movement in the overall Standard & Poor's (S&P) average rather than a single stock or industry sector within the S&P.
- Providing certain financial services to the U.S. government, U.S. financial institutions, and foreign official institutions while playing a major role in operating and overseeing the nation's payments systems.
- Serving as a lender during crises in recent years, not only to domestic banks but also to a broad range of other players, including foreign banks, insurance companies, corporations, state and local governments, and to an increasing extent the federal government.

MONETARY POLICY

For much of its existence the powers of the Federal Reserve were limited to regulation of the banking system combined with monetary policy decisions, including directly setting interest rates for its loans to banks (i.e., the discount rate) and open-market operations, which can result in changes to the supply of money. These were adequate tools for achieving its mission until recent years. However, the banking and resulting economic crisis of 2008–2009, as well as the COVID-19 public health and resulting economic crisis of 2020, have caused the Fed to engage in a number of large and unprecedented actions. As a result, another set of legislation may be coming after the COVID-19 crisis passes.

During the 2008–2009 banking crisis, the Fed engaged in unprecedented loans to both U.S. and foreign banks and insurance companies. It purchased several trillion dollars in U.S. Treasury securities in direct intervention into credit markets for the first time. It funded the rescue of American International Group (AIG), as well as the mortgage guarantee companies, Fannie Mae and Freddie Mac. Both Fannie Mae and Freddie Mac were private sector entities, not formally guaranteed by the federal government. However, the systemic risk associated with letting them fail was deemed too high so the Fed intervened. The Fed even guaranteed money market funds. These actions were designed to stabilize the financial system, support the economy, and hold down interest rates on U.S. debt. For the most part, they were effective but also set a troubling precedent.

As a result of the COVID-19 crisis, the Fed reversed its previous efforts to dispose of its sizeable Treasury holdings purchased in 2008 and 2009 and started again to purchase trillions of additional U.S. debt. It also engaged in a new unprecedented effort to purchase corporate, state, and local debt in order to help stabilize businesses and prop up troubled states and localities. Its willingness to purchase Treasury debt was engaged in seemingly without limit.

Irresponsible past fiscal policy, relatively weak economic growth, and increased market volatility have caused the Fed to engage in these unprecedented actions because it has largely used up the traditional tools in its toolbox. For example, the Fed discount rate was lowered to 0-.25% in 2020. In addition, federal fiscal policy (i.e., taxes and spending) has stimulated demand while adding substantially to the nation's debt burdens.

In fact, several Fed chairs understood the imprudence of recent fiscal policies and expressed concern regarding the need for Congress and the president to work together to address our current unsustainable fiscal path, which has been made much worse by COVID-19. For example, Fed Chairman Ben Bernanke used his first conference in 2011 to warn that the U.S. deficit was "not sustainable" and told political leaders they had to address it "as quickly and effectively as they can." As recently as November 2019, Fed Chairman Jerome Powell said, "The federal budget is on an unsustainable path, with high and rising debt. Over time, this outlook could restrain fiscal policymakers' willingness or ability to support economic activity during a downturn." These statements contrast with Fed Chairman Alan Greenspan's statement in 2001: "The time has come, in my judgement, to consider a budgetary strategy that is consistent with a preemptive smoothing of the glide path to zero federal debt or, more realistically, to the level of federal debt that is an effective irreducible minimum." At that time, we were experiencing budget surpluses expected to continue for more than 10 years. Those days are gone! In February 2020, former Chairman Alan Greenspan said, "Unless we bring those extraordinary budget deficits under control, history tells us this is going to be a much more rapid rate of price increases than we've seen." And that was before the adverse impact of COVID-19!

INFLATION: AMERICA'S ACHILLES HEEL

Inflation represents a sustained increase in the general price level of goods and services in the economy over a period of time. When inflation rises, each unit of currency buys fewer goods and services and the impact is compounded over the years, much like interest but with an opposite effect. Inflation represents an accelerated decrease in the purchasing power of money and a loss of real value to anyone holding the currency. Inflation penalizes savers and anyone living on a fixed income (e.g., seniors) while encouraging consumer borrowing. During periods of inflation, insurance companies experience loan withdrawals from whole life insurance policies and banks experience Certificate of Deposit withdrawals. Both happened during the Carter years. Inflation is particularly harmful to persons with significant savings in currency (e.g., bank accounts and Certificates of Deposit), especially today when interest rates paid are below the prevailing inflation level. The result is that savers may collect in effect a "negative" interest rate because interest paid annually is less than inflation, so interest received does not compensate for loss in value due to inflation. This is further complicated by the fact that the interest paid on savings is taxable, further reducing the return. As has been said, "inflation is the cruelest tax of all" since it is invisible to many and levied without consent.

The opposite of inflation is deflation, which represents a sustained decrease in the price level of goods and services. It has the opposite effect compared to inflation. The only time the U.S. experienced deflation was during the 1920s and 1930s. Deflation caused massive unemployment then because companies faced falling prices and cut workers to protect profits. The Federal Reserve has stated it will take all necessary action to ensure deflation does not occur again.

As shown in the below graphic from the Federal Reserve Bank of St. Louis, inflation has varied considerably in the U.S. but has not been a significant problem recently. Today the Fed has set a 2% annual target for inflation.

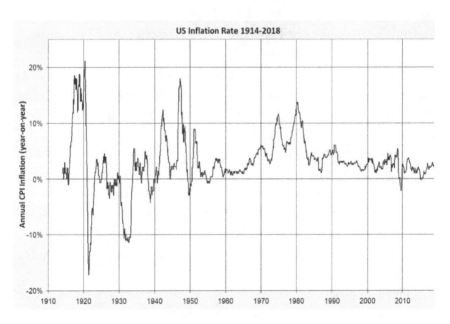

From a human behavioral perspective, if people fear that the value of money will decrease, they will tend to spend it more quickly. They will have less of an incentive to save unless interest rates rise consistently with, or in excess of, inflation. A noted, rising interest rates substantially increase the interest costs to the federal government. This is compounded when debt levels are also increasing.

An example of rampant and destructive inflation happened during the German Weimar Republic after WWI. At that time, paychecks were spent within days to avoid a complete loss value because prices were escalating rapidly. The resulting economic chaos caused considerable political instability, enabling Hitler to seize power and impose authoritarian control to get "the railroads running back on time" and restore order. He stoked nationalism and sought retribution for the tough terms imposed on Germany at the end of WWI. He retook the coal-rich Ruhr from France and Belgium. The ultimate result was WWII and huge human and economic destruction, as well as the horrific genocide imposed on Jews and other so-called "undesirables."

Returning to inflation-related issues, there are two types of inflation, demand pull and cost push. Demand pull is best described as too much money chasing too few goods and other items. It can be controlled by taking money out of the system through the Fed selling bonds in exchange for bank balances or cash. This drives up interest rates, which also reduces economic growth and demand.

The second type of inflation is cost push, which typically comes from increases in wages and/or commodity prices. One example is the energy crisis of 1973 when the price of oil went from $2 ($11.50 in today's dollars) to more than $35 ($109 in today's dollars) a barrel in 1980. The result was unprecedented "stagflation," slow economic growth combined with high inflation. In order to control inflation, the Fed reduced the money supply, which drove up interest rates, reduced economic growth, and reduced demand for oil. It also resulted in much higher unemployment. From a personal standpoint, my wife and I purchased a home McLean, VA in early 1981 and had a double-digit mortgage rate, as compared to today's historically low mortgage rates.

There is a generally accepted mathematical formula in economics that illustrates the key relationships between the supply of money and other variables that the Fed open-market operations deal with when acting to control interest rates and inflation. Specifically, the money supply, people's expectations regarding further inflation, and the future value of money, which impact their willingness to hold wealth in cash, save, and spend it. I have included a discussion of this formula in Appendix A for readers who want to better understand how these variables relate and why the Modern Monetary Theory (MMT) is inconsistent with this long-accepted formula.

THE DOLLAR'S IMPORTANCE AS A RESERVE AND TRADING CURRENCY

Today, approximately 60% of all central bank reserves and international trade transactions are denominated in dollars, making the dollar the world's largest reserve and trading currency. Being a reserve and trading currency helps to lower trade transaction costs and the cost of borrowing for the U.S. To become a leading reserve and trading currency, a currency must be freely traded and stable in value so that businesses can rely on the value of the payments they will receive in the future when engaging in transactions. The dollar's role as the primary trading currency is also supported by the Fed's development of the American electronic money transfer system (i.e., "Swift System") coupled with the Fed's efficient check processing services that are used to execute trade and financial transactions around the globe.

This primacy trading role of the dollar is also instrumental in imposing economic sanctions on both countries and individuals. For example, when the Fed refuses to serve a targeted country or individual as a result of economic sanctions, the target has to resort to alternative means for engaging in transactions. In the case of Iran, it resulted in a significant decline in the Rial (Iranian currency), reducing imports and driving up import prices, increasing inflation, reducing oil export revenues, and causing a serious recession.

The Chinese RMB or Yuan has risen to about 15% of global trade transactions. The RMB's rise, to date, has come largely at the expense of the Japanese Yen, the Euro, and British Pound. This may change in the future as China rises and the value of the dollar becomes less reliable due to increased uncertainty regarding growing ratios of U.S. debt held by the public/GDP (gross domestic product), and its adverse impacts on economic growth and job creation. For the Chinese RMB or Yuan to become a major reserve currency, its economy will have to continue to grow, inflation will need to remain low, confidence in political stability within China will have to increase, and their exchange controls will need to be removed. This is certainly possible, and indeed probable, before 2040. This, combined with China's development of its own electronic, digital "Swift System" denominated in RMB/Yuan, could enable China to impose its own economic sanctions. This could become a greater threat if the dollar's value becomes unreliable and subject to devaluations as the British Pound did during the immediate post-WWII period.

In times of economic or other uncertainty, investment capital tends to flow to stable reserve currencies. Today the dollar enjoys that reputation and is the "go-to" currency of choice during times of stress like 2008 and 2009 and today. This factor, combined with the Fed's huge purchases of Treasury securities, results in lower interest rates than otherwise would be the case in a fully "free market" absent direct intervention by the Fed. For example, during the banking and economic crisis of 2008–2009 many investors sold nondollar-denominated assets and bought dollar-denominated treasuries and other assets because they feared their nondollar-denominated assets would lose value compared to the dollar. This brought down dollar interest rates considerably then, and they have remained low ever since. However, as the British experienced after WWII, this "go-to" role and high-stability reputation will not always apply to the dollar unless America gets its financial house in order so the Fed does not have to keep employing extraordinary measures on a recurring basis, including self-dealing in Treasury securities.

These lower interest rates hold down, for the time being and absent inflation, the cost of financing the federal government's growing debt burdens. At the same time, it has the perverse effect of discouraging much-needed and long-overdue fiscal reforms. The MMT will only serve to further discourage action to address our large, known, and growing fiscal imbalances. As a result, and as discussed below, it is downright dangerous and serves to threaten the very existence of America as we know it!

Importantly, when excess inflation eventually reoccurs, the impact on the interest cost of the federal budget would be immediate and substantial. For example, since 2007 the U.S. debt held by the public has grown such that if rates were to return to the pre-crisis level, the interest rate paid on our public debt would increase about 4%, causing an immediate $800 billion in interest costs for the federal budget. That amounts to about a 20% overnight increase in federal spending for which we get nothing! And with every one percent rate increase, the interest costs rise another $200 billion based on today's debt levels. Unless something is done to restore federal fiscal responsibility, the Fed will continue to be pressured to keep rates low by buying U.S. debt, further increasing the inflation impact risk and the potential for a future interest cost shock.

MODERN MONETARY THEORY (MMT)

Fiscal irresponsibility has become so popular in some groups that a few economists have attempted to cloak it in academic respectability by espousing a new "Modern Monetary Theory." It basically states that deficits and debt levels do not matter as long as the U.S. can borrow in dollars and unless we experience excess inflation. Under that theory, the government should simply spend and "print money" while the Fed continues to purchase more Treasury securities. However, as discussed below, the unproven MMT is likely to result in excess inflation and higher interest rates over time and possibly much worse outcomes.

Some call it post-Keynesian economics, which is ironic because the political system has misused and misrepresented Keynesian theory for its own irresponsible and political purposes for some time now. Specifically, John Maynard Keynes, the prominent British economist, did not support running continuous deficits during times of economic growth, peace, and absent national emergency as we have for many years since WWII. Keynes believed the federal budget should be balanced over the economic cycle and debt should be used to stimulate the economy only in periods of collapsing demand such as what occurred in the 1930s. As a result, Keynes would understand the origins of MMT better than most from his perspective of having witnessed the misuse and misrepresentation of his original theory to achieve partisan and ideological ends.

As discussed previously, based on our current path, inflation will likely be our next serious challenge over time. In fact, if America fails to change course after the COVID-19 crisis passes, and the MMT gains acceptance, a spike in interest rates triggered by inflation will happen. It is not a matter of if; it is a matter of when and by how much. This is one of the reasons why I and many others, including Fed Chair Jerome Powell and former Treasury Secretary Larry Summers, do not accept the MMT.

The MMT reminds me of the time that I was on the Charlie Rose Show with Noble Prize-winning economist Paul Krugman. He asserted then that deficits and debt levels do not matter in the U.S. because we can just mint trillion-dollar coins to fund them! I thought that was "fluid logic" that did not pass a "straight face or common-sense test." When pressed to provide the historical and economic basis for such a theory, he could not do so. Fortunately, his theory did not gain any traction. Unfortunately, the new version of the trillion-dollar coin concept seems to be the MMT. Both represent counterfeit concepts.

The MMT is based, in part, on a misinterpretation of the Japanese debt experience. It is true that Japan has a much larger public debt/GDP level than the U.S., but Japan is very different from the U.S. in many ways. First, the calculation of publicly reported Japanese and U.S. public debt levels is not done on a comparable basis. Second, Japan's economic growth rate has been anemic for years as their debt burdens rose. Third, Japan's Nikkei stock market performed poorly for many years and fell precipitously when it became clear that they intended to borrow excessively starting in the late 1980s. Fourth, Japan has a much higher personal savings rate than America's, which has cushioned the economic impact somewhat. Fifth, a significant majority of Japan's debt is funded within Japan, but such is not the case for the U.S. Sixth, the Japanese consider it patriotic to invest in their government's debt even when it pays a negative interest rate. Finally, Japan is not a superpower with responsibility for supporting the world's largest reserve currency and global security, including Japan's security.

In her recent book, *The Deficit Myth* (Hachette Book Group, 2020), Dr. Stephanie Kelton, who is arguably the leading proponent of the MMT, notes that "money should no longer be viewed as a store of value." Dr. Kelton was also a senior economic advisor to Senator Bernie Sanders' (I-VT) presidential campaign. As a result, the MMT might help to explain why Senator Sanders was not concerned with explaining the cost of his "Medicare for All" or "free" college for everyone plans!

Anyone who has taken Economics 101 knows that the value of money is based on confidence in the issuer and the ability of the person who accepts it to exchange it to purchase both tangible and intangible assets and to satisfy debts. If the U.S. said it would not concern itself with maintaining the dollar's value and that it intends to borrow without limit, it would not be long before confidence in the dollar would plummet. This would result in a significant decline in the U.S. dollar's role as a reserve currency, and the void would likely be filled by China, the European Union, and others, thereby giving them enhanced borrowing and sanctions power. As the dollar devalued, the result would be higher prices and inflation in the U.S., especially for imported goods and services.

The resulting decline in confidence would likely result in a reduction in cash balances and an increase in the speed (velocity) of money flow within the U.S. (see Appendix A for a further explanation), which would drive prices up further, translating into more inflation.

Given the above, we might not have an immediate problem *if* inflation stayed low and the MMT was employed today. However, it would eventually result in excess inflation, higher interest rates, and many other future problems. What would policymakers do then? How would they regain confidence and stability without doing irreparable harm, not only to the U.S. but also to the rest of the world as well? Finally, if the reserve currency void due to the decline of the dollar was not filled quickly by others, global trade would plummet. The possibility of a return to the world of the 1930s will loom large.

But let me appeal to common sense. What independent banker, investor, or other person would continue to lend to a borrower who declared there was no limit to how much they would borrow regardless of the purpose, and they were not concerned with the value of their currency? Few, if any. Let's face it; the Fed is not an independent banker! And how many foreign traders are likely to want to use the dollar as their primary exchange currency when America demonstrates such a cavalier attitude? A dramatically fewer number than today. When markets understand this and when a modest increase in inflation becomes a reality, a flight from the dollar will eventually happen. As the word spreads, the flight from the dollar would likely be sudden and dramatic. It could even spark a "sell panic." After all, markets are often driven by emotion. We saw that a lot in 2007–2009 and in 2020.

One more point: As inflation takes hold it creates its own momentum for increased borrowing. Why? Because the borrower wants to borrow as much as possible and repay in deflated (i.e., less valuable) dollars. This benefits the borrower but cheats the lender or investor. Soon lending and investing stop. The result will be reduced economic growth with higher and accelerating interest rates and a general reduction of willingness to lend or invest over time. Simply put, the destruction of independent capital markets.

The new MMT also reminds me of three age-old sayings. First, "Good money (of reliable value) soon drives out bad (of unreliable value)." Second, "A fool and their money are soon parted." Finally, "Money does not grow on trees."

In summary, the MMT ignores the lessons of history and rejects the time-tested formula we discussed earlier and will discuss further in Appendix A. In addition, it destroys the trust that is necessary for any financial system to function properly and assumes that the U.S. will always maintain the confidence of investors even if the dollar's value is at significant risk of being seriously eroded by inflation.

Why do U.S. policymakers think we can maintain investor confidence when the U.S. has failed to demonstrate we can put our own financial house in order? When confidence is lost, a collapse of the dollar would likely happen quickly and result in rapid increases in interest and inflation rates, significant reductions in economic growth, much higher unemployment levels, a dramatic decline in equity markets, and a significant increase in both corporate and personal bankruptcies.

Stated differently, it would be the end of the post-WWII "golden era" of progress that has benefited both the U.S. and many others worldwide. The result of all of this would not just be a serious U.S. recession, but also a worldwide depression. It is not prudent and it is not a risk worth taking, especially given the rise of China, changing security threats, growing U.S. political divisions, and the mounting debt held by the public/GDP levels. America needs to wake up and learn from history, others, and long-established principles rather than trying to invent new theories to justify a continuation of irresponsible practices.

Keep in mind that the U.S. status as a superpower is based first and foremost on economic strength. If we lose that, then our military, diplomatic, and cultural influence over time will wane and our superpower status will be lost. That is not a future we should be seeking for our country and our families. That is why I and many others reject the "free lunch theorists" who are promoting the MMT. As happened with the misrepresentation of the Keynesian theory, MMT provides an excuse for weak politicians to further delay needed reforms that will put our nation on a more prudent and sustainable path. That is not just inappropriate; it is also irresponsible and downright dangerous.

CHAPTER 11

AMERICA'S GREATEST ECONOMIC AND NATIONAL SECURITY THREAT

As noted in Chapter 3, major powers come and go, and until now, none has stood the test of time. Will America? Helping to answer that question is the purpose of this book.

A modern-day superpower needs to have global economic, diplomatic, military, and cultural strength and impact. History tells us that economic power is by far the most important of these factors because it enables the others. Economic power brings diplomatic power, enables military capability, and increases cultural influence. At the same time, when relative economic power recedes, history also tells us that it is followed by a decline in the relative diplomatic power, military capability, and cultural influence. In some cases, the exceptional power ceased to exist, like Rome. Therefore, relative economic power is a leading indicator and the most critical factor.

There are three primary factors that serve to drive economic growth. They are: availability of financial capital for investment, human capital for working hours and skills, and innovation for creativity and productivity. As discussed previously, geographic factors can also play a role in a country's economic potential and relative security. For example, the U.S. has exceptional access to three great bodies of water and a number of major inland waterways.

Since its inception, the United States has grown from a relatively small and fledgling nation to a global superpower. Its geography and demography worked to help fuel its economic growth for much of its existence. In addition, its stable, if not always effective, political system combined the "rule of law" and personal freedoms and helped to attract both financial and human capital to America. America's market-based economy and entrepreneurial spirit also helped to fuel innovation and productivity increases.

While the geographic boundaries of the U.S. have not changed in the past 60 years, its demography and relative financial position have changed considerably. From a financial perspective, with the sole exception of debt accumulated to win WWII, the U.S. largely followed George Washington's admonition to "avoid excessive debt" for all periods from its inception until recent years. However, we have lost our way in recent years, especially since 2003.

The following graphic demonstrates how federal finances, as defined by debt held by the public/GDP, have spun out of control in recent years. It also shows what the nonpartisan Congressional Budget Office (CBO) projected our future might look like as of January 2020, which was BEFORE COVID-19 hit us! Debt held by the public/GDP escalated from about 79% to more than 106% and rising as of June 30, 2020 due primarily to COVID-19. As a result, the numbers now are much worse than depicted below.

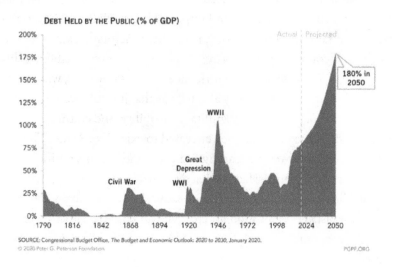

DEBT HELD BY THE PUBLIC (% OF GDP)

SOURCE: Congressional Budget Office, *The Budget and Economic Outlook: 2020 to 2030*, January 2020.
© 2020 Peter G. Peterson Foundation

PGPF.ORG

In addition to the rapid increases in debt held by the public/GDP since 2003, even after we defeat COVID-19, the country faces annual deficits in excess of $1.5 to $2 trillion for as far as the eye can see. And that assumes we return to modest economic growth and avoid "wars" and other "national emergencies." And these increasing structural deficits and mounting debt burdens have several adverse implications, including allowing economic growth and reducing job opportunities, thereby contributing to an "economic decline loop." First, deficits and increasing debt burdens serve to "crowd out" investment capital that could be put to more productive use in the private sector, which has been the primary source of growth and innovation in our market-based economy. Second, they reduce the ability of the government to make prudent investments that can help to create more growth and opportunity in the future (e.g., basic research, critical infrastructure). Third, they serve to put additional pressure on defense and other discretionary spending, which can reduce our national security and compromise other federal programs. Finally, they increase the likelihood of a fiscal and economic crisis in the future.

So what is a reasonable level of debt held by the public/GDP? Economists differ on this, but there is a broad-based consensus that the level chosen by the European Zone members is a reasonable and sustainable level. Their fiscal sustainability target is 60% of public debt/GDP. At the end of 2019, less than half its members have met this target and the average for the EU is 84.2%. The biggest problem countries in 2020 were Greece (178%), Italy (137%), and Portugal (120%). On the other hand, Germany was at 61.2% and Sweden, a country with very generous social insurance programs, was at 35.4%. As noted herein, the U.S. is far above the European average and our debt/GDP is growing rapidly!

Appendix B includes a summary of three academic studies on sovereign public debt/GDP ratios and their impact on economic growth. It also includes an overview of the "debt brake" approach used by Sweden and Switzerland to control public debt/GDP as a means to increase economic growth and ensure fiscal sustainability.

The sad but simple truth is that America has become addicted to spending, deficits, and debt. It is understandable to run deficits in time of a declared war, a serious recession, or national emergency; however, running them when the economy is growing, when we are at peace, and when we do not face any major national emergencies is irresponsible, unethical, and even immoral. This is especially true when such deficits significantly exceed the growth rate of the economy and are primarily attributable to higher interest costs without any new government initiatives or investments. The result is higher debt held by the public/GDP, which is a drag on economic growth and a threat to our superpower status. That is where we were headed before COVID-19, and it is projected to continue after we defeat the virus, but with higher deficit levels and debt burdens.

As former Fed Chair Paul Volcker said in 2005, "Baby boomers have been spending like there is no tomorrow. Big adjustments will inevitably come." It was true then and is even truer today. The "baby boom" generation (people born between 1946 and 1964 inclusive) are on track to be the first generation in American history to fail to discharge their stewardship responsibilities to later generations. By that I mean to leave the country better off *and* better positioned for the future. Such is clearly not the case at present in connection with financial/fiscal, environmental, and selected other matters of critical importance.

I have been concerned about the nation's long-term financial outlook for many years dating back to my time as one of two public trustees for Social Security and Medicare (1990–1995). In fact, my fellow public trustee, Stan Ross, and I included a warning regarding the longer-term financial challenges facing these programs in our first published Public Trustees Report in 1991, and we continued to include those warnings in our subsequent annual reports. Even when the U.S. was running a budget surplus in 2001, I testified in Congress that we were likely to face large and growing deficits in the future, due primarily to known demographic trends and rising health care costs. And this was at a time when some were projecting surpluses for as far as the eye could see and were saying we might even pay off the national debt! Unfortunately, I was correct and they were way wrong!

Later, I spoke out publicly regarding the three irresponsible fiscal actions that took place in 2003, which were discussed in Chapter 6 of this book. And when Congress and the president failed to act, I engaged in a range of actions over several years that were designed to increase transparency and enhance public engagement regarding the large and structural financial and fiscal challenges facing America. These actions included pushing for and eventually achieving enhanced financial reporting in the U.S. government's consolidated financial statements, including a new Statement of Social Insurance and a new Statement of Fiscal Sustainability. It also included many congressional testimonies and the instigation and execution of a "Fiscal Wake-up Tour" in partnership with the Concord Coalition, the Heritage Foundation, The Brookings Institution, the Committee for Economic Development, and other groups.

Since the inception of the audit requirement under the Chief Financial Officers Act in the 1990s, great progress has been made in connection with financial management matters in most of the federal departments and agencies. However, the U.S. Government Accountability Office (GAO) has been unable to express an opinion on the consolidated financial statements of the U.S. government, primarily due to the inability of the Department of Defense to undergo a successful audit. Nonetheless, due to my concerns regarding the fiscally irresponsible actions that occurred in calendar year 2003, I included the following "emphasis paragraph" in the audit report for the U.S. government's consolidated financial statements for the Fiscal Year Ended September 30, 2004, which I signed:

"While we are unable to express an opinion on the U.S. government's consolidated financial statements, several key items deserve emphasis in order to put the information contained in the financial statements and the Management's Discussion and Analysis section of the Financial Report of the United States Government into context. First, the federal government reported a $412.3 billion unified budget deficit and a $568 billion on budget deficit in Fiscal Year 2004, representing approximately 3.6 percent and 4.9 percent of gross domestic product (GDP), respectively. Importantly, a significant majority of this deficit was unrelated to the conflicts in Iraq and Afghanistan and additional homeland security costs. Second, the U.S. government's reported liabilities and unfunded social insurance and other obligations grew by over $13 trillion in Fiscal Year 2004, primarily due to enactment of the new Medicare prescription drug benefit, and now are over $43 trillion, representing close to four times current GDP. In addition, while the size of the nation's long-term fiscal imbalance grew significantly during the fiscal year, the retirement of the "baby boom" generation is closer to becoming a reality. Given these and other factors, it seems clear that the nation's current fiscal path is unsustainable and that tough choices by the president and Congress will be necessary in order to address the nation's large and growing fiscal imbalance."

Fortunately, Gene Dodaro, my successor as U.S. Comptroller General, whom I selected to serve as GAO's chief operating officer (COO) during my tenure, has included language along the above lines in every GAO audit report since the original insertion. This is just one example of how some of the transformational changes that occurred during my tenure as head of GAO have stood the test of time. Unfortunately, very few people read the U.S. Government's Annual Financial Report, including members of Congress, cabinet officials, and the press, even though an Executive Summary is provided each year.

It is important to understand that the federal government's financial statements are prepared on an accrual basis. This is consistent with private sector practices and represents the most sound economic basis for financial reporting. Cash-based budget deficits that most governments focus on are misleading and can be easily manipulated. For example, not counting the accrued cost of the very generous retirement benefits that are not funded until many years later results in a huge difference between cash and accrual-based results. To illustrate, in Fiscal 2019 the cash-based federal budget deficit was $0.984 trillion compared to the accrual-based net cost (deficit) of $1.445 trillion. That is a $461 billion or 47% difference! In addition, the federal government had a negative net worth of $22.95 trillion as of the end of Fiscal 2019. This represents the difference between the federal government's reported assets and liabilities on the balance sheet as of September 30, 2019. Importantly, this number does not include a number of items that would make the negative net worth number much worse. For example, it does not include the $59.1 trillion in Social Security and Medicare Trust Fund debt and other unfunded benefits as of September 30, 2019. It is also important to note that the United States does not report "whole of government" financial information (i.e., combined federal, state, and local) like some other countries. Finally, from a transparency and accountability perspective, New Zealand is probably the "gold standard" for financial and performance reporting at the present time. The U.S. has made progress since the early 1990s on financial and performance reporting, but it still has a way to go.

Given America's deteriorating financial condition, I worked with a number of prominent nonprofits (e.g., Brookings Institution, Committee for Economic Development, Concord Coalition, and Heritage Foundation) on a nonpartisan basis to go to the American people with the facts and truth about the nation's finances. The resulting Fiscal Wake-up Tour drew the attention of a number of media outlets, including the premier national news program *60 Minutes*. They followed the tour to several cities and interviewed me in my Comptroller General's office for about three hours. The result was a segment that appeared twice in 2007 and included the following quote by me:

> "The greatest threat to America is not someone hiding in a cave in Afghanistan or Pakistan; it's our own fiscal irresponsibility."

The first person to call me after that program ran was H. Ross Perot Sr. He was very complimentary and said he wanted to help. I had always admired Ross Perot for his patriotism, courage, commitment, and entrepreneurial ability. For the record, while I admired him and what he stood for, I was a Bush (41) presidential appointee in 1992 and voted for President Bush in that election.

In 1992, while running for president, Ross Perot said, "The budget should be balanced, the Treasury should be refilled, the public debt should be reduced and the arrogance of public officials should be controlled." He famously used a number of simple charts and graphs in a series of infomercials in 1992. I am fortunate to have one of his original signed charts that he gave me. Later, in 2012, Ross Perot wrote a $200,000 check to the Comeback America Initiative that underwrote the cost of the $10 Million a Minute Tour, which will be discussed in Chapter 13. He, like Pete Peterson, was the type of person who put his money where his mouth was and spent his time where his heart was. They were both great men who will not be forgotten.

During the early stages of my public communications efforts, I got heat from some on Capitol Hill, including the Chairman of the Senate Budget Committee Pete Domenici (R-NM), for the additional press attention to our nation's fiscal and financial challenges. I did not let that bother me and had no problem explaining my actions. After all, as U.S. Comptroller General, I had to sign the opinion on the audited financial statements of the U.S. government every year. This meant that I was arguably in the best position to address longer-range fiscal and financial issues and, in fact, as a CPA, I believe that I had a professional and ethical responsibility to do so. This seemed to satisfy any who complained, including Senator

Domenici, who later apologized to me and said he thought that what I was doing was appropriate.

The *60 Minutes* segment also resulted in the production and limited distribution of the award-winning documentary *I.O.U.S.A.* This entertaining and educational film by Patrick Creadon was purchased and promoted by the Peter G. Peterson Foundation, of which I served as its first CEO after leaving GAO. In January of 2010, *Comeback America: Turning the Country Around and Restoring Fiscal Responsibility* was published by Random House. That book achieved national best-seller status for nonfiction, and an updated paperback version was published in October 2010. The paperback version included a supplement that addressed the Affordable Care Act (ACA), which was passed in March of 2010. As noted in Chapter 7, the Simpson–Bowles Commission was created in the spring of 2010 and reported its findings and recommendations in December of 2010. It did good work which, for the most part, has yet to result in concrete action by Congress.

Over time, many traditional public officials whose responsibilities related to fiscal matters began to echo concerns about our nation's fiscal outlook, including current and former Office of Management and Budget (OMB) and CBO directors, treasury secretaries, Fed chairs, and other prominent persons. My warning about the dangers of our nation's growing debt burdens and their potential national security implications also began to draw the attention of some other important and nontraditional players. Most notably, in 2010, the Chairman of the Joint Chiefs of Staff Admiral Mike Mullen said, "The most significant threat to our national security is our debt." It was true then, and it is even truer today, especially given changing security threats and our deteriorating financial position and fiscal outlook.

Despite the alternative history depicted in such books, shows, and films as *The Man in the High Castle*, the U.S. is not likely to ever be defeated by military means due to our geographic location, military capabilities, and significant nuclear stockpile. However, that does not mean we will stay exceptional and that we can continue to pursue our current fiscally irresponsible ways when we defeat COVID-19.

As Fed Chairman Jerome Powell said in May 2020, "The time to get on a sustainable fiscal path, which really just means that the economy is growing faster than the debt, and that means you've got to control the growth of the debt, and the time to do that is when the economy is strong." That is a true statement, and it relates to our structural deficits and rising debt held by the public/GDP levels. However, Congress and the president have failed to follow this advice from Chairman Powell, me, and many others in the past. Can we really expect them to do so in the future? Or will they continue to play Wimpy and say, in effect, "I'll gladly pay you Tuesday if you give me a hamburger today." Tuesday allegedly being the day when tough choices will be made and the hamburger being additional spending and a continuation of an imprudent and unsustainable fiscal policy. Given the continued punting by policymakers, the time may have come for a Fiscal Responsibility Amendment to the Constitution. More on this topic in Chapter 14.

In May 2020, Treasury Secretary Steven Mnuchin said, "One of the reasons I do feel comfortable with us spending all this money is because interest rates are very low. And we're taking advantage of long-term rates." That may be true, but what is the money being used for and how long will interest rates stay low? To put things into perspective, if interest rates were to return to pre-2007 levels, that would result in additional interest costs on federal debt of $800 billion per year! Interest costs already represent the fastest-growing recurring expense in the federal budget. And what do you get for interest, NOTHING! If interest rates rise from historic lows, and they have started to do so, the problem will get worse.

History shows that if investors lose confidence in the ability of the U.S. government to put its own finances in order, it will get much worse and very fast! Do we really want to take that chance? Do we really want to risk the future of our country, children, and grandchildren? I, for one, am not willing to do so, even if it means some pain and sacrifice today in order to create a better tomorrow. As they say, "No pain, no gain!"

It is also important to understand who owns U.S. debt and how significant the related interest costs are, as compared to the overall federal budget. Japan has a much higher public debt/GDP level than the U.S. does; however, most of Japan's debt is funded by the Japanese. The U.S. has become increasingly dependent on foreign lenders and the Federal Reserve to buy its debt. This is not a prudent or sustainable long-term strategy. In addition, a much higher public debt/GDP level in Japan has imposed a heavy cost on Japanese economic growth and equity markets.

As of June 30, 2020, the U.S. had $26.48 trillion in total federal debt, of which $20.53 trillion was debt held by the public and $5.95 trillion related to debt held by various intragovernmental trust funds (e.g., Social Security and Medicare). Shockingly, due to the rise in debt and the decline in the economy as a result of COVID-19, debt held by the public as of June 30, 2020 was 106% of GDP and total federal debt was 136% of GDP!

As the below graphic shows, as of March 2020, 39% of U.S. public debt was held by foreign governments, with Japan having the largest holdings and China being a close second.

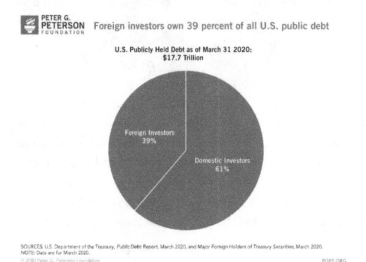

PETER G. PETERSON FOUNDATION   Foreign investors own 39 percent of all U.S. public debt

U.S. Publicly Held Debt as of March 31 2020:
$17.7 Trillion

Foreign Investors 39%

Domestic Investors 61%

SOURCES: U.S. Department of the Treasury, *Public Debt Report*, March 2020, and *Major Foreign Holders of Treasury Securities*, March 2020.
NOTE: Data are for March 2020.
© 2020 Peter G. Peterson Foundation   PGPF.ORG

Some people have asserted that having so much of our debt held by foreign governments represents a threat to U.S. national security. They assert that a foreign government individually (e.g., China) or in collusion with others could demand immediate repayment of their U.S. debt. That is not accurate. However, they could decide to "dump" (sell) their holdings and discontinue buying new issuances. This could serve to change the supply-and-demand equation and drive up interest rates, thereby compounding our interest expense and debt held by the public/GDP challenge. In this regard, China recently decided to reduce its holdings of U.S. Treasury securities.

What is surprising to most people, as shown in the graphic below, is that the largest single holder of U.S. public debt as of September 30, 2019 was the U.S. Federal Reserve. It held about $4 trillion, as compared to about $2.4 trillion being held by Japan and China combined at that time!

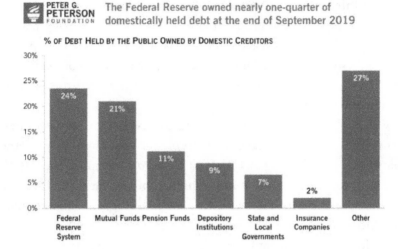

And, as shown in the below graphic, the Federal Reserve's holdings have increased dramatically since then as a result of COVID-19. Does this sound like self-dealing to you? It sure does to me.

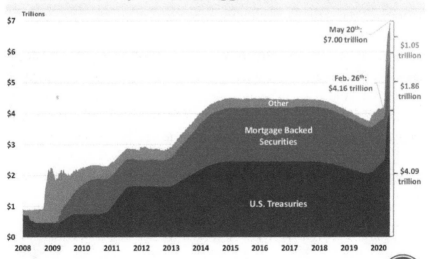

At a minimum, while it provides some short-term help, it serves to aid and abet irresponsible and unsustainable fiscal policies. Shockingly, some "liberal" politicians even use the temporary and artificially low interest rates as a reason to spend even more and further mortgage our collective future. But how long will these low rates last when we return to a more normal market-based system?

Why is the Federal Reserve buying so many Treasury securities? Because the Fed has a mandate to promote economic growth and employment. This buying of U.S. debt helps to accomplish these goals in the short term, but it may result in higher interest rates and inflation over time, thereby adversely impacting their third goal of maintaining stable prices over time.

The federal government has also increased spending dramatically as a result of COVID-19. This additional spending is an attempt to use fiscal policy to help stem the adverse economic impact while helping individuals, businesses, and other levels of government. Through buying the bulk of new Treasury issuances, the Fed helps to keep Treasury rates low. The Fed's actions change the supply-and-demand equation for treasuries since there may not be enough demand for new Treasury issuances absent Fed intervention, especially since China recently decided to reduce its holdings in Treasury securities. While this approach may be necessary during a short-term financial or public health crisis, it is not a prudent or sustainable approach over time.

What about interest costs? As noted in the below graphic, the single fastest-growing projected cost in the federal budget before COVID-19 was interest. And as I said before, what do you get for interest? Nothing!

As noted below, interest costs on debt held by the public (also known as net interest) and its related percentage of the federal budget has fluctuated widely over the years. As you can see, net interest costs were already headed up before COVID-19, and they will increase further because of the impact of the virus.

Total Deficit, Primary Deficit, and Net Interest

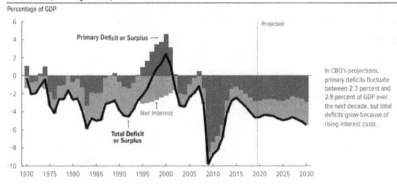

Source: Congressional Budget Office.

Primary deficits or surpluses exclude net outlays for interest.

When October 1 (the first day of the fiscal year) falls on a weekend, certain payments that would have ordinarily been made on that day are instead made at the end of September and thus are shifted into the previous fiscal year. All projections presented here have been adjusted to exclude the effects of those timing shifts. Historical amounts have been adjusted as far back as the available data will allow.

GDP = gross domestic product.

Interest payments on the U.S. national debt are on the rise again

Fiscal year net interest on the national debt ...

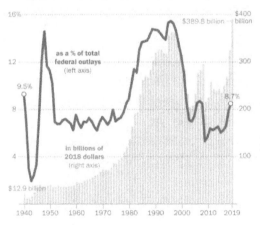

Note: Fiscal year 2019 figures are estimates.
Source: Office of Management and Budget; Federal Reserve Bank of St. Louis;
Bureau of Economic Analysis (U.S. Department of Commerce).

PEW RESEARCH CENTER

All of the above charts and graphs were based on projections before COVID-19. Therefore, what are some of the fiscal implications post-COVID-19? The below graphic shows the estimated impact as of April 2020.

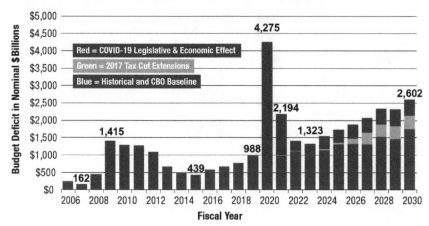

THE 2020 BUDGET DEFICIT IS CURRENTLY PROJECTED TO REACH $4.2 TRILLION

Chart: **Manhattan Institute** / Source: Estimated using Jan. 2020 CBO baseline and historical data, CBO bill scores, and author estimates of economic costs as of April 2020.
By Brian Riedl, Manhattan Institute (@Brian_Riedl)

As you can see, COVID-19 is not just a one-year financial hit; it is expected to add to our financial and fiscal challenges far into the future.

In summary, the U.S. was on an imprudent and unsustainable fiscal path before COVID-19 and that path has been made worse by the virus. The real key metrics of fiscal sustainability are debt held by the public/GDP and interest as a percentage of the budget. If the information presented in this chapter coupled with warnings by a number of prominent individuals does not convince you that we are on a "burning platform," then I do not know what will. Tough choices need to be made after we get past this public health challenge, and the sooner we do it, the better.

CHAPTER 12

INCREASING SECURITY THREATS

Security means different things to different people. From my perspective, I define the term very broadly to include economic security, national security, and personal security. One of the things I remember from my college psychology class is Maslow's Hierarchy of Needs. Under that theory, the most basic human need is self-preservation, and the ultimate human desire is self-actualization. That made a lot of sense to me and is generally consistent with the basic principles and values on which the U.S. was founded.

As noted in Chapter 4, America's original founding principles included such issues as individual liberty and opportunity, personal responsibility and accountability, rule of law, and equal justice under the law (for many but not all at that time). America was and is a land of opportunity where a person with a good education, a positive attitude, a strong work ethic, and solid moral and ethical values has virtually unlimited opportunity for self-actualization. At the same time, our nation's Founders also realized that certain important matters that were of broad societal interest had to be dealt with by the government at the federal level to varying degrees. These included such matters as to "establish Justice," "insure domestic Tranquility," and "provide for the common defence" (see the preamble of the U.S. Constitution).

Establishing justice is addressed at all levels of government, with the ultimate foundation being the U.S. Constitution and the ultimate arbiter being the U.S. Supreme Court. Insuring domestic tranquility is also addressed by all three levels of government. It includes actions by state (e.g. National Guard and state police) and local governments (e.g., police), as well as the federal government (e.g., FBI). In rare circumstances, it can also include actions by other federal agencies and even the nationalization of the National Guard by the president. Importantly, U.S. law, including civil rights legislation, is designed to provide equal opportunity and, in some cases, to encourage affirmative action to achieve desired societal outcomes. At the same time, the government cannot ensure equal results.

Providing for the "common defence" is addressed by the federal government through the military and the various intelligence agencies (e.g., CIA, NSA, and DIA). While these are the traditional federal entities that most Americans think of when discussing national security, the topic also involves a range of other agencies that help to promote our national interests from a diplomatic and economic perspective (e.g., State, UN, Treasury, Fed, Commerce, and USTR).

Let's start with economic security. As discussed earlier in the book, the U.S. had gone from about 50% of global GDP in the immediate aftermath of WWII to about 24% in 2019 and declining. The U.S. is still ranked number one in nominal GDP, but China is ranked number one in Purchasing Power Parity (PPP)-based GDP and the gap is growing. According to the International Monetary Fund (IMF), the U.S. still has a well-above-average GDP per capita ($65,111 in 2019) and is far ahead of China ($10,098 in 2019) in that regard, resulting in a ratio of 6.5:1. The gap shrinks considerably when you consider PPP-based per-capita GDP whereby, according to the IMF, in 2020 the U.S. was estimated to be $67,426 and China at $20,984, resulting in a ratio of 3.2:1, or less than half the nominal GDP ratio.

Trade is a key consideration in economic security matters. Promoting trade was a key concept after WWII to help better connect countries, provide more individual opportunity, and raise standards of living around the world. As President John F. Kennedy said, "A rising tide lifts all boats."

According to the CIA Fact Book, the U.S. is the second-biggest exporting country, exceeded only by China, and Germany, Japan, and South Korea are the other top-five exporting countries. On the flip side, the U.S. is the biggest importing country, with China, Germany, Japan, and France rounding out the top five. Germany has the largest global trade surplus, followed by Japan, China, Netherlands, and South Korea. The U.S. has the largest global trade deficit, followed by the UK, India, Canada, and Turkey.

From a bilateral perspective, according to the U.S. Census Bureau, in 2019 Mexico was the top U.S. trading partner, followed by Canada, China, Japan, and Germany. Trade with the European Union as a whole exceeds U.S. trade with China. The U.S. has trade deficits of various magnitudes with each of these entities in 2019, and the trade deficit with China is the largest. The U.S. has trade surpluses with some countries (e.g., Netherlands, UAE, Australia, Belgium, and Singapore), but they are not of significant magnitude when compared to overall U.S. trade levels.

The primary global exports from the U.S. are machinery (e.g., computers), mineral fuels (e.g., oil), electrical machinery, aircraft, and vehicles. The primary global imports into the U.S. are machinery (e.g., computers), electrical hardware (e.g., mobile phones), vehicles including automobiles, minerals, fuel and oil, and pharmaceuticals. Do you notice some significant overlap in these? In part, the overlap results in U.S. and other consumers having more choices (e.g., automobiles) as a result of global trade. The overlap is due in part to U.S. companies deciding to outsource certain manufacturing overseas, especially to China, due to lower labor costs along with weaker worker protections and environmental rules.

Importantly, certain countries have a greater abundance of natural resources and food production capabilities than others. For the first time in many decades, the U.S. is now an oil-exporting nation. In fact, due to fracking and other technological developments, North America is now energy-independent for the first time in a very long time. Most major nations are not energy-independent, including most European nations, China, and India. Russia is a clear exception as the second-largest oil-exporting nation in the world.

The U.S. is currently self-sufficient from a food, water, and even energy perspective, given North American reserves. This is very important from both an economic and national security perspective. However, the U.S. is not self-sufficient when it comes to certain rare earth metals and materials needed to produce certain pharmaceuticals. These rare earth metals and minerals can be critical in the production of electronic equipment, airplanes, and weapons systems. Being dependent on a competitor nation for critical materials when we could in the future be in conflict with that nation is not a good idea. In addition, as we saw in the case of the COVID-19 experience, being unduly dependent on foreign countries for certain items (e.g., PPE) is not a good idea. Thus, the U.S. needs to reconsider some of its current sourcing, production, and distribution strategies in light of economic, public health, and national security considerations.

As has been noted, the U.S. represented about 50% of global GDP in the immediate aftermath of WWII. The U.S. assumed a leadership role in every major global institution and sought to promote free trade between nations. In

1947, the General Agreement on Tariffs and Trade (GATT) was adopted. It involved 23 nations (i.e., Australia, Belgium, Brazil, Burma, Canada, Ceylon, Chile, China, Cuba, Czechoslovakia, France, India, Lebanon, Luxembourg, Netherlands, New Zealand, Norway, Pakistan, South Africa, Southern Rhodesia, Syria, the UK, and the U.S.) and was the first major global trade agreement. It resulted in a substantial reduction in tariffs and trade barriers between the respective countries and eliminated certain preferences.

There were a number of GATT trade rounds since the original 1947 agreement. The 1994 round included the creation of the World Trade Organization (WTO). The WTO is the international organization that regulated trade between nations, and resolves trade disputed between nations. However, its enforcement mechanisms can be lengthy and, in the opinion of many members, are inadequate.

Today, a vast majority of countries in the world are members of the WTO, including China which joined in 2001, and some countries are observers who are seeking accession (e.g., Algeria, Belarus, Bhutan, Bosnia-Herzegovina, Ethiopia, Iran, Iraq, Libya, Serbia, Somalia, South Sudan, Sudan, Syria, and Uzbekistan). Only three nonmember countries are not seeking admission to the WTO (i.e., Eritrea, North Korea, and Turkmenistan).

The WTO divides countries into two groups; that is, developed and developing nations. Developing nations are granted additional flexibilities in connection to the timing for full implementation of the agreement and can be eligible for technical assistance. Interestingly, China is currently considered to be a developing nation in the WTO. This is a matter of significant controversy among developed nations, especially the U.S.

U.S. trade strategy has changed over the years, especially during the Trump administration. The North American Free Trade Agreement (NAFTA) was a hotly debated issue during the 1992 presidential election campaign. President Bush and Governor Clinton supported it, and Ross Perot was strongly opposed to it. In fact, in one of his most famous lines from the presidential debates that year, Perot said that NAFTA would result in a "giant sucking sound" of jobs leaving America for Mexico due to its lower wages, weaker worker and environmental protections, and close proximity to the U.S. Ultimately, NAFTA passed in 1994 and was signed into law. Looking back, it did result in an outsourcing of jobs to Mexico and a more than tripling in trade between the three countries. Years later, that was renegotiated during the Trump administration. The resulting United States, Mexico, and Canada Agreement (USMCA) was passed and signed into law in early 2020.

Prior to the Trump administration, there was a significant amount of attention given to negotiating multilateral trade agreements. One of the biggest ones that had been concluded in 2015 was the Trans-Pacific Partnership (TPP). This agreement involved 12 nations (i.e., Australia, Brunei, Canada, Chile, Japan, Malaysia, Mexico, New Zealand, Peru, Singapore, the U.S., and Vietnam) that bordered the Pacific Ocean. It removed tariffs and standardized business practices between the participating countries. Collectively, the 12 countries involved in TPP produced about 40% of the world's total GDP, which exceeded NAFTA. It also recognized that Asia represented the region of the world that was expected to have the greater economic growth than the global average in the twenty-first century. Importantly, China was not part of that agreement. President Trump withdrew from the TPP after assuming office and stated that he would seek to replace it with a number of bilateral agreements.

In theory, as an economic "big dog" with that largest consumer market, the U.S. would have more leverage if it negotiated bilateral rather than multilateral agreements. This may well be true, but it takes a lot longer to cover as many countries. More importantly, this type of bilateral mercantilism approach removes the U.S. from its post-WWII historic role as the primary leader in promoting global free trade. And who is now trying to fill the gap created by the change in the U.S. position? China!

In the aftermath of WWII, the U.S. was the major diplomatic power. It had a leadership position in all major international institutions and had the most embassies around the world of any country. The Soviet Union became the chief ideological, military, and diplomatic rival to the U.S. during the Cold War and had the second-most embassies around the world. It also played an important role in most major international organizations. Fast forward to 2019, and China had the most diplomatic missions around the world, followed by the U.S., France, Japan, and Russia.

China has been actively seeking to increase its diplomatic influence around the globe for a number of economic and national security reasons. First, it is actively seeking to gain access to critical natural resources (e.g., oil, natural gas, critical materials). Second, it is seeking to expand markets for Chinese goods. Third, it is seeking to leverage diplomatic influence in major international institutions (e.g., the UN). Finally, it is seeking to gain access to potential military bases for its global expansion plans.

While the U.S. is an exceptional country with a proud history that had far more than its share of visionary leaders at its creation, the biggest deficit the U.S. seems to have today is a leadership deficit. In addition, while China has always looked to the long term and has used strategic planning as an integral part of its approach to achieve its objectives and desired outcomes, the U.S. has tended to be more myopic and still lacks a comprehensive strategic plan that is future-focused, results-oriented, and resource-constrained.

One key aspect of China's current strategic plan is their "Belt and Road Initiative" (BRI). As shown below, the BRI is designed to create a modern-day "Silk Road" over land and sea. It is clear that the BRI is about much more than gaining market access and shares, securing trade routes, energy supplies and other critical materials, and exporting Chinese industrial capacity to faraway construction projects. The BRI is a key part of Chairman and President Xi Jinping's grand foreign policy and design to increase China's influence both in its neighborhood and far beyond it.

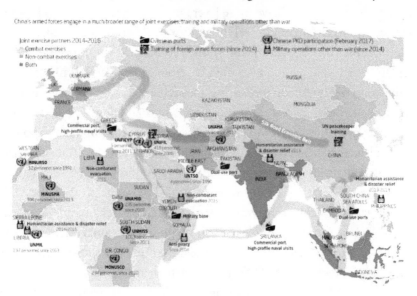

In fact, Xi has made several things clear. First, the BRI is a long-term project. Second, as the above *Defense Business Board (DBB)* graphic shows, the BRI is global in scope and involves both land and sea initiatives.

Finally, it is not limited to economic and diplomatic goals; it also has military and cultural components.

The BRI is not without controversy. It is focused on building major infrastructure projects (e.g., railroads, pipelines, and ports), primarily in poor developing countries, and mostly with Chinese labor. In most cases it involves what appears to be very favorable terms; however, if the country cannot make the required payments on time, China can take control of the project. In addition, some projects come with conditions (e.g., Chinese military vessel access to ports in strategic locations). One possible example of this is in Sri Lanka, which is directly off the coast of India, another emerging power that borders China.

The U.S. and other countries are becoming increasingly concerned about the ever-expanding BRI. At the same time, words alone will not get the job done when China is bringing billions of dollars in economic development support to the table. In addition, while China is increasing foreign aid, the U.S. has not, and foreign aid is likely to come under increasing scrutiny and pressure due to domestic fiscal challenges that have been exacerbated by COVID-19.

One example of this is Djibouti, which already hosts military bases for the U.S., China, Japan, France, Germany, Italy, and Spain. That small country is on the horn of Africa, which is of great strategic importance from a shipping standpoint. Just next door, Eritrea hosts a military base for Israel, and Russia is seeking to have a base there.

At the end of WWII, the U.S. and the Union of Soviet Socialist Republics (USSR or the Soviet Union) were the only two countries with major military forces, and the U.S. was the only country with an atomic weapon. Europe was divided, with the Soviets controlling and occupying Eastern Europe while the Soviets, U.S., Britain, and France occupied Germany.

The Soviet Union successfully tested their first atomic bomb in 1949, and the arms race was on. NATO was formed in 1949 to counter the threat of a possible Soviet invasion into Western Europe from the East. NATO's initial members were Belgium, Canada, Denmark, France, Iceland, Italy, Luxembourg, the Netherlands, Norway, Portugal, the UK, and the U.S. Each of these countries pledged to defend each other in the event of an attack. NATO has expanded over the years to include 30 countries, including some former members of the Warsaw Pact.

The Warsaw Pact was created in 1955 immediately after West Germany joined NATO. The Pact was formed as a counterweight to NATO. Its initial members were Albania, Bulgaria, Czechoslovakia, East Germany, Hungary, Poland, Romania, and the USSR. The only major military action by the Warsaw Pact was the invasion of Czechoslovakia. Albania withdrew from the Warsaw Pact in 1968, and it ceased to exist in 1991, shortly before the dissolution of the USSR in December of 1991.

After the USSR dissolved in 1991, both the U.S. and Russia reduced their military forces, and so did the other NATO and former Warsaw Pact countries. While the size of conventional forces has declined for many countries, such is not the case for all countries, with China and India being clear exceptions. In addition, while the U.S. was the only nation with an atomic weapon at the end of WWII, the nuclear family has expanded significantly to include the following in 2020, listed by the estimated size of their nuclear arsenals:

- Russia
- United States
- France
- China
- United Kingdom
- Pakistan
- India
- Israel
- North Korea

Iran and possibly other countries are seeking to join the nuclear family, but the U.S. and many other countries are seeking to prevent further proliferation of nuclear weapons. Russia and the U.S. each has more nuclear weapons than all of the other nuclear nations combined. Each also has enough to destroy the other and much of the rest of the world several times. Then the real question is? How many nuclear weapons are enough, especially when you hope that none will ever be used again?

Unfortunately, most past nuclear agreements between the U.S. and Russia have not stood the test of time. In fact, the only major nuclear agreement that is still in force is the New START Treaty, which is set to expire in February 2021. It can be extended for another five years if both sides agree to do so.

As mentioned previously, the U.S., Russia, and most other nations have reduced the size of their militaries after the Cold War ended in 1991. The single major exception is India. While the total number of military personnel in China has actually declined since 1991, its military capabilities and relative global position have increased significantly. In 2020, the five largest standing military forces in the world based on active duty personnel are: China, India, U.S., North Korea, and Russia.

How does the above relate to annual defense spending? As noted below, the U.S. spends more on defense than China, India, North Korea, Russia, and several other nations combined, based on publicly reported numbers in nominal U.S. dollars.

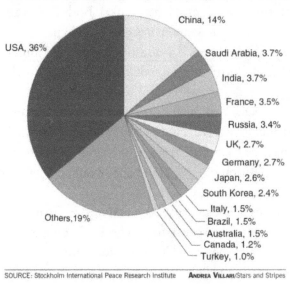

Global Military Spending in 2018

China, 14%
USA, 36%
Saudi Arabia, 3.7%
India, 3.7%
France, 3.5%
Russia, 3.4%
UK, 2.7%
Germany, 2.7%
Japan, 2.6%
South Korea, 2.4%
Italy, 1.5%
Brazil, 1.5%
Australia, 1.5%
Canada, 1.2%
Turkey, 1.0%
Others, 19%

SOURCE: Stockholm International Peace Research Institute   ANDREA VILLARI/Stars and Stripes

While the above figures may be accurate, they are very misleading. That is because China, Russia, North Korea, and other countries have conscription while the U.S. has an all-volunteer force. As is discussed in Chapter 17, that all-volunteer force is very, very expensive. In addition, purchasing power varies widely across the globe, including in connection with weapons systems. As a result, when you consider the difference in the cost of maintaining an all-volunteer force and the difference in PPP, China has probably already passed the U.S. in defense expenditures, and the gap is growing. As mentioned in Chapter 2, in the aftermath of COVID-19, Chairman and President Xi announced that he would be increasing his country's defense budget due to increasing security threats while we are openly talking about cutting our defense budget. More on this later in the book.

While reasonable people can and do differ, when you consider the total land, sea, air, space, and cyber capabilities of these countries, I would rank the top five militaries in the world in 2020 as follows: U.S., China, Russia, India, and France. On a trend basis, China and India are rising and Russia is slipping. One of the primary reasons for China's and India's rise is their growing economies, and the primary reason for Russia's relative decline over time is its weaker economy, which is overly dependent on its energy sector; its declining population; and its aging military platforms (e.g., ships, planes, tanks). Both Russia and China are investing in more modern weapons systems (e.g., hypersonics, unmanned vehicles, space, and cyber). In addition, the 2020 proclamation by Russian President Putin that he would not commit to the nonuse of nuclear weapons in a conventional military conflict is also an indication that Russia's conventional capabilities are far from what they used to be. At the same time, Russia still has the largest nuclear arsenal in the world, which is a matter of concern from a variety of perspectives, including the possible acquisition of nuclear or other weapons of mass destruction (WMDs) by rogue nations or terrorist groups.

What about personal security? As mentioned in Chapter 2, about 50% of Americans live from paycheck to paycheck and do not have significant savings. In addition, as noted in Chapter 9, there are growing gaps between the so-called "haves" and "have nots" in America. Furthermore, the huge fiscal imbalances in the nation's finances and the impending insolvency of Social Security, Medicare, and other so-called "trust funds" represents additional economic threats to those who rely on government social insurance and social safety net programs. These facts and other factors represent a direct threat to the economic security of Americans.

If our growing societal gaps are not closed and our nation's finances are not put into order, we could be facing a major economic crisis in the future that would not only adversely impact the economic security of millions of Americans, but it would also likely present major domestic tranquility problems for our nation. Those domestic tranquility problems would be much more severe than those that occurred after the deaths of the Rev. Martin Luther King Jr. and Senator Robert F. Kennedy in the summer of 1968. We must take both collective and individual steps to avoid that.

CHAPTER 13
AMERICANS ARE AHEAD OF THE POLITICIANS

I have long believed that most Americans know you cannot spend more money than you make, charge the difference to your credit card, self-deal in your own debt, and not face a day of reckoning at some point in the future. This was the first hypothesis for the $10 Million a Minute Tour discussed below.

The second hypothesis was that, contrary to the belief of most politicians, Americans can handle the truth and accept tough choices if they are part of a goal-oriented plan that is based on principles and values that unite rather than divide Americans.

During my more than 40-year career, it has become clear to me that we need more leadership rather than "laggardship" from our political leaders! By laggardship I mean failing to look ahead, see the trends and challenges facing the U.S., and take affirmative steps to capitalize on opportunities before they expire and mitigate the risks before they reach crisis proportions and impose very serious economic hardships on tens of millions of Americans. Laggardship is the opposite of leadership, and unfortunately it has become far too prevalent in government today, especially in connection with fiscal matters.

PERSONAL BACKGROUND AND QUALIFICATIONS

I have always been concerned with fiscal issues since I became an adult. This is a result of my profession as a CPA, the teachings of my father, and because of my love for history and this country. My 40+ year professional career has spanned the private, public, and nonprofit sectors. My interest and activities regarding fiscal matters and the financial condition of the country increased when I headed the Pension Benefit Guaranty Corporation (PBGC) and when I served as Assistant Secretary of Labor for Pensions, Health, and Other Employee Benefit Programs, which I was appointed to by President Reagan in 1987. These were my first two government executive positions, and they both involved pension and health care matters. As discussed in Chapter 8 of this book, unfunded pension and retiree health care obligations represent the biggest financial challenges at the federal, state, and local level.

In 1990, President Bush (41) appointed me as one of two public trustees for the Social Security and Medicare Trust Funds. I had the pleasure of serving with Stan Ross, who had been a Commissioner of Social Security for President Carter, for five years. Stan and I committed from Day 1 to conduct our affairs in a professional, objective, fact-based, nonpartisan, nonideological, and nonpersonal manner. We also agreed to advise the public of the serious long-range financial challenges facing the combined Social Security and Medicare Hospital Insurance (HI) programs. These pension and health care social insurance programs, like PBGC, have adequate assets to pay current benefits but face huge unfunded liabilities and obligations and major cash flow deficits in the future. Stated differently, they could pay benefits today, but when their "Trust Funds" went to zero, they could not pay full pension or disability benefits or make all health care payments when due. In 1991, the estimated dates that the combined Social Security and Medicare HI Trust Funds were expected to become exhausted were 2045 and 2005, respectively. The 2020 Trustees Report projected these Trust Funds would become exhausted by 2035 and 2026, respectively, but that was prior to the impact of COVID-19. In June 2020, the Congressional Budget Office (CBO) estimated that the Trust Fund exhaustion dates would be accelerated by three years to 2032 and 2023, respectively, as a result of COVID-19.

In 1998, President Clinton appointed me as Comptroller General of the United States and head of the GAO. In that position, I was the de facto Chief Auditor and Chief Performance and Accountability Officer for the federal government. I also served as Chair of the Inter-governmental Audit Forum for federal, state, and local accountability organizations. In this position, I became intimately familiar with the myriad of performance, accountability, and financial challenges facing the federal, state, and local governments. During my tenure as Comptroller General, I undertook a number of institutional and individual efforts to help policymakers and the public understand the serious challenges that we faced over time. For example, when I became Comptroller General the federal government had a surplus. However, due to known demographic trends and rising health care costs, I knew that Social Security, Medicare, and the federal government as a whole would face serious financial challenges that needed to be addressed. As noted in Chapter 11, surpluses turned to large and growing deficits and mounting debt burdens starting in 2002, and the three actions that took place in 2003 convinced me that things were spinning out of control. COVID-19 has made what was a bad situation much worse.

During the period 2008 to 2013, I served as the first CEO of the Peter G. Peterson Foundation (2008–2010) and as the Founder and CEO of the Comeback America Initiative (CAI) (2010–2013). These two nonprofits were focused on public education and engagement regarding our fiscal challenges. During my tenure, the Peterson Foundation was primarily focused on outlining the federal fiscal challenge. However, CAI was focused on federal, state, and local fiscal challenges, and also sought to engage the public directly on a range of "sensible solutions" to address them.

Unfortunately, by 2012, federal, state, and local leaders had failed to do enough to defuse our ticking debt bomb, so I decided to go on the road and interface directly with the people regarding these challenges and potential ways to address them. Thus, the $10 Million a Minute Tour was born.

$10 MILLION A MINUTE TOUR

As shown in the below CAI map, the $10 Million a Minute Tour was a national bus tour conducted by CAI in 2012. It went 10,000 miles, crossed 27 states, and involved public events in 16 states, including 11 swing states. It also included two unprecedented more than half-day engagements with representative groups of voters in two swing states, and ended with a public event at the National Press Club in Washington, D.C.

$10 Million-a-Minute Tour Destinations & Events

The purpose of the Tour was to help raise awareness regarding the nature and extent of our nation's fiscal challenge in an effort to increase attention to these matters both during the 2012 campaign cycle and after the elections. It was also designed to test the two hypotheses noted above.

The first question one might ask is, what does $10 Million a Minute mean? It relates to the fact that, at the time of the tour, the nation's total liabilities and unfunded promises were going up by about $10 million a minute, or about $5.2 trillion a year! Shockingly, the number is going up faster now due to COVID-19.

The $10 million a minute number was calculated by considering the annual deficit, plus increases in civilian and military pension and retiree health care costs, plus the growth in traditional liabilities, plus the increase in unfunded social insurance obligations (e.g., Social Security and Medicare), which were by far the biggest numbers. The total of these numbers was dubbed the "financial burden" and was much bigger than the debt held by the public or the debt subject to the debt ceiling limit (which includes debt held by the public and intergovernmental debt held by government trust funds). As an example, debt held by the public at the time in 2012 was about $11.6 trillion, up from $3.4 trillion in 2000. Debt subject to the debt ceiling was about $16.1 trillion, up from $5.7 trillion in 2000, and the total financial burden was about $70 trillion, up from about $20 trillion in 2000. In 2020 the financial burden was approaching $100 trillion prior to COVID-19, or almost five times the size of the entire U.S. economy. Is that number big enough to get your attention? If not, it is about $303,000 for every man, woman, and child in the U.S. Now do I have your attention?

While I led the Tour, I was accompanied by a number of my dedicated and capable staff from the CAI, some representatives of organizations who were allies of CAI, and our trusted bus driver from Premier Transportation out of Tennessee. Our bus was wrapped with the $10 Million a Minute Tour logo, and my name was nowhere on the bus. Why? Because this was about an important issue and not personalities, whoever they may be. The bus had previously been used by The Eagles, Mitt Romney, and John Edwards, among many others. We were joined in certain cities by other prominent people, including former Governor Ed Rendell (D-PA), former Senator Sam Nunn (D-GA), Governor Terry Branstad (R-IA), Senator Ron Johnson (R-WI), former Senator George LeMieux (R-FL), former presidential candidate Ross Perot (I-TX), former Office of Management and Budget (OMB)/CBO Director and former Vice Chair of the Federal Reserve, Alice Rivlin (D-DC), and many others.

The Tour included events at major economics and press clubs (e.g., The New York Economic Club, The National Press Club), major colleges and universities (e.g., St. Anselm's, Yale, Penn, Pitt, Ohio State, University of Denver, TCU, Elon), and civic organizations (e.g., Rotary and Kiwanis Clubs). Most importantly, it included two very special events. The first was in a swing congressional district outside of Cleveland, OH, which was in a swing state in the north. The second was in a swing congressional district in Springfield, VA, which was in a swing state in the South. In total, the Tour went nonstop for six weeks.

We had a number of alliance partners to CAI who participated in various aspects of the Tour. They included the Committee for a Responsible Federal Budget, The Committee for Economic Development, the Common Sense Coalition, the Concord Coalition, No Labels, Rebellious Truths, and the Can Kicks Back.

These groups were all nonprofits who cared about the issue. Importantly, they included people from different generations, different parts of the country, and with a broad range of political affiliations.

Representatives from various well-known think tanks also participated on the Tour (e.g., Brookings Institution, Heritage Foundation). The Tour received national and local media attention (e.g., ABC, CNN, Fox Business, USA Today, and various state and local publications).

The Tour was well received at every stop. The only potential problem was defused at the very first event at St. Anselm's College in Manchester, NH when Senator Bernie Sanders' (I-VT) attempt to disrupt the Tour failed. Most importantly, as you will discover in the balance of this book, my hypothesis that the American people were ahead of the politicians was proven to be true. This served to reinforce my view that the biggest deficit we have in America with regard to solving the fiscal and many other major public policy challenges we face was and is a leadership deficit that is complicated by hyperpartisanship and a significant ideological divide in Congress that results in stalemate all too often. It is leadership that evidently does not adequately know history or understand the laws of economics and finance.

Last but not least, the Tour was made possible when H. Ross Perot Sr. wrote a $200,000 check to underwrite the cost. Several other prominent and caring individuals also contributed to the cost of the Tour. These individuals were from different parts of the country with a range of political affiliations.

Ross was the first person to call me after my 2007 appearance on *60 Minutes* where I stated that the greatest threat to America's future was its own fiscal irresponsibility. He cared deeply about the country and the need to put the nation on a more prudent and sustainable fiscal path. This was a big part of why he ran for president in 1992 and 1996. While he did not win a single electoral vote, he helped to make fiscal responsibility a priority for President Clinton and the Republican House that resulted from the 1996 elections. This political combination and resulting fiscal choices created the conditions for strong economic growth and resulted in budget surpluses in Fiscal 1998–2001.

I was honored to know Ross Perot. He was a true patriot, a great family man, and a very successful entrepreneur. I was fortunate to have the opportunity to do a joint C-SPAN–*USA Today* interview with him when the Tour was in Dallas. We did the interview in his office in Plano, TX. The entrance to his office featured bronze statutes of his grandchildren, and his office was adorned with family photos, as well as patriotic paintings and memorabilia. That said a lot about the man. Later I found out that our interview was his last extended public interview. Ross died in June of 2019. He will be missed, and may he rest in peace.

TWO VERY SPECIAL EVENTS

CAI contracted with America Speaks to recruit two representative groups of voters who were willing to commit more than half a day on a Saturday to hear about our nation's fiscal challenge and provide their views on possible solutions. By a representative group of voters, I mean about 150 to 175 participants in each session reflected a cross section of voters based on age, race, gender, income, and political affiliation. This was important in order to assess the relative reliability of the related results.

I partnered with Belle Sawhill, former associate director of the OMB, from the Brookings Institution for the first event and with Alice Rivlin, former director of the CBO and OMB, and former vice chairman of the Fed, from the Brookings Institution for the second event. Both of them were very capable and respected professionals who cared about the issue. The three of us were also friends. Alice Rivlin was a great public servant who passed in 2019. She will be missed.

Both of these events were structured exactly the same way in order to be able to compare the results from the two groups. The sessions began with an overview PowerPoint presentation by me and my co-presenter. Each person attending had a briefing booklet and other supporting material. We had technical experts around the room who could answer any questions as a supplement to — and not a substitute for — asking a question directly to me or my co-presenter. In addition, each person was provided with a handheld and confidential electronic voting device whereby they could quickly provide their views on a series of questions relating to all of the topics we discussed.

Both sessions included sections on the following topics:

- The "Burning Platform" Case
- Fiscal Goals, and Guiding Principles and Values
- Budget Process and Controls
- Social Security
- Medicare, Medicaid, and Health Care
- Defense
- Government Transformation
- Political Reforms

Presentations were made on all of the above topics in order. The presentations were followed by a question-and-answer session. After the presentations had been made, and all questions had been answered, participants were asked to use their handheld confidential voting devices to express their opinions. The results were then aggregated by a representative of America Speaks and presented to the participants. This real-time approach proved to be very effective. In addition, the result of this effort served to confirm both of my hypotheses.

As a result of this effort, we achieved between 77% and 97% agreement on the issues and packages of illustrative reforms that were presented to the participants. This chapter will focus on the first two topics noted above. The other topics will be covered in selected chapters in the remainder of this book.

What do I mean by a "burning platform?" This is a key concept to help achieve the needed understanding and support to make any kind of major transformational change happen. Namely, you need to convince a significant majority of the affected parties that the "status quo" is unacceptable and unsustainable, and that the future is likely to be worse if you do not make needed changes. You also need to convince them that doing nothing is not a viable option and that it is prudent to act sooner versus later. This is particularly true when you have large, known, and growing problems that do not present an immediate crisis.

We reviewed the growth in the size and scope of the federal government over time. We then showed how the federal government had lost control of the budget and that most of the annual budget was comprised of "mandatory spending" and was on "auto pilot." We also reviewed trends in federal revenues, spending, deficits, and debt burdens over time. This provided a historical context up to 2012. We then showed a number of projections regarding the future from authoritative sources (e.g., GAO, CBO, Social Security, and Medicare Trustees). Keep in mind that the situation in 2012 was bad, but we are much worse off in 2020, and the projections forward are much worse than they were in 2012, especially after COVID-19. As a result, while they understood the problem then and supported needed actions, I am confident they would be even more concerned and supportive now with the right kind of leadership and engagement approach.

After discussing the above matters, we then asked the participants whether they felt that we were on a "burning platform" from a fiscal perspective. More than 95% of both groups answered in the affirmative. We then asked them whether they thought it was prudent to act sooner versus later. More than 90% of both groups answered in the affirmative. Finally, we asked them whether they thought "putting our fiscal house in order" should be a top priority for Congress and the president. More than 90% of both groups answered in the affirmative. Keep in mind that this was after passage of the Affordable Care Act (ACA) in early 2010 and after the unsuccessful conclusion of the Simpson–Bowles Commission in late 2010.

After building the "burning platform" case, we turned to discussing appropriate fiscal goals and metrics. This included a discussion of the difference between deficits and debt. Simply stated, deficits are the difference between the total amount of spending each year as compared to the total amount of revenue for the year. Debt for the purpose of this exercise was the sum total of all past deficits and surpluses (e.g., debt held by the public). We also discussed how to measure the total economy (i.e., GDP). We acknowledged that sometimes deficits are necessary or even appropriate (e.g., wars, serious recessions or depressions, national emergencies). We also noted that not all debt is bad (e.g., debt incurred to win wars that benefit multiple generations, and investments in things like basic research and infrastructure that have economic merit and benefit multiple generations). Finally, we discussed the types of fiscal metrics that some other countries and systems use to help achieve "fiscal sustainability." These included "balanced budget" requirements, like most states, debt ceilings, like the U.S. federal government, and public debt/GDP limits, like the Eurozone, New Zealand, Sweden, and Switzerland. We had a more detailed discussion of why debt held by the public/GDP might be the most appropriate metric since, as discussed in Chapters 11 and 14, "balanced budget" provisions can be gamed and the federal debt ceiling limit has not been effective.

After reviewing and discussing all of the above material, more than 80% of the participants in both groups felt that the correct fiscal goal would be to achieve a level of debt held by the public/GDP of 60% by

2025 and in a manner that is sustainable over time. This is the same level of debt/GDP used by the Eurozone countries.

After agreeing on an overall fiscal debt held by the public/GDP target, the discussion turned to what an appropriate mix of prospective spending cuts to prospective revenue increases should be. In doing so, we reviewed past and projected spending and revenue trends. We discussed how additional economic growth will generate additional revenues at current tax rates and that a reduction in deficits, through spending cuts and/or tax increases, would result in reduced interest costs. We also noted that by achieving a reasonable and sustainable debt held by the public/GDP ratio, we can achieve higher economic growth, create more jobs, have more budget flexibility, avoid a debt crisis, and enhance the economic and national security of the U.S.

Based on these factors and after a thorough discussion, more than 80% of both groups agreed that achieving a 2:1 projected spending reductions to projected revenue increases ratio, excluding interest, would be appropriate. Keep in mind that at that time interest was the federal government's fastest-growing recurring expense, and it still is today.

Now that we had built the burning platform, decided on an appropriate fiscal sustainability goal, and an appropriate ratio of prospective spending cuts to revenue increases, we turned to discussing appropriate principles and values that should guide our overall reform effort. I have always believed that in making tough transformational changes, in addition to having a goal, you should also have a set of principles and values that will bring people together. After all, change is tough, especially if it involves spending cuts and tax increases in a situation where an immediate crisis does not compel the action.

After a thorough discussion, more than 85% of the participants in both groups agreed on the following six principles and values to guide the overall reform effort:

- Pro-Growth
- Socially Equitable
- Culturally Acceptable
- Mathematical Integrity

- Politically Feasible
- Meaningful Bipartisan Support

"Pro-growth" was the first key principle, because with additional growth comes additional opportunity, which can result in more jobs, additional federal revenues (e.g., taxes), and reduced federal spending (e.g., welfare). It is also an appropriate principle because our fiscal goal is based on debt held by the public/GDP. Therefore, if we can grow the GDP denominator (the economy) faster than the debt numerator (accumulated deficits), we will still be making progress. This is what we did between 1945 and 1980 with great success; however, things have changed a lot since then, and we have clearly lost our way since 2003.

"Socially equitable" is an appropriate principle because, while we are an opportunity-based society, we need a solvent, sustainable, and secure social safety net for those who are truly in need. At the same time, we do not want public policies and programs to discourage work, marriage, and other important societal relationships.

"Culturally acceptable" is an appropriate principle because there is a limit as to how large the federal government should get and how much the federal government should tax based on our desire to have strong economic growth, an adequate national defense, and be competitive with other nations. These limits may change over time based on societal changes and our relative position as compared to other countries, but the truth remains that the private sector is the primary driver of economic growth and innovation.

"Mathematical integrity" means that the estimation of the economic, fiscal and other impacts of the reforms needs to be based on transparent and reasonable assumptions, proven economic theories, and credible and consistent methodologies with appropriate contextual sophistication. This is an appropriate principle because government is infamous for having its own accounting methods, politicians are noted for making overly rosy economic forecasts, and the media can be biased and is typically not adept at providing appropriate contextual sophistication.

"Politically feasible" means that the overall reform package needs to be able to pass the House and Senate, and be able to be signed by the president. Although theoretically if the president vetoed the legislation, his/her veto could be overridden by a two-thirds vote of each House of Congress, such a supermajority override is unrealistic. From a practical perspective, any major fiscal reform package will be controversial and will need to have the president's support to become law. In fact, the president will have to use his/her "bully pulpit" extensively to help sell it to the American people, a pulpit that only the president has. Finally, while the House only requires a majority vote, under normal Senate rules at least 60 Senators must support consideration of a piece of legislation for it to go to the floor for debate and an ultimate vote. Importantly, this 60-vote requirement is suspended in connection with budget reconciliation bills. Therefore, it is highly likely that any major fiscal reform package would be considered as part of the annual budget reconciliation process.

Finally, any major fiscal reform package must have meaningful bipartisan support. This principle may seem to be redundant with the politically feasible principle, but it is much more. While it is possible to pass legislation along a straight party-line vote, such legislation would not be deemed to be fair by the American people. In addition, given the close margins in the House and Senate and periodic changes in control of each, not having meaningful bipartisan support would likely result in the reform package being undone, in whole or part, over time, by a future Congress.

Now that we have established that a "burning platform" exists, determined a "goal," and established some principles and values to guide the determination of a fiscal reform package, it is appropriate to address the other six elements that were the subject of these two special events. We will do so in the next several chapters.

CHAPTER 14

BUDGET PROCESS AND CONTROLS

The first topic we had the two representative groups of voters address in 2012 after building the "burning platform" case and agreeing on a goal and set of principles and values, was the budget process and need for additional controls. We had already achieved more than 90% agreement that the nation had lost control of its finances. Therefore, it goes without saying that the budget process and controls that are in place have failed.

The following January 2020 graphic from the Congressional Budget Office (CBO) demonstrates the loss of fiscal discipline in recent years. Importantly, the below projection figures are before the impacts of COVID-19.

Total Deficits and Surpluses

Percentage of GDP

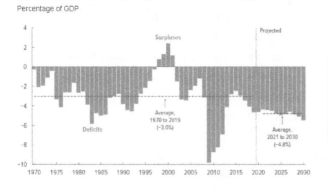

Deficits as a percentage of GDP are projected to rise from 4.6 percent in 2020 to 5.4 percent in 2030. They exceed their 50-year average throughout that period.

Source: Congressional Budget Office.

When October 1 (the first day of the fiscal year) falls on a weekend, certain payments that would have ordinarily been made on that day are instead made at the end of September and thus are shifted into the previous fiscal year. All projections presented here have been adjusted to exclude the effects of those timing shifts. Historical amounts have been adjusted as far back as the available data will allow.

GDP = gross domestic product.

In addition to running sizeable deficits, Congress has lost control of spending. As noted in Chapter 6, in 1912 Congress controlled 97% of all federal spending annually, and the only expense it did not control was interest. Due to the expansion in the size and scope of government and the implementation of many mandatory spending programs (e.g., Social Security, Medicare, Medicaid, agricultural subsidies) since then, the amount of annual federal spending controlled by Congress has fallen to about 29% in 2019, down from 35% during the 2012 $10 Million a Minute Tour, and the percentage is expected to continue to fall in the future per the CBO. Stated differently, as of 2019, Congress had written a "blank check" for 71% of the annual budget, and that percentage was growing despite huge and increasing budget deficits and debt levels!

Before we discuss sensible solutions, it is appropriate to provide an overview of the current federal budget and appropriations process. By law, the president is supposed to present an annual proposed budget to Congress by the first Monday in February each year. The proposed budget is for one year and typically includes a number of policy proposals and the projected impact on revenues, spending, deficits, and debt levels over the next 10 years. In many cases, especially when the opposite political party from the president controls one or both Houses of Congress, the president's budget is deemed to be "dead on arrival." In effect, the president's budget is a bid (a proposal), and Congress has to decide what to do (a disposal).

Both Houses of Congress have budget committees, and they normally have the director of the Office of Management and Budget (OMB) testify on the president's overall proposed budget. The Senate and House budget committees will then draft and vote on a budget resolution that includes top-line numbers for discretionary spending (i.e., the part of the budget that is not on autopilot and is subject to annual appropriations and spending caps). This resolution must be approved by both Houses of Congress but, unlike most legislation, it does not require the president's signature. The budget resolution is supposed to be completed and acted on by April 15 of each year. The budget resolution sets the overall level of spending that is then used by the Senate and House Appropriations Committees to determine detailed spending levels based on 12 major categories of federal spending (e.g., Agriculture, Defense, Homeland Security, and Legislative Branch). The 12 respective appropriations subcommittees then take testimony from all the respective agencies before deciding on appropriations legislation. Each subcommittee votes on its assigned category, and the resulting legislation then proceeds to the full appropriations committee for consideration. Once the full committee agrees on a bill, typically with some amendments, it is sent to the full Senate or House for action. Once the House and the Senate each passes and reconciles any differences for each of the 12 appropriations bills, the bills are sent to the president for his/her signature. If the president signs the bill it becomes law. If he/she vetoes it, then Congress must either override the veto via a two-thirds vote to override the president's veto or send the president another bill that he/she will sign.

The above process continues until all 12 appropriations bills have been signed into law. That is supposed to happen well in advance of the beginning of the fiscal year, which is October 1. However, in many years, Congress does not get its job done on time and has to pass a Continuing Resolution for any appropriations that have not been passed pending passage of a final bill. A Continuing Resolution essentially funds the applicable federal agencies at the same level as the prior year. If the president and Congress cannot agree on a Continuing Resolution, the applicable agencies will be shut down for all but essential services until an appropriations level is agreed to and signed into law. Shutdowns represent a failure of the budget process and are very costly and disruptive. In the vast majority of cases, some services are not provided and contracts are not issued, while once the differences are resolved, federal employees are paid retroactively and the pending contracts are issued. As a result, there are major adverse productivity impacts, but typically little, if any, actual financial savings. In fact, this can even result in additional costs due to contract termination clauses and other factors!

With increasing frequency, Congress fails to pass all 12 appropriations bills by the beginning of the fiscal year. This results in one or more Continuing Resolutions. In addition, if a number of appropriations bills have not been acted on, this typically results in an Omnibus Budget Bill that includes all remaining appropriations bills and possible other legislation. If there are differences between the Senate and the House, as with all legislation, they must be reconciled. The resulting budget reconciliation bill is acted on and sent to the president for his/her signature. Importantly, budget reconciliation bills do not require 60

Senators to agree to consider the bill before debating and only require a simple majority vote. As a result, the budget reconciliation process is likely to be the vehicle that is used in connection with any major fiscal reform legislation.

The above-described annual process has not worked very well over the years. In fact, Congress has only been able to pass all 12 appropriations bills and have them signed into law by the president by the end of the fiscal year four times in the past 68 years. As a professor, that is an F minus if you ask me! In addition, there have been a number of "Shutdowns" as a result of a failure to pass related legislation, including three between 2013 and 2019 that involved the furlough of hundreds of thousands of federal employees. Clearly the current system is broken and needs major reforms.

So what types of reforms might be in order? During the $10 Million a Minute Tour, we achieved more than 80% support from both groups for a reform package that included the following three items:

- **No Budget, No Pay:** This was the most popular reform element, and it was almost universally supported. Under this reform, Congress would not be paid if it failed to pass a budget and all 12 appropriations bills by the beginning of the fiscal year (i.e., October 1). If it failed to do so, which it has failed to do in all but four of the last 68 years, pay for Congress would be suspended until it had passed all the appropriations bills either individually or through an omnibus bill. Importantly, unlike what happens with federal workers in a typical shutdown, Congress would not receive any retroactive pay after they pass the required appropriations bills.

    Passing annual appropriations bills is the only express and enumerated responsibility that both Houses of Congress have every year under the Constitution. Rather than federal workers and U.S. citizens suffering the consequences for the failure of Congress to do its job, the members should be held accountable. One way to do so is by adopting this No Budget: No Pay concept. The State of California was having problems passing its annual appropriations bills on time and, as a result,

143

passed a provision like this. Guess what? They have not had a problem since!

Due to the 27ᵗʰ Amendment, which requires that any changes in congressional pay need to be effective in the next Congress, adopting the above would require that the change be implemented during the following Congress. That is a small price to pay. As they say, better late than never.

- **Recapture Control Over the Budget:** The second proposal related to reducing the amount of the budget that is on autopilot. Under the proposal, the only items that would not be subject to an annual appropriation cap would be Social Security and interest on the federal debt. Based on 2019 figures, that would mean mandatory spending would be reduced from 71% of the budget to about 33%. Other current mandatory spending programs would not be eliminated, but they would no longer be given a "blank check."

    The reason for the two exceptions is pretty simple. Social Security is the most popular federal program, and its expenditures, unlike Medicare and Medicaid, can be calculated with a reasonable degree of certainty given the nature of the related programs. In addition, just as in 1912, you cannot cap interest expense although self-dealing in your own debt can hold the costs down for a while until the market realizes what is going on. All the more reason to act sooner rather than later to put our nation's finances in order.

- **Reform Budget Controls:** As you can clearly see from the below U.S. government graphic, the current debt ceiling concept has not constrained the growth in the size and scope of the federal government nor has it caused Congress and the president to make the needed structural reforms to our nation's spending and tax practices. Stated differently, the current debt ceiling approach has been a failure. In addition, as noted in Chapter 8, the debt ceiling has been suspended until July 31, 2021. That turned out to be fortuitous for Congress and the president, given the huge amount of additional spending resulting from COVID-19.

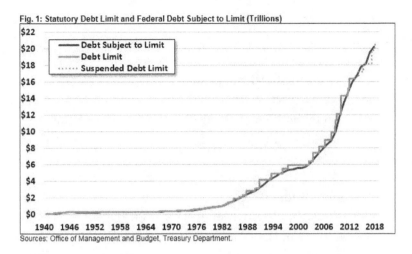

Fig. 1: Statutory Debt Limit and Federal Debt Subject to Limit (Trillions)

Sources: Office of Management and Budget, Treasury Department.

We are the only major industrialized nation in the world that has a debt ceiling. Most other nations focus on debt/GDP approaches. As a result, under this proposal the debt ceiling would be eliminated and a public debt/GDP limit would be imposed. In 2012, the proposed limit was 60% by 2025 with automatic enforcement mechanisms on both the spending side and the tax side if the limit is violated. However, given the dramatic escalation of debt held by the public/GDP, that limit needs to be reconsidered. A more appropriate target might be to achieve 90% of public debt/GDP by a certain date (e.g., 2030), with interim milestones while retaining automatic enforcement mechanisms if the milestones are not met. Given how badly things have spun out of control since 2012 and the impact of COVID-19, it is also appropriate to pursue a Constitutional Fiscal Responsibility Amendment through the normal congressional legislative process or the alternative states adoption process as authorized under Article V of the Constitution. More on this subject later in this chapter.

The second aspect of the third element dealt with "pay-as-you-go rules." Namely, when you are in a hole, the first thing you need to do is quit digging! Contrary to the claims by some, you cannot dig your way out of a hole, you must climb out of it! Under this concept, absent a supermajority vote by both the House and Senate (e.g., 60%), any proposed tax cuts or spending increases would have to be offset to ensure that they did not make our debt/GDP situation worse. And to safeguard against some assertions like "the tax cuts or spending increases will pay for themselves," there would be a "show me test." Namely, the public debt/GDP limits would still have to be met. Therefore, this in essence provides a "belt and suspenders" approach to help ensure fiscal responsibility.

While the above three reforms are the only ones that were submitted for consideration by both representative groups of voters during the $10 Million a Minute Tour, the following three budget reforms should also be considered.

- **Biannual Budgets:** Given the failure to pass timely annual budgets and since most states budget on a biannual basis, the federal government should move to biannual budgets as well. This would save a considerable amount of time in the year the budget was not being acted on, and that time could be used for increased congressional oversight and, as appropriate, legislative activities.

- **Separate Operating and Capital Budgets:** Most states also have separate operating and capital budgets. They seek to "balance" the operating budget while providing flexibility to borrow for worthwhile capital projects (e.g., basic research, critical infrastructure) whose costs and benefits should be spread over many years. The federal government currently has a "unified" federal budget that combined these two items. As a result, it serves to constrain the willingness and ability to enact much-needed and economically meritorious investments. By adopting this approach in combination with the debt held by the public/GDP approach discussed above, we can achieve a better balance between investment and fiscal issues.

- **Flat Earth Fiscal Forecasting:** It is time to recognize that 10-year (flat earth) fiscal forecasts for both tax and spending legislative proposals are inadequate. Given known demographic trends, rising health care costs, changes in the economy, mounting debt burdens, and other factors, the longer-term fiscal implications of major legislative proposals need to be disclosed before any related votes. As a result, we must look over the horizon and beyond 10 years when considering major fiscal legislation.

CONSTITUTIONAL AMENDMENT

It should be clear the federal government has lost control of the nation's finances, and neither political party is dedicated to fiscal responsibility. It should also be obvious that past statutory budget controls have not worked and, while they can help if properly designed and implemented, they can be suspended or repealed through legislation. Therefore, given the seriousness of our situation and the stakes involved, I believe the time has come to adopt a fiscal responsibility constitutional amendment.

This amendment would not be focused on achieving a "balanced budget" because that type of approach is not appropriate at the federal level and, as noted in Chapter 8, it has been ineffective at the state level. Therefore, the related constitutional amendment should focus on getting debt held by the public/GDP to a reasonable and sustainable level and not exceeding it in the future, absent extraordinary events (e.g., a formal declaration of war by Congress).

Article V of the Constitution provides two means to adopt a constitutional amendment. The traditional route, which has been used for all 27 Amendments to date, is for both the House and the Senate to pass a proposed amendment by a two-thirds majority and then three-quarters of the states would have to ratify it. This is the preferred approach, but it is not the only approach. The nation's Founders also realized that federal elected officials could become so out of touch and out of control that they may not act on certain issues. For example, ones that limited their ability to tax and spend without limit or that set term limits. To remedy this, Article V also provides a state-led option. Under this option, two-thirds (34 currently) of the states would call for a Constitutional Convention to consider one or more amendments and three-quarters of the states (currently 38) would have to ratify any proposed amendment(s) resulting from the Convention.

Several groups have been supporting this option, including the Center for State Led National Debt Solutions. I serve on the Advisory Board of CSNDS (www.csnds.org). To date, they have achieved 28 of the 34 required state resolutions calling for a single-issue state-led Constitutional Convention that would propose a federal Fiscal Responsibility Amendment for ratification by the states. I hope that this effort is successful.

Success can be achieved in two ways. First, by forcing Congress to act in order to avoid a state-led Constitutional Convention as was the case in connection with the 17th Amendment (i.e., direct election of Senators). Alternatively, for a single-issue Convention to be held that produces an appropriate amendment for adoption by the states. Under both of these approaches the president has no official role although he/she could use his/her "bully pulpit" to encourage action and adoption. Under the second state-led approach, Congress has no role other than setting the time and place for the Convention. We need action on this matter sooner versus later. After all, the fuse on our debt bomb is getting shorter every day, and only God knows when it might go off.

Now that we have addressed needed budget reforms and controls, let's move on to address specific programs and policies that need to be reviewed and revised. We will start with Social Security.

CHAPTER 15

SOCIAL SECURITY

Social Security is the most popular and arguably the most important social insurance program in the United States. While the U.S. has been a leader in many things since its founding, including creating the greatest political document in history (i.e., the U.S. Constitution), it was not the leader in establishing social insurance programs.

Germany was the first country to establish such a retirement income program for seniors. The German social insurance program was established by Otto Von Bismarck in 1889 and provided a modest pension to individuals who reached the age of 70. At the time, the average life expectancy at birth was 40! Given these facts, I like to say that Bismarck was a brilliant politician. He made a "liberal" type promise that was fiscally "conservative."

When Bismarck, who was a political "conservative," originally proposed the program in 1881, he was accused of being a "socialist." In reply he said, "Call it socialism or whatever you like. It is the same to me." Later, when President Franklin Delano Roosevelt, who was a political "liberal," proposed an American Social Security program, he was also called a socialist. Needless to say, he did not care and is the only American president to be elected four times. That cannot ever happen again due to the 22nd Amendment, which limits presidents to two terms, the model that George Washington voluntarily established at the beginning of the American republic.

Germany later reduced its retirement eligibility age to 65 in 1916, which was during WWI. At that time, German life expectancy at birth was about 47. German life expectancy at birth today is about 81.

The U.S. adopted its Social Security system, which had and still has three elements, in 1935. First, it is a retirement income program for individuals who work at least 40 quarters and meet the age eligibility requirements. Second, it is a survivor's insurance program for children of persons who were eligible for Social Security retirement benefits but died. Senator Lindsey Graham (R-SC) was a prominent beneficiary of this program when he was a child and after both his parents died. Third, it is a Disability Insurance (DI) program for individuals who have met the work requirements but become disabled before becoming eligible for Social Security retirement benefits.

The initial eligibility age for full Social Security retirement benefits was 65. However, eligible individuals could take early retirement at age 62 with a reduced monthly benefit based on life expectancy. In 1935, life expectancy at birth in the U.S. was almost 62, as compared to 61 in Germany.

The initial benefit levels were fairly modest and "progressive." By progressive, I mean that the relative benefit level for lower-income workers was higher than that of higher-income workers. Stated differently, lower-income workers received a higher percentage of their pre-retirement wages than higher-income workers did.

The initial Social Security program covered most of the population but excluded government workers at all levels of government. As was the case in Germany in 1879, government workers had their own pension plans.

The initial combined Social Security program was financed with a payroll tax of 1% that was imposed on both the employee and the employer up to a wage base cap of $3,000 per year. (That is equivalent to about $53,400 in today's dollars.) The tax began in 1937, and the first benefit payments were made in 1940. While the benefit schedule was deemed to be progressive, the payroll tax system was regressive. By that I mean that the relative tax burden on lower-wage workers was greater than the relative burden on higher-wage workers. This was especially true for workers who made more than $3,000 per year in wages.

Both the payroll tax rate and the payroll tax cap have increased significantly over the years. The payroll tax rate on both employers and workers has been increased periodically, and in 2019 it was 6.2%, as compared to the original rate of 1%. This represents a 520% increase. As noted in the Social Security Administration graphic below, the payroll tax cap increase has been even more dramatic and grew to $132,900 in 2019, or about a 4,330% increase. Unlike the payroll tax rate, which has remained constant since 1990, the wage base cap is indexed and increases every year.

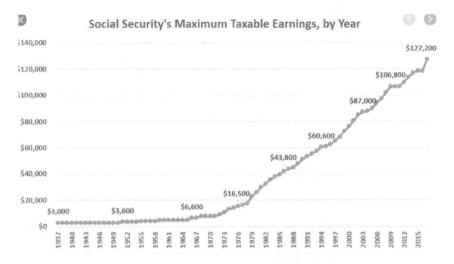

The Social Security and Medicare programs both have several "trust funds." They are very different from the typical trust funds in the private sector. For example, the typical pension trust fund in the private sector is a separate and distinct legal entity that has to be managed for the exclusive benefit of its participants and beneficiaries. Private-sector trust funds have fiduciaries that are responsible for investing the money prudently, solely in the interests of and for the exclusive purpose of paying benefits to plan participants and beneficiaries, and to avoid conflicts of interest. Like other federal government trust funds, the Social Security and Medicare Trust Funds are not separate and distinct legal entities. They do not have fiduciary responsibility provisions or conflict of interest rules. In addition, any cash flow surplus must, by law, be invested in U.S. government securities or securities that are backed by the full faith and credit of the U.S. government. Historically, these trusts have only invested in U.S. Treasury securities.

Given the above, government trust finds are more like intragovernmental accounting devices, or as I call them, the "trust the government funds." Believe it or not, the federal government does not consider the trillions of dollars in government bonds held by these trusts to be a liability of the U.S. government, and those amounts are not counted in the debt held by the public figure that is shown on the balance sheet of the U.S. government. Those amounts are, however, subject to the debt ceiling limit, which has been suspended until July 31, 2021.

In my view, this accounting treatment is wrong. After all, the government took employees' and employers' payroll taxes, spent them on other government expenses, and replaced the amounts with U.S. government bonds that are guaranteed by the 14th Amendment of the Constitution, as to both principal and interest. As a result, the trust funds should be treated as separate and distinct legal entities and the debt shown as an asset (investment) for the trust fund and a liability in the U.S. government's financial statements. Unfortunately, too many traditional economists and politicians do not support this. After all, they would rather continue to ignore the trillions in trust fund debt and continue to just focus on the lower debt held by the public/gross domestic product (GDP) ratio. For example, at the end of Fiscal 2019, the debt held by the public/GDP ratio was 78% and the debt subject to the debt ceiling limit was 105%. That's a big difference!

However, to a certain extent this gap is just a timing difference. Why? Because when the Social Security and Medicare programs run cash flow deficits, as they are now, the trust funds have to cash in some of their Treasury securities to pay benefits on time. In order to do so, the U.S. government has to borrow from the public, either domestically or internationally, to generate the cash for payments. As a result, when the trust funds go to zero (i.e., est. 2032 for the combined Old-Age and Survivors Insurance and Disability Insurance (OASDI) Trust Funds after COVID-19), all of the related trust fund debt will have been converted to debt held by the public, assuming that the federal government continues to run deficits. You can bet on that! That is enough discussion on trust funds and accounting issues.

The financial condition of the Social Security system has varied over the years. As noted previously, Social Security taxes began in 1937, while the first benefits were not paid until 1940. This helped to cover "startup costs" and provide an adequate amount of funds to pay full promised benefits in a timely manner. However, the Old-Age and Survivors Insurance (OASI) Trust Fund, which pays Social Security retirement and survivors income benefits, began to experience serious financial challenges in 1974. The Trust Fund balance declined every year and would have declined at an even more rapid rate in 1980–1981 if the payroll tax rate had not been changed to provide a higher amount to the OASI program versus the DI program.

In October of 1982, the OASI Trust Fund balance was down to $10 billion, which was about $1 billion less than was needed to pay full OASI benefits on time in November. As a result, OASI borrowed from both the DI and Medicare Hospital Insurance (HI) Trust Funds in order to be able to make payments on time. These loans harmed the financial status of the DI and HI programs, but the loans were later repaid with interest.

President Reagan was made aware of the projected financial problems relating to Social Security when he assumed office. As a result, in 1981 he and Congress agreed to establish a National Commission on Social Security Reform. The president and the Senate and House leaders were each given five appointments to the Commission, which included sitting members of the House and Senate, as well as prominent business leaders, labor leaders, and Social Security experts. The Commission was headed by Alan Greenspan, who would later be appointed Chairman of the Federal Reserve by President Reagan. It was therefore informally known as the Greenspan Commission.

The Commission's work lasted more than one and a half years, and its final report was issued in January 1983, not long after the extraordinary lending measures noted above were taken. The Commission made a number of recommendations to restore the financial integrity of the OASI Trust Fund. Their major recommendations included the following:

- Revised and accelerated the scheduled gradual increase in the payroll tax rate that would ultimately reach 6.2% in 1990.
- Taxed a portion of Social Security benefits for higher-income beneficiaries.
- Revised and increased the tax basis for the self-employed.
- Covered nonprofit and new federal employees while prohibiting withdrawals of state and local employees who were already covered under the program.
- Changed the basis of calculating cost-of-living increases (COLAs) to a calendar year basis.

Most of the above recommendations involve revenue increases rather than benefit adjustments. Importantly, the Commission did not recommend changes in the retirement eligibility age.

President Reagan worked with Speaker of the House Tip O'Neill and other congressional leaders to enact Social Security reform in April of 1983. Those were the days of bipartisan action for the greater good. The resulting legislation relied heavily on the work of the Greenspan Commission and included many of its recommendations. It also included gradually increasing the normal retirement age from 65 beginning in 2000 to 67 in 2022. It did not, however, index the normal retirement age to increases in life expectancy or change the early retirement age.

Life expectancy in the U.S. today is about 79, as compared to about 81 in Germany. For comparison purposes, the current German normal retirement eligibility age is 65 plus nine months, and it is being gradually increased to 67 by 2029.

While the Social Security Reform Act of 1983 solved the immediate financial crisis and stabilized the system for many years, it did not adequately consider the impact of demographics on the longer-term financial position of the Social Security system, namely, increasing life spans among the overall population and lower birth rates among American women. Therefore, when I was one of two Public Trustees, along with former Commissioner of Social Security Stan Ross, we noted in our first Public Trustees Report in 1991 that Social Security's long-range financial challenge had not been solved and that additional reforms would be needed to restore Social Security's long-range financial integrity. We also noted that the next reform package should consider the demographic factors that were not adequately considered in the 1983 reforms. Namely, that the goal should be to restore the financial integrity of the program for 75 years and make sure the related reforms considered changes in the dependency ratio and other factors beyond the 75-year period. For example, when I was born in 1951, there were 16 persons working per Social Security beneficiary. Today that ratio is below 3:1 and is projected to decline to 2:1 and possibly lower by no later than 2040. As has been said, demographics are destiny!

Based on the 2020 Annual Social Security Trustees Report, the combined OASDI Trust Fund is expected to go to zero in 2035. However, that was before COVID-19. Because of COVID-19 unemployment increased dramatically, which resulted in fewer payroll tax revenues, more people retiring, and more people seeking disability benefits. In June 2020, the Congressional Budget Office (CBO) estimated that the combined

OASDI Trust Funds are expected to be exhausted in 2032, or three years earlier, due to COVID-19.

Importantly, just because the "Trust Fund" goes to zero does not mean that Social Security is out of money, but it would have an immediate cash flow problem. As a result, Social Security would not be able to pay full benefits when due. For example, based on the 2020 Social Security Trustees Report, if no action is taken, Social Security retirement income and survivors benefits would have to be cut about 24% in order to make income and expenses match. That might not be a big problem for well-off individuals, but it would be a huge problem for poor and near-poor individuals.

In reality, there are separate trust funds for the OASI and the DI program. Looked at separately, based on the 2020 Social Security Trustees Report, the OASI Trust Fund goes to zero in 2034 and DI not until 2065. However, historically these programs have been looked at jointly and have lent to each other in the past when they faced "cash flow" problems. As a result, the combined OASDI Trust Fund exhaustion date of 2035 is the one that most people focus on. As noted previously, the 2035 date is now expected to be 2032 as a result of COVID-19. The below graph from the 2020 Social Security and Medicare Trustees Report shows the rapid increase and decline in these trust funds.

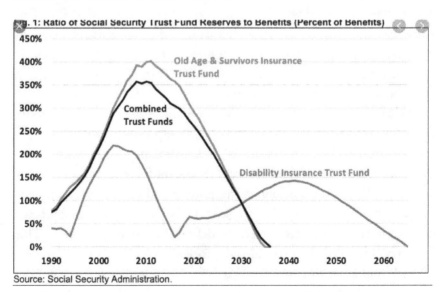

Fig. 1: Ratio of Social Security Trust Fund Reserves to Benefits (Percent of Benefits)

Source: Social Security Administration.

There have been other past attempts by presidents to reform Social Security after the historic 1983 agreement. In the late 1990s President Clinton wanted to reform Social Security as one of his legacies. He worked with AARP and the Concord Coalition to hold three public forums to build support for a reform effort. I was selected by AARP and the Concord Coalition to be a "truth teller" presenter at the forms. I was selected, in part, because I was a CPA, a political independent, and a former public trustee of Social Security and Medicare. At that time I was a partner with Arthur Andersen LLP and a potential candidate for Comptroller General of the United States. The forums went well and I engaged in a couple of meetings at the White House to discuss potential reform packages. Unfortunately, due to President Clinton's personal indiscretions and the subsequent impeachment process, he had to abandon this effort. I believe strongly that the type of reforms he would have proposed then are similar to what will ultimately be adopted when the president and Congress eventually address Social Security reform. The only problem is that the changes will need to be more significant, and there will be less transition time due to the delay.

President George W. Bush (43) also tried to reform Social Security in 2005 after his reelection. President Bush, Vice President Cheney, and other top Bush administration officials engaged in a number of public forums. Their reform proposal was, however, very different from what President Clinton had in mind. In effect, the Bush (43) administration wanted to convert the Social Security program from a monthly defined benefit approach where the government bore the investment risk to a defined contribution program without a promised monthly benefit and where the individual bore the investment risk. While many people could theoretically achieve more retirement income under that approach depending on the investment results and other factors, it ignored the second word in the program's name, which was "Security." President Bush's approach did not allow any distributions or borrowing prior to retirement. In addition, it resulted in a $2 trillion cash flow (i.e., transition obligation) due to the conversion from a defined benefit to defined contribution system. This had to be addressed if you decided to proceed.

It is important to remember that Social Security is the foundation of a three-legged retirement income security system that also includes private pension/retirement savings plans and personal savings arrangements. Social Security benefits were intended to be supplemented by the other two legs to create an adequate amount of income throughout a person's retirement years. Social Security provides a defined monthly benefit that is indexed to inflation and does not cease until the person dies. Most private-sector retirement plans and personal savings arrangements do not share all these features.

According to a 2020 report from the Social Security Administration, the following represents the facts regarding the importance of Social Security benefits to retirees:

- Nearly nine out of ten individuals age 65 and older receive Social Security benefits.
- Social Security benefits represent about 33% of the income of the elderly.
- Among elderly Social Security beneficiaries, 50% of married couples and 70% of unmarried persons receive 50% or more of their income from Social Security.
- Among elderly Social Security beneficiaries, 21% of married couples and about 45% of unmarried persons rely on Social Security for 90% or more of their income.

Given the above facts, President George W. Bush's (43) effort to reform Social Security fell flat. As a result, after numerous public events, he abandoned his reform efforts. Unfortunately, no president since then has tried to reform Social Security. This is very frustrating for three reasons:

- Social Security is much easier to reform than Medicare and health care.
- There are ways to reform Social Security that will exceed the expectations of all generations of Americans.
- The sooner we reform Social Security, the fewer the reforms that are needed and the more transition time we have.

Why do I say that we can exceed the expectations of all generations of Americans? Because my experience over many years has shown that seniors fear that their benefits will be cut significantly and younger people do not even think they will receive Social Security. Realistically, current seniors' benefits will not be cut much, if at all, for two reasons. First, it would not be fair. Second, it would not be politically feasible since seniors vote a lot more than young people do.

Given the above, it is possible to reform Social Security in a way that phases changes in over time and exceeds the expectations of every generation of Americans. I call that a win! So what are we waiting for?

POSSIBLE REFORMS

The following package of reforms achieved 77% support from both representative groups of voters during the $10 Million a Minute Tour:

- **Raise the Retirement Eligibility Ages:** Gradually increase both the early and normal retirement ages for Social Security by two years to 64 and 69, respectively, over 20 years and then index the eligibility ages to increases in life expectancy. This proposed reform recognizes changes in the nature of the economy and longer life spans. The increase would be accompanied by special early retirement provisions for persons who work in certain manual labor fields.
- **Raise the Taxable Wage Base Cap:** Increase, but do not eliminate, the taxable wage base cap to equal 90% of wages, consistent with the Reagan years. This reform recognizes the growing gap between the "haves" and "have nots." It is in lieu of raising the payroll tax rate, which would be regressive.
- **Modify the Benefit Formulas:** Change the initial benefit formula to provide somewhat higher benefits for lower- and lower-middle income workers and somewhat lower benefits for upper-income workers but do not make it a means-tested program. This proposed reform increases the progressivity of the benefit structure under Social Security while maintaining a broad-based and virtually universal social insurance program.
- **Increase the Minimum Benefit:** Increase the minimum benefit level for lower-income workers and survivors to ensure they would

not be in poverty. This proposed reform is intended to ensure that workers with at least 35 years of work do not live in poverty during their retirement years.

The above reforms were designed to make the program solvent, sustainable, and secure indefinitely, including beyond the 75-year horizon the Social Security trustees are required to consider. In addition to the above reforms, certain other reforms should also be considered, including the following:

- **Change Cost-of-Living Adjustment:** Modify the basis for the cost-of-living adjustment to better reflect price increases for seniors. This reform recognizes basket of goods for seniors is different from the population as a whole, and the cost-of-living adjustment (COLA) should reflect that difference.
- **Implement a Supplemental Savings Account:** Add an automatic and supplemental savings program (e.g., 2–3% of pay) on top of a reformed base defined benefit program. This reform recognizes the need to increase the national savings rate and provide an efficient and effective means for individuals to supplement their Social Security benefit in retirement. This automatic savings vehicle could be attached to a number of existing public and private savings and investment vehicles, including private-sector plans and the Federal Thrift Savings Plan for federal employees. Individuals would only be able to take distributions for death, disability, or retirement reasons, although there could be limited loan provisions prior to any of those events in certain hardship situations.

From time to time some presidents, including President Trump in 2020, talk about temporarily suspending or cutting the payroll tax for Social Security, and possibly Medicare, to help stimulate the economy during a recession. While this action might help to stimulate the economy and generate additional jobs and income tax revenues as compared to the status quo in the short term, it would have a significant adverse effect on the financial condition and trust fund exhaustion dates for these programs.

The nature and extent of the impact would depend on the amount and duration of the actual payroll tax cut.

As noted previously, Social Security benefits are not guaranteed by the Constitution of the United States. In a 1960 decision, *Flemming v. Nestor*, the Supreme Court ruled that Congress can alter, or even terminate, Social Security benefits. The same concept applies to Medicare, Medicaid, and other mandatory spending programs. There is, however, a difference between what can be done legally versus politically.

In summary, Social Security is a critically important social insurance program with several dimensions. It has help to dramatically reduce the poverty rate among seniors and has provided valuable income assistance to survivors and the disabled. The above collective reforms would help to ensure that Social Security is modernized while making it solvent, sustainable, and secure indefinitely. So what are we waiting for? It is time to get on with it!

CHAPTER 16

MEDICARE, MEDICAID, AND HEALTH CARE

While interest costs are the fastest-growing expense in the federal budget, health care, represents the fastest-growing programmatic expense. This includes Medicare, Medicaid, civilian, military, and veterans' health care, as well as subsidies under the Affordable Care Act (ACA). According to the Congressional Budget Office (CBO), these items amounted to more than $1.3 trillion in Fiscal 2019, and the related costs were growing faster than the economy (i.e., gross domestic product [GDP]). In addition, according to the Joint Committee on Taxation, the federal government lost about $273 billion in tax revenues in Fiscal 2019 due to tax preferences (also known as "tax expenditures" since they serve to reduce revenues) relating to health care (e.g., individual tax exclusion for employer-provided coverage, ACA premium tax credits). CBO also noted that net federal outlays amounted to $4.4 trillion and total federal tax preferences amounted to $1.4 trillion in Fiscal 2019. Therefore, health care represented about 29.5% of all federal spending and 19.5% of all federal tax preferences in Fiscal 2019.

Health care also represents the biggest programmatic challenge for state and local governments, as well as for many private and nonprofit sector employers. As a result, it is essential that we reform the nation's health care system in order to ensure access, quality, affordability, and sustainability while also improving the competitive posture of American businesses that compete globally.

MEDICARE

After several prior attempts by President Harry Truman and others, Medicare and Medicaid were finally enacted into law in 1965 as part of President Johnson's "Great Society" programs. Former President Harry

Truman joined President Lyndon Johnson at the signing ceremony in the White House.

Medicare was intended to cover 80% of health care costs for persons ages 65 and over, as well as for individuals under the age of 65 who were permanently disabled. Medicare is run by the federal government and is funded through a combination of payroll taxes, individual insurance premiums, and federal government funding (i.e., general revenues).

Medicare initially included two programs. First, the Hospital Insurance (HI) program, which is funded primarily by payroll taxes imposed on both workers and their employers initially up to the Social Security taxable wage base cap (see Chapter 15), which has now been eliminated. Second, the Supplementary Medical Insurance (SMI) program, which is funded by individual premiums and federal funding.

Over the years Medicare has been reformed to add Medicare Advantage (Part C) in 1997 and Medicare Prescription Drug Plans (Part D) in 2003. Medicare Advantage is a type of Health Maintenance Organization (HMO) operated by private-sector insurers.

The federal government has tended to significantly understate the cost of health care programs over time. For example, in 1967, the House Ways and Means Committee said the entire Medicare program would cost $12 billion in 1990. The actual cost in 1990 was $98 billion. In 1987, Congress projected that Medicaid — the joint federal–state health care program for the poor — would make special relief payments to hospitals of less than $1 billion in 1992. Actual cost: $17 billion.

While it is important to understand the estimation errors from the past, it is also important to know that cost estimation has improved significantly over time. The following graphic demonstrates how Medicare has become a larger portion of the federal budget over time, and that trend is expected to increase in the future.

The below graphic demonstrates the projected increase in Medicare costs as a percentage of the economy (GDP) over time, broken down by the three main Medicare programs. As you can see, physician and other services (e.g., durable medical equipment) are expected to be the fastest-growing Medicare costs in the future. Durable medical equipment includes such things as walkers, wheelchairs, electric chairs, and beds.

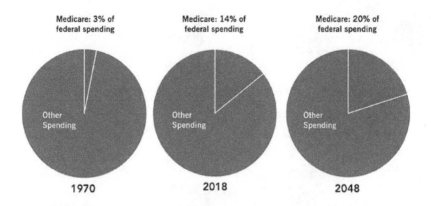

SOURCES: Office of Management and Budget, *Budget of the United States Government, Fiscal Year 2020*, March 2019; and Congressional Budget Office, *The 2018 Long-Term Budget Outlook*, June 2018. Compiled by PGPF.
NOTE: Pies represent total spending.
© 2019 Peter G. Peterson Foundation   PGPF.ORG

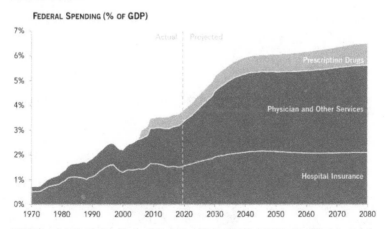

SOURCE: Centers for Medicare and Medicaid Services, *2020 Annual Report of the Boards of Trustees of the Federal Hospital Insurance and Federal Supplementary Medical Insurance Trust Funds*, April 2020.
NOTE: The figures shown above are based on gross Medicare spending.
© 2020 Peter G. Peterson Foundation   PGPF.ORG

The distribution of costs for Medicare has changed over time and is expected to continue to change in the future. As the below graphic shows, an increasing percentage of the cost of Medicare is coming from the general funds, which means costs would be primarily paid for by income tax revenues, and that trend is expected to continue in the future.

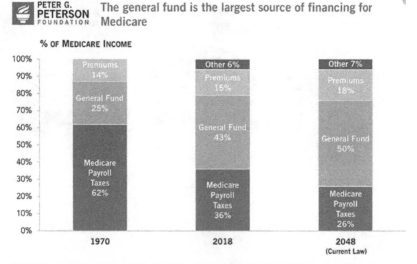

PETER G. PETERSON FOUNDATION — The general fund is the largest source of financing for Medicare

% OF MEDICARE INCOME

1970
- Premiums 14%
- General Fund 25%
- Medicare Payroll Taxes 62%

2018
- Other 6%
- Premiums 15%
- General Fund 43%
- Medicare Payroll Taxes 36%

2048 (Current Law)
- Other 7%
- Premiums 18%
- General Fund 50%
- Medicare Payroll Taxes 26%

SOURCE: Centers for Medicare and Medicaid Services, The 2019 Annual Report of the Boards of Trustees of the Federal Hospital Insurance and Federal Supplementary Medical Insurance Trust Funds, April 2019. Compiled by PGPF.
NOTES: "Other" includes proceeds from the taxation of Social Security benefits, which help to finance Medicare Hospital Insurance costs, as well as drug fees and state transfers. Medicare income does not include interest income. Numbers may not sum to 100% due to rounding.
© 2019 Peter G. Peterson Foundation   PGPF.ORG

Unfortunately, as we have previously discussed, general tax revenues have been far short of the amounts needed to pay for general fund expenses, and this is projected to continue in the future.

As noted previously, Medicare was expanded in 2003 to include prescription drug coverage (Part D). At the time it added an estimated $8 trillion in new unfunded obligations to Medicare. Based on the 2019 consolidated financial statements of the U.S. government, the estimated unfunded obligations for this program have not changed. Based on the 2019 consolidated financial statements, the estimated unfunded obligations of Medicare HI (Part A) were $5.4 trillion and for Medicare SMI (Part B) were $28.8 trillion, for a total unfunded Medicare unfunded obligations of $42.2 trillion. These unfunded promises represent costs that are being passed on to future generations. For comparative purposes, the total unfunded obligations for the combined Social Security programs (OASDI) in the 2019 consolidated financial statements were $16.8 trillion. Therefore, Medicare's unfunded obligations were 2.5 times greater than Social Security! This serves to reinforce the fact that it will be much easier to reform Social Security than Medicare.

Medicare Advantage was created in 1997. Medicare Advantage represents an "all-in-one" Medicare program that is offered by a number of private-sector insurance companies. Under this program, Medicare beneficiaries can choose Medicare Advantage in lieu of traditional Medicare Parts A, B, and D. The insurance companies must offer the minimum Medicare benefits but can offer more. Medicare pays the insurance companies a standard amount that is not risk-adjusted, and their financial results depend to a great extent on the relative health condition of the persons they insure. Medicare beneficiaries continue to pay their applicable Part B and Part D premiums to Medicare rather than the insurance company.

The below graphic shows how the Medicare Advantage program (Part C) has become more popular over time. It is expected to become even more popular in the future.

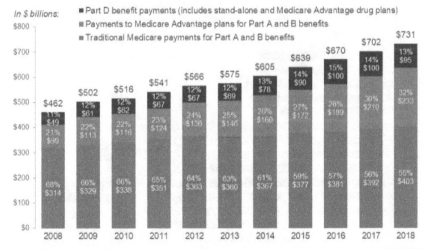

Medicare Benefit Payments for Traditional Medicare and Medicare Advantage, 2008-2018

SOURCE: KFF analysis of Medicare spending data from the 2009-2019 Annual Report of the Boards of Trustees of the Federal Hospital Insurance and Federal Supplementary Medical Insurance Trust Funds, Table II.B1.

Medicare programs have two "Trust Funds" (i.e., Medicare Part A, and Medicare Parts B, C, and D) along the lines of the Social Security Trust Funds. The only one of these that is projected to become exhausted is the HI-Part A Trust Fund that is funded primarily through a 1.45% payroll tax imposed on both workers and employers on all wages. Unlike Social Security, there is no wage base tax cap for Medicare HI-Part A. Based on the 2020 Medicare Trustees Report, the HI-Part A Trust Fund is expected to run dry in 2026. At that point, Medicare in only projected to have about 89 cents in revenue for every dollar of expenses, and that ratio of revenues to spending is projected to decline thereafter. As a result, the day of reckoning for Medicare Part A will come before it does for Social Security.

The below graph shows how that estimated date of HI Trust Fund exhaustion has varied over time. The significant increase in 2010 was primarily attributable to additional tax revenues and reduced provider reimbursement costs resulting from the Affordable Care Act (ACA) in 2010. As noted above, the 2020 Medicare Annual Trustees Report estimated a 2026 exhaustion date. Importantly, this estimate was before COVID-19 hit. In June 2020, the CBO estimated the Medicare HI Trust Fund exhaustion date would be accelerated by three years to 2023 due to COVID-19 — just three years away!

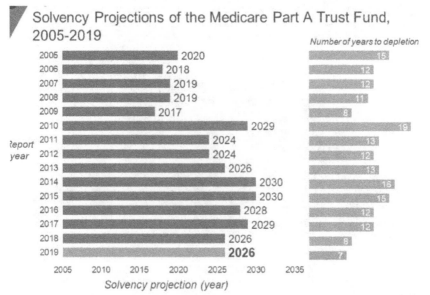

Solvency Projections of the Medicare Part A Trust Fund, 2005-2019

SOURCE: Intermediate projections from 2005-2019 Annual Reports of the Boards of Trustees of the Federal Hospital Insurance and Federal Supplementary Medical Insurance Trust Funds.

MEDICAID

Medicaid is a combined federal and state health care program designed to provide basic health insurance coverage for low-income workers who are not otherwise eligible for Medicare. It is run by the states in accordance with federal guidelines, and the federal government and the states share in the cost. Covered participants pay no premiums and little to no coinsurance costs. The ACA gave states the opportunity to expand Medicaid coverage to a larger portion of the lower-income population, with the federal government picking up any extra costs for several years, and the states would assume their normal portion thereafter. Many states took this option, which resulted in short-term gain and longer-term pain. This is the typical approach for many government fiscal decisions. It is also the opposite of what it takes to get into shape and restore fiscal sustainability.

As the below graphic shows, Medicaid is the third-largest mandatory spending program, behind Social Security and Medicare.

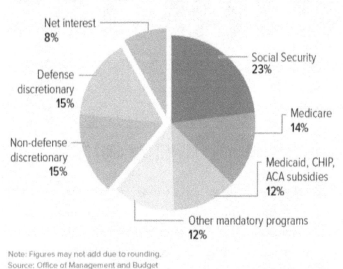

Federal Spending, FY 2019

Net interest 8%

Defense discretionary 15%

Non-defense discretionary 15%

Social Security 23%

Medicare 14%

Medicaid, CHIP, ACA subsidies 12%

Other mandatory programs 12%

Note: Figures may not add due to rounding.
Source: Office of Management and Budget

CENTER ON BUDGET AND POLICY PRIORITIES I CBPP.ORG

Like other health care programs, Medicaid costs are growing faster than the economy and other parts of the federal budget. Medicaid is also the only federal program that covers long-term care. Long-term care provides a broad range of services and support (e.g., bathing, dressing, eating, light cleaning) to meet the everyday living needs of individuals with various impairments. Most long-term care expenses do not relate to medical care.

As noted in the below CBO graphic, Medicaid is expected to comprise an increasing portion of the nation's economy in the future.

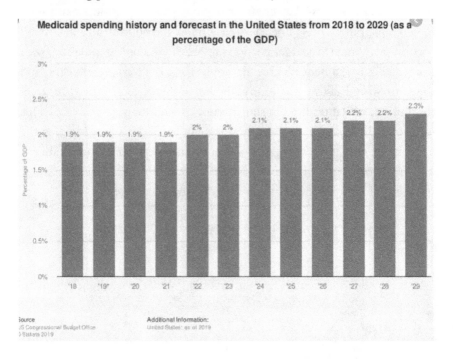

Medicaid spending history and forecast in the United States from 2018 to 2029 (as a percentage of the GDP)

Source
US Congressional Budget Office
Statsta 2019

Additional Information:
United States: as of 2019

CIVILIAN MILITARY AND VETERANS HEALTH CARE

The federal government is the nation's largest employer, with more than 2 million civilian employees, more than 1.3 million active duty military, and more than 800,000 members of the Guard and Reserves. As is true with virtually all other employers, the federal government offers health insurance to all of its full-time workers. There are separate systems for military versus civilian personnel.

Unlike most private-sector employers, the federal government offers very generous and costly retiree health care benefits to both civilian and military personnel. Many state and local governments have followed suit. Given the financial challenges facing all levels of government, these benefits are likely to come under increased scrutiny and will be reformed over time.

The federal government also offers health care coverage to eligible veterans through the Department of Veterans Affairs (VA), which provides a range of health care, disability, and other services to eligible veterans. As the below VA graphic shows, the VA spent about $201 billion in Fiscal 2019, and its budget has increased in recent years.

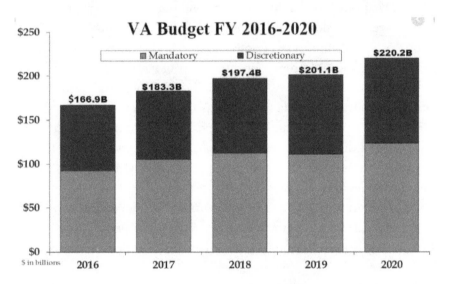

AFFORDABLE CARE ACT (ACA)

After much debate and considerable controversy, the ACA was enacted into law in 2010. The ACA had three primary goals:

- Make affordable health insurance available to more people. The law provides consumers with subsidies ("premium tax credits") that lower costs for households with incomes up to 400% of the federal poverty level.
- Expand the Medicaid programs to cover all adults with income below 138% of the federal poverty level. This expansion was voluntary, and not all states have expanded their Medicaid

programs due to concerns over the longer-term cost of this federal-
and state-funded program.

• Support innovative medical care delivery methods designed to
lower the overall costs of health care.

The ACA generally retained the existing structure of Medicare,
Medicaid, and the employer-based market, but some insurance practices
were changed dramatically. For example, insurers were required to accept
without charging based on preexisting conditions or demographic status
(except age). In order to try and combat "adverse selection," whereby a
disproportionate number of persons with serious health conditions would
seek coverage and a disproportionate number of younger and/or healthier
individuals would not, the ACA mandated that individuals buy insurance
(or pay a penalty). The penalty varied based on income and was capped at
a little over $2,000 per year. It also mandated that insurers cover a list of
"essential health benefits." Needless to say, the government's definition of
"essential" was far more extensive and expensive than what most Americans
would consider to be a "basic" health care plan.

Individuals who obtained coverage under the plan and who were up
to 400% of the federal poverty level were eligible for premium subsidies.
This subsidy is in the form of a refundable tax credit that varies based on
level of income.

The ACA was expected by most to result in a significant increase in
federal spending. However, the related legislation included a number of
tax increases and a reduction in Medicare provider reimbursement rates.
In total, the sponsors of the ACA asserted that the law would expand
coverage dramatically and reduce the federal budget deficit by about $600
billion over 10 years. There were significant differences between what
various groups estimated the actual cost would be. The nonpartisan CBO
estimated that it would reduce the budget deficit by about $143 billion
over 10 years.

The ACA withstood an attack on its constitutionality when in 2012
Chief Justice John Roberts, a President George W. Bush (43) appointee,
voted to retain it based on Congress' power to tax. In doing so, he equated
the penalty for not obtaining the required coverage to be a tax. Ironically,
the individual penalty (tax) for not obtaining the required coverage was

later rescinded effective in 2019. It is too early to tell what impact this will have on overall coverage levels and possible "adverse selection" over time.

As noted in the below graphic, according to a Commonwealth Fund study, the percentage of uninsured declined significantly between 2012 and 2018. Much of this came as a result of the expansion of Medicaid. However, 12% of the population remained uninsured.

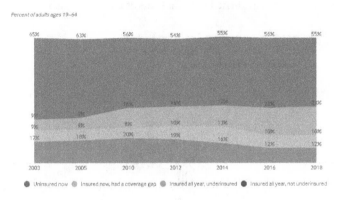

Percent of adults ages 19–64

Uninsured now ● Insured now, had a coverage gap ● Insured all year, underinsured ● Insured all year, not underinsured

OVERALL HEALTH CARE

Health care represents a large and growing part of the American economy. As noted in the below Center for Medicare and Medicaid Services (CMS) graphic, total health care costs have grown from 5% to about 18% of GDP since 1960.

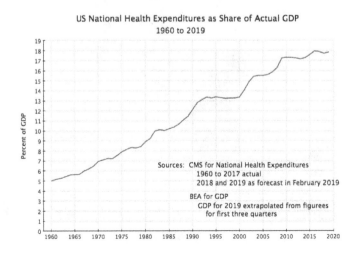

US National Health Expenditures as Share of Actual GDP
1960 to 2019

Sources: CMS for National Health Expenditures
1960 to 2017 actual
2018 and 2019 as forecast in February 2019

BEA for GDP
GDP for 2019 extrapolated from figurees
for first three quarters

As noted in the below graphic, total health care costs are expected to continue to grow as a percentage of the economy (GDP). The primary reasons are demographics and excess health care cost growth. The primary demographic variables are longer life spans and a higher percentage of elderly as compared to the overall population. The excess cost growth is due to a variety of factors, including the predominant fee-for-service reimbursement model and the lack of a budget cap on health care spending.

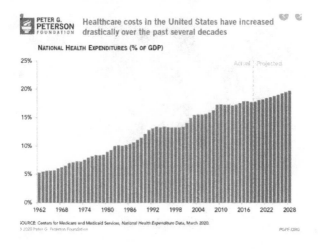

As shown in the below graphic, the U.S. spends a much higher percentage of its economy (GDP) on health care than any other industrialized nation and roughly twice the average for countries that are members of the Organization for Economic Cooperation and Development (OECD).

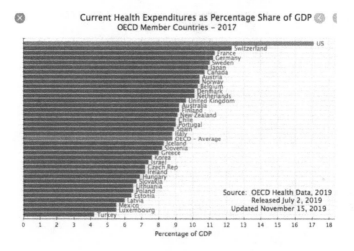

One of the reasons the U.S. spends so much on health care is that health care is one of three major American systems that fails the three-pronged test for success and sustainability. Namely, for any system to be both successful and sustainable over time, it must meet three tests. First, it must have properly designed incentives that encourage positive behavior and discourage abuse. Second, it must have adequate transparency (e.g., cost and quality) to help consumers make informed decisions and to facilitate accountability. Third, there must be adequate accountability for those who abuse the system and rewards for positive behavior. The current U.S. health care system fails all three of these tests. That's called a strikeout! Our K-12 education system and our current political system, especially at the federal level, also fail this basic test.

High health care costs impact employers and individuals as well. For example, the fastest-growing component of total compensation cost for employers is health care. Higher health care costs can result in reduced employment opportunities and compressed wages. Higher health care costs also put U.S. producing companies at a comparative disadvantage to foreign producing companies who are domiciled in countries with single-payer systems. In addition, health care costs represent the single largest reason for personal bankruptcies.

Two other factors also contribute to excessive health care costs. First, health care is where the money is and, as a result, there is a lot of fraud, waste, abuse, and mismanagement in the system. For example, the Department of Health and Human Services estimated that there was $104 billion in improper payments in Medicare and Medicaid alone during Fiscal 2019. In addition, the payments system in the U.S. is very burdensome, resulting in much greater administrative costs.

Although the U.S. dedicates the highest percentage of its GDP to health care and has the highest per capita health care costs, the U.S. has below-average outcomes in connection with health care. For example, according to the American Public Health Association's (APHA) America's Health Rankings, in 2014 the U.S. was ranked 34th in the world on life expectancy at birth. The top three countries were Japan, Andorra, and Singapore.

The U.S. also has well above-average infant mortality and medical error rate statistics. As my wife says, "With health care you pay your money and take your chances. There are no guarantees." I have experienced this firsthand. When I was Comptroller General, I had a bad cycling accident that broke several of my ribs and separated my collarbone from my shoulder. The orthopedic surgeon for two of Washington, DC's professional sports teams operated on me. Unfortunately, the procedure was not very successful, and I now have a separated shoulder held together by a titanium plate. I can still play golf, tennis, and pickleball, but the doctor said I am not allowed to play contact basketball, football, or hockey! In addition, shortly after the first surgery I had to go back in for a second operation to clear out an infection that I got in the hospital! More seriously, four years ago my mother died of an infection that she contracted in the hospital. I miss her.

MEDICARE FOR ALL

Senator Bernie Sanders (I-VT) and others have called for a "Medicare for All" single-payer program. These programs and their related costs vary by individual proposal. For example, Sanders' proposal is intended to provide virtually universal coverage for all U.S. residents (legal and illegal) through a federal health care program that covers all medically necessary services (very broadly defined), including long-term care. Unfortunately, there is no independent and authoritative estimate of the related cost to the federal government or the overall impact on the health care system. Senator Sanders has asserted that it would save about $450 billion a year in total health care costs to the economy, although he acknowledges that the distribution of costs between the government (i.e., taxpayers) and individuals would be very different.

The Medicare for All concept, as well as the topic of health care as a whole, is likely to be a major public policy issue in upcoming elections and for years to come. This is fully understandable given the importance of health care from both a macro (total economy) and micro (individual) economic, public, and personal health, and overall competitiveness, perspective.

POSSIBLE REFORMS

Now that we have an overview of our health care challenge, it is appropriate to review the health care reform options that were presented to the representative groups of voters during the $10 Million a Minute Tour in 2012. The following package of reforms achieved more than 80% support from both groups:

- **Universal Health Care:** Provide a universal level of basic health care insurance for all legal residents where the federal government is the single payer while using the public and private health care system to deliver services. Basic health care would include preventive, wellness, and catastrophic care. Catastrophic coverage would consider the income and/or wealth of the individual or family unit. Illegal residents would still be eligible for emergency care. Employers would be able to purchase supplemental insurance for their employees and retirees, as is the case in the United Kingdom, Canada, and other countries with universal health care. Importantly, the government would provide additional health care for the poor, the disabled, and veterans.

- **Evidence-Based Payments:** Require all government health care practice payments to be evidence-based.

- **Limit Health Care Tax Exclusion:** Phase out the individual tax exclusion for employer-provided and paid health care in excess of the cost for the basic coverage level noted above.

- **Malpractice Reform:** Reform medical malpractice laws, including providing a "safe harbor" for approved procedures as determined by a qualified and independent medical board.

- **Implement a Budget Cap:** Impose an annual budget for all federal health care spending while allowing employers and individuals the flexibility to spend what they want (e.g., for supplemental coverage). No government should write a "blank check" for health care. Importantly, there are effective checks and balances on health care spending by employers and individuals. These effective checks and balances do not exist in government at this time.

- **Modify Subsidies:** Make federal government premium subsidies more income-based.

- **Reform Medicaid:** Fund Medicaid through block grants to states based on a uniform definition of eligibility and an allocation formula that considers differences in the size of the eligible population and in medical costs by region. Allow states the flexibility to cover more people if they so desire at their own expense.

In addition to the above package of reforms, several other possible reforms should be considered. They include, but are not limited to, the following:

- **Prescription Drugs:** Ban advertising for prescription drugs like most other industrialized nations. Allow for expanded negotiation of prescription drug pricing beyond the Department of Veterans Affairs. Allow for a regulated system of prescription drug importation.
- **Home Health Care:** Allow for more home health care under government programs versus institutional services.

CONCLUSION

Health care is a critically important issue with multiple dimensions. It is a huge fiscal challenge for governments at all levels, a major competitiveness challenge for employers, and a major public and personal health issue. It is also a subject of great equity, security, and affordability concern to individuals of all ages. We must take steps to reform and rationalize our current health care system in a manner that ensures universal coverage for basic and essential services, provides flexibility with regard to services beyond the basic and essential level, ensures that the poor, disabled, and veterans have appropriate levels of care beyond the basic and essential services, and is both affordable and sustainable over time. Doing so needs to be a top policy priority. It is also essential in order to put the nation on an equitable and sustainable fiscal path.

CHAPTER 17

DEFENSE TRANSFORMATION: TOOTH VS. TAIL

To the Department of Defense's (DoD's) credit, ever since Defense Secretary Robert McNamara introduced the Planning, Programming, Budgeting, and Execution (PPBE) system to the department in the 1960s, it has led most federal departments and agencies in long-range planning from a security versus business perspective. That is good, but the truth is most federal agencies do a poor job of long-range planning. The PPBE was supplemented by the National Security Strategy in later years. In that regard, the latest National Security Strategy (NSS) includes the following three priorities:

- Build a More Lethal Force
- Strengthen Alliances and Attract New Partners
- Reform the Department for Greater Performance and Affordability

The above three goals seem reasonable, involve more than military might, and need to be considered in light of the "burning platform" elements described below and elsewhere in this book. Most importantly, while the NSS words sound good, all related actions need to be consistent with the words. In some cases, this means that the president and Congress must provide the needed leadership and support necessary to achieve these priorities. That has clearly not always been the case, especially in these challenging times.

BURNING PLATFORM

The DoD is on a "burning platform," and significant transformational change is needed in order to better position the U.S. to meet changing security threats in the twenty-first century. By burning platform I mean that the status quo is unacceptable and unsustainable and major reforms

177

are needed if the U.S. wants to maintain its superpower status in the future. The following are the three main drivers that have created the "burning platform:"

- **Changing Security Threats:** For the first time in more than 25 years, the U.S. has a new and growing peer competitor: China. Unlike the former USSR and the current Russian Federation, China has a large and growing economy and a hybrid economic system that includes both state-owned enterprises (SOEs) and private-sector firms. In addition to terrorism and nonstate actors, the twenty-first century has also broadened the security threat domains to include cyber, space, and viruses (bio). COVID-19 demonstrated the threat a virus pandemic can represent both to the overall population and the economy and to our military readiness capabilities (e.g., USS Theodore Roosevelt CVN-71). In addition, most of America's current military might is represented by various manned platforms that are more vulnerable to various new weapons (e.g., hypersonic missiles and unmanned vehicles).

- **Growing Fiscal Pressures:** The growth of mandatory spending programs, deficits, and debt held by the public/gross domestic product (GDP) represent a threat to future DoD funding. COVID-19 has served to increase these threats and will also serve to increase pressure for additional nondefense discretionary spending that will put even more downward pressure on future DoD budgets.

- **Business Transformation Needs:** Despite more than 20 years of various efforts, the DoD has failed to reduce its bloated bureaucracy and expanding overhead structure. The DoD has also been unable to rationalize its military compensation structure, especially in connection with current and deferred benefit programs. It has six direct items and shares seven government-wide items on the U.S. Government Accountability Office's (GAO's) "High Risk List." Most of these items have been on the list for more than 20 years!

As a member of the Defense Business Board (DBB), a Professor at the U.S. Naval Academy, the immediate former Comptroller General of the United States and a graduate of the National Defense University's Capstone program for flag officers, I have a multidimensional perspective regarding the above matters.

To help make the case, a number of graphics can be helpful. Unless otherwise noted, the source for the information in the graphics is the DBB, of which I am a member.

As noted earlier, the leading indicator for a country's military capabilities is its economic power, including the strength of the country's industrial base and the strength and stability of its currency. Military capabilities tend to rise when a country's relative economic power grows, as is the case with China, and tends to fall when a country's relative economic power declines, as is likely to be the case in the U.S. based on our current path, especially after COVID-19.

Based on World Bank data, China has already passed the U.S. in Purchasing Power Parity (PPP)-based GDP. China was 18.58% of PPP-based global GDP in 2018 and the U.S. represented 15.02%. India represented 7.69% and is expected to pass the U.S. before 2050. Asia also represents the fastest-growing global region with regard to GDP.

U.S. debt held by the public/GDP is projected to exceed the all-time WWII era high by no later than the end of Fiscal 2021. The following graphic illustrates that debt held by the public/GDP was already expected to rise significantly before COVID-19. That coronavirus alone caused debt held by the public/GDP to jump by at least 25% in Fiscal 2020. The following graphic does not include that significant increase.

Mandatory spending continues to absorb greater portions of the U.S. budget and GDP, thereby putting additional pressure on defense and nondefense discretionary spending. As the following graphic shows, mandatory spending was projected to grow much faster than defense and nondefense discretionary spending before COVID-19. In addition, nondefense discretionary spending was expected to grow faster than defense spending, and COVID-19 will only increase that gap. Interest was projected to grow more than four times faster than defense before COVID-19, and that multiple has increased as a result of the virus. Interest rates represent an "Achilles heel" for America because they cannot be

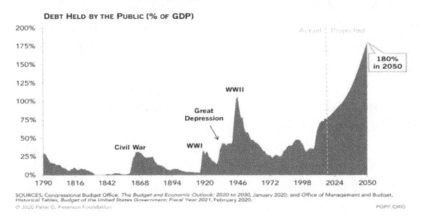

US Debt to GDP

DEBT HELD BY THE PUBLIC (% OF GDP)

Actual | Projected

180% in 2050

WWII

Great Depression

Civil War

WWI

SOURCES: Congressional Budget Office, *The Budget and Economic Outlook: 2020 to 2030*, January 2020; and Office of Management and Budget, *Historical Tables, Budget of the United States Government: Fiscal Year 2021*, February 2020.

© 2020 Peter G. Peterson Foundation

PGPF.ORG

entirely controlled over time. History demonstrates that interest rates and payments can spiral out of control at inopportune times. While interest rates are currently low, in large part because of the unprecedented intervention by the Federal Reserve, history tells us that such will not always be true, and it is not prudent to think that it will be.

Social Security, Health Care, And Interest Explain 82% of Spending Growth

2018-2028 Spending Growth

Non-Defense Discretionary 6%

Defense 5%

Other Mandatory 7%

Net Interest 21%

Medicaid/ACA/CHIP 10%

Social Security 27%

Medicare 23%

Source: CRFB calculations based on Congressional Budget Office data
Numbers may not add due to rounding

CRFB.org

Given increased mandatory spending and the changing security environment, the percentage of the federal budget and the economy (GDP) dedicated to defense spending has declined significantly in recent decades and is expected to continue to decline. The below DBB graphic, which shows DoD spending as a percentage of GDP, was prepared before COVID-19 which, as previously noted, is already resulting in calls to increase nondefense discretionary spending at the expense of defense spending.

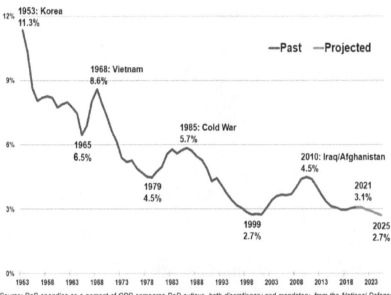

Source: DoD spending as a percent of GDP compares DoD outlays, both discretionary and mandatory, from the National Defense Budget Estimates for FY 2020 (Table 7-7) and projected GDP from OMB's Economic Assumptions for the FY 2021 Budget.

As the below graphic shows, even President Trump was calling for decreases in projected defense spending prior to COVID-19. Part of the decrease relates to the planned exit from Afghanistan and a lowering of troop levels in Europe, both of which should have happened many years ago. As previously noted, the COVID-19 experience is likely to increase pressure for further reductions.

In order to put things into perspective, it is important to understand where our main rivals stand with regard to current military capabilities. China is that main rival, and the below DBB graphic illustrates the relative capabilities of both countries' conventional military capabilities in 2019. The U.S. had almost 20 times the number of nuclear weapons as China (i.e., more than 6,000 versus about 300); however, China has enough to deter a

PETER G. PETERSON FOUNDATION — The largest spending cuts under the president's budget are to non-defense discretionary and the major health programs

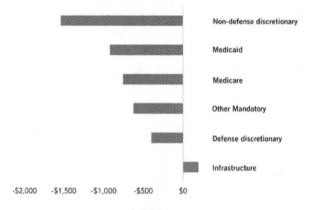

TEN-YEAR CHANGE IN OUTLAYS (BILLIONS OF DOLLARS)

- Non-defense discretionary
- Medicaid
- Medicare
- Other Mandatory
- Defense discretionary
- Infrastructure

-$2,000   -$1,500   -$1,000   -$500 $0

SOURCE: Office of Management and Budget, *Budget of the United States Government: Fiscal Year 2021, February 2020.*
© 2020 Peter G. Peterson Foundation   PGPF.ORG

nuclear attack. Russia and the U.S. still have not learned the meaning of the word "enough." Both nations should be seeking to dramatically reduce their nuclear stockpiles to save money and reduce the threat from terrorism or a nuclear accident and waste disposal.

The U.S, spends considerably more than any other nation in the world on defense on a nominal dollar basis. However, using a nominal dollar basis for comparison can be very misleading. Two key factors need to be considered when comparing defense spending beyond nominal dollar amounts. First, the domestic purchasing power differs significantly between countries. Therefore, considering PPP figures is appropriate. The below DBB graphic shows how China has almost caught up to the U.S. in defense spending on this basis and is expected to pass the U.S. within the next five years.

Importantly, the above projection was before COVID-19. As noted previously, Chinese Chairman and President Xi has pledged to increase China's defense spending even further after COVID-19 while the U.S. is openly talking about reducing its spending.

There is a second key factor that needs to be considered when comparing U.S. military spending to China, Russia, and selected other nations. Namely, the U.S. has an all-volunteer force, and China and Russia have conscription. The cost of maintaining an all-volunteer force is multiple times greater than conscription. As a result, the combination of the PPP difference and the differential in manpower costs means that China has already passed the U.S. in relative defense spending and the gap is growing. In addition, the defense spending gap with Russia is not nearly as great as the typical nominal dollar comparison.

Great Power Military Spending in PPP

*If China continues to increase military spending at the same rate, China will pass the US in military spending PPP by 2025

With regard to compensation costs, the below DBB graphic depicts the life-cycle costs of our all-volunteer force.

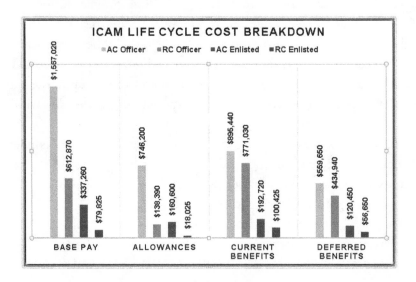

In order to convert the above life-cycle costs into annual costs, you need to know the average service period for the categories of military personnel shown in the graph. The average years of service are divided into the life-cycle costs, and the resulting annual total compensation costs are as follows:

Category	Avg. Years of Service	Avg. Annual Cost
Active Duty Officer	7	$533,000
Active Duty Enlisted	5	$160,600
Reserve Officer	7	$282,400
Reserve Enlisted	5	$51,500

The above figures include total compensation cost, such as current cash pay, allowances, education and training, current benefits (e.g., health care, commissary), deferred benefits (e.g., pensions and retiree health care), and veterans' benefits.

As noted by the graphic, current and deferred benefit costs for the military are more than twice the ratio that exists in the private sector. In addition, the average tenure in the military is much shorter than first responders at all levels of government (e.g., police, fire, EMS). It is also important to keep in mind that not all military personnel are placed in harm's way, although all have an important role to play in keeping the nation secure.

In another disturbing trend, while the defense budget has risen in recent years, the total size of the active duty military force has decreased, as shown in the below DBB graphic.

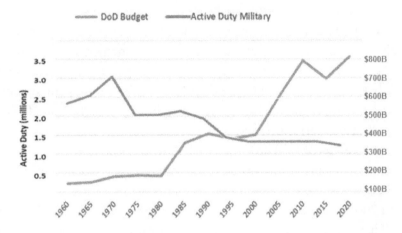

Historical View: DoD Budget vs Active Duty Force

In addition to an increase in total compensation costs for active duty personnel, a reason for the reduction in the size of active duty forces is the dramatic growth in overhead (tail) in the Pentagon, to the detriment of our warfighting capability (tooth). The below DBB graphic demonstrates that dramatic growth in the tail.

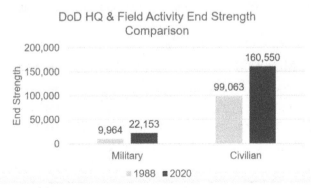

Overall, DoD HQ personnel counts have increased by over 67% since 1988

DoD HQ & Field Activity End Strength Comparison

The sad but simple truth is that the "tail" was already too big in 1988, and it is much bigger today. We must cut the tail in order to sharpen our teeth. In doing so we must also do a much better job of determining which positions should be held by military versus civilian and contractor personnel. We also need to review and reconsider the appropriate length of time for certain temporary assignments (e.g., program managers for major military weapons systems procurements). It is clear that the status quo is both unacceptable and unsustainable.

The DoD has a history of major challenges in the weapons systems acquisition and contracting areas. In the past, too many weapons systems have been planned based on wants in response to past threats rather than needs based on current and future threats. In addition, too many systems proceeded into production before the key technologies had matured. The result was cost overruns, delays in getting capabilities to our forces, and performance problems. These were evident in connection with a number of weapons systems during my tenure as Comptroller General, including the F-22, V-22, and the Joint Strike Fighter (F-35).

In 2009 Congress passed the Weapons Systems Acquisitions Reform Act. That legislation was based on a lot of GAO "best practices" and "lessons learned" work over many years. This legislation and the subsequent implementation efforts resulted in significant improvement in the DoD's weapons systems acquisition outcomes.

In 2016, Congress passed additional acquisition reform legislation that was designed to delegate more responsibility for less "risky" weapons systems acquisitions to the various military services. This was intended to expedite delivery of these systems to our forces. While many services have taken advantage of this option, it is too soon to tell what the outcomes will be.

Finally, the DoD has always had problems in connection with services contracts. Most of these contracts are labor-hour contracts. As a result, contractors get paid for the work they do rather than the results they achieve. Among other things, the DoD needs more personnel with the expertise to effectively manage the cost, quality, and performance of these contracts.

To put things into perspective, it is important to understand that while the U.S. military is the strongest, most capable, most experienced, and most respected fighting force in the world, the DoD does a relatively poor job when it comes to cost effectiveness, efficiency, and accountability. For understandable reasons, the DoD has always made its "warfighting" and related "readiness" metrics its highest priority. This is the "mission" side of the DoD and deserves a grade of "A." However, the "mission support" side of the DoD is important too. Unfortunately, it has not been as high of a priority and, as a result, it deserves a grade of "D."

GAO'S HIGH RISK LIST

While the DoD is number one in warfighting capability, it also has more items on GAO's High Risk List than any other department, and that is not good. By "High Risk," GAO means programs, policies, functions, or activities that are at higher risk of fraud, waste, abuse, mismanagement, and/or not being able to successfully achieve the relevant mission on a sustainable basis. As noted below, the DoD has six direct High Risk areas and shares seven government-wide High Risk areas for a total of 13 out of GAO's 35 High Risk Areas in 2019. No other department comes close.

DoD Specific High Risk Areas
1. DOD Weapon Systems Acquisition
2. DOD Financial Management
3. DOD Business Systems Modernization
4. DOD Support Infrastructure Management
5. DOD Approach to Business Transformation
6. DOD Contract Management

DoD Shared (Government Wide) High Risk Areas
1. Government-wide Personnel Security Clearance Process
2. Ensuring the Cybersecurity of the Nation
3. Ensuring the Effective Protection of Technologies Critical to U.S. National Security Interests
4. Strategic Human Capital Management
5. Improving the Management of IT Acquisitions and Operations
6. US Government Environmental Liability
7. Improving and Modernizing Federal Disability Programs

Progress has been made on a number of the above items, including in the acquisitions area and in preparing for a full financial statement audit. However, it will take a number of years for the DoD to be able to effectively address these issues. In order to do so, getting these items off the High Risk list will need to be a top priority for the department and for congressional oversight. That means it needs to be a top priority for the secretary and deputy secretary and the relevant congressional committees of jurisdiction. It also means that the current chief management officer (CMO) position needs to be reformed in order to make it successful.

POSSIBLE REFORMS

The following package of reforms received more than 80% support from both representative groups of voters as part of the $10 Million a Minute Tour:

- **Require Consideration of Cost in All Defense Planning:** Defense officials must give greater consideration to cost when determining its requirements. Such requirements need to be based on credible current and future threats. In addition, the affordability and sustainability of the proposed acquisitions need to be considered up front, including consideration of ongoing operating costs and likely future funding levels.
- **Right-size Current Force Structure, Footprint, and the Pentagon Bureaucracy:** The U.S. needs to withdraw as soon as possible from Afghanistan and move to rationalize and reprioritize military bases both internationally and domestically in light of credible current and future threats and likely resource levels. The Pentagon's bureaucracy needs to be significantly reduced. In my view, if the Pentagon bureaucracy were 50% smaller, the Pentagon would be much more effective from a business perspective. There are way too many layers, players, and hardened silos within the Pentagon. This became glaringly clear to me during my Capstone experience and time serving as a member of the DBB.
- **Reform Current Acquisition and Contracting Practices:** In addition to rationalizing and reprioritizing weapons systems acquisitions based on credible current and future threats in light of expected resource levels, the way in which those systems are

procured needs improvement. Weapons systems specifications need to be "nailed down" in order to effectively plan and execute on time and within budget. Changes in specifications result in delays, cost overruns, and performance problems. In addition, contracts for both systems and services need to achieve a better risk and reward balance between the contractors and the taxpayers.

- **Modernize Current Compensation and Benefits Practices:** Military pay needs to give more consideration to the relative value and risk of various positions. In addition, the total compensation package needs to be reviewed and rationalized in a manner that enables the U.S to attract and retain a capable force in an affordable and sustainable manner. This includes considering the appropriate mix of active duty and reserves. It also includes a reassessment of the proper mix between cash compensation and current and deferred benefits. Current deferred benefits are very generous, and many military personnel and members of Congress have no idea how expensive they are.

Rationalizing the size and structure of the military will not be easy because there are a number of forces at play. President Eisenhower warned about the power and influence of the "military/industrial complex." In doing so he was referring to the wants of military leaders combined with the desires of the major military contractors. In 2019, the top five U.S. military contractors, according to *Investing News Network*, were Lockheed Martin, Boeing, Northrop Grumman, Raytheon, and General Dynamics. These companies not only gained from supplying the U.S. military with equipment and technology, but they also provided equipment to a number of U.S. allies via foreign military sales. In fairness, these companies care about the national security of the U.S., but they are also in business to make a profit, and they have a fiduciary duty to their shareholders.

There is also a key four-letter word that comes into play when discussing the "rightsizing" and transformation of the DoD. That word is "jobs." This is not only a concern for the country as a whole and for individuals; it is also a key concern for members of Congress. Specifically, military bases mean jobs, and government contracting in their states and districts means jobs. The contractors have recognized this and have used it as part of their marketing strategy to Congress for a number of major military weapons systems. For example, when I was Comptroller General of the United States, I became aware that contractors, including subcontractors, for the F-22 were present in 49 of 50 states! I will not mention the 50th state to avoid embarrassment. As a result, Congress can be an obstacle to rightsizing when the interests of the states and districts they represent conflict with what may be in the broader national interest. In fairness, this situation exists in other aspects of government as well (e.g., U.S. Postal Service).

In addition to the above items that were presented to the representative groups of voters, the following five items should also be considered:

- **Modernize Information Systems:** The DoD needs to implement a modern, integrated, and secure management information system. Currently, the DoD has thousands of nonintegrated legacy information systems, many of which are long outdated. The failure to have an upgraded system results in a lack of timely, accurate, and useful information to make informed decisions on a day-to-day basis. It also represents a major obstacle to the DoD being able to achieve an opinion on its consolidated financial statements in a timely manner. Importantly, the annual audit process is about a lot more than obtaining an opinion on financial statements. It can also result in the identification of significant savings that generate a positive return on investment while promoting continuous improvement.

- **Reform the Chief Management Officer (CMO) Position:** This position needs to be restructured in order to make it effective. The position and related office needs to focus full-time on addressing major enterprise-wide business transformation challenges, including items on the GAO's High Risk List, rightsizing the Pentagon, restructuring the defense agencies, and rationalizing the compensation and benefits system. The DBB issued an extensive report on this topic in June 2020 that outlines several options and other issues that need to be pursued on a priority basis. I was one of four members of the DBB who was on this DBB CMO-related task force.

- **Revise Governance Structure for Defense Agencies:** The various defense agencies in the DoD are huge businesses. Some of these agencies are mission-related (e.g., Defense Intelligence Agency, Defense Logistics Agency), and some are mission support-related (e.g., Defense Finance and Accounting Services, Defense Contracting Agency, Defense Health Agency). In total, these agencies represent about $160 billion in annual spending. The time has come to review and revise the governance structure of these agencies to reflect their size and nature.

- **Implement Guaranteed Budget Allocation:** Given the importance of national defense and the fact that it is one of the express and enumerated responsibilities in the Constitution that cannot be delegated to the states, the DoD should, at a minimum, receive a stated percentage of GDP (e.g., 3.25% of the expected GDP for the current year and the next two years) in appropriations that it can count on for planning purposes. It should also be able to seek additional funding based on clear and credible threats to national security interests. By that I mean the interests of the U.S. and not nation-building exercises for other countries. These additional funding amounts should be based on a business case and considered each year. In addition, Other Contingency Operations (OCO) funds, if any, should only be used for such operations and not as a way to supplement the base budget.

- **Pursue Mandatory Public Service:** The U.S. should also pursue a mandatory public service requirement for younger Americans on a prospective basis. The service commitment could be met in a variety of ways (e.g., military, civilian government at all levels, nonprofit sector). Military service would require a shorter commitment (e.g., two years) than other types of service. Meeting this commitment could also be tied to college/technical school assistance and/or student loan relief.

All of the above items would help to strengthen the military capabilities of the United States in a rational and affordable manner.

However, we must not forget that national security involves much more than military capabilities; it also involves intelligence, diplomacy, and a range of other activities. Finally, as noted previously, economic strength is the most important factor of all. It is a historical and proven leading indicator as to both the rise and fall of military powers.

CHAPTER 18

REFORMING GOVERNMENT

The federal government has grown dramatically in size and scope since its founding in 1789. The growth has been particularly dramatic since 1913, as discussed in Chapter 6. Some of this growth clearly makes sense, given changes in society and the very different role the U.S. has played in the world beginning in the twentieth century. However, not all of it does. The plain and simple truth is that the federal government has grown dramatically, has promised too much, and needs to restructure.

As discussed in Chapter 4, two of the key founding principles for our nation were to have a limited but effective federal government, and for that government to be financially responsible. In fact, the 10th Amendment clearly states that "The powers not delegated to the United States by the Constitution, nor prohibited by it to the States, are reserved to the States respectively, or to the people." For many decades, even during times of peace, the largest expenditure by the federal government was for defense. That made sense because it was an express and enumerated responsibility of the federal government under the U.S. Constitution that could not be delegated to the sovereign states. That has changed dramatically beginning in the 1960s. In addition, the new Constitution was needed in order to give the federal government adequate authority to be able to service the Revolutionary War debt.

There are several ways to view the size of the federal government. One is by how much it spends as compared to the entire economy. Another is by how many departments, agencies, and other governmental entities that it comprises. And still another is the size of the total federal force. No matter which of these measures you use, the federal government has grown dramatically over the years.

Regarding the amount of federal spending as a percentage of the economy, as shown in the chart below, which was prepared by the CATO Institute, it grew from 2% in the early twentieth century to 21% in Fiscal 2019. It is projected to continue growing, based on Congressional Budget

Office (CBO) data from even before COVID-19. The estimated spending for Fiscal 2020 is close to 40% due to the effects of COVID-19. Before COVID-19, the CBO estimated that recurring federal spending would be more than 25% of GDP by 2040 and climbing based on current programs and policies.

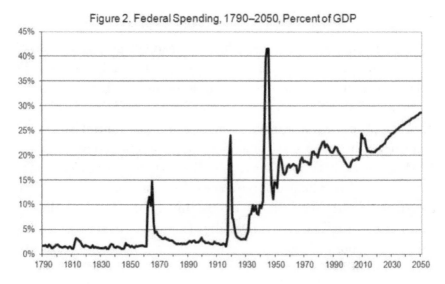

Figure 2. Federal Spending, 1790–2050, Percent of GDP

Interestingly, when you look at federal spending today, far less than half of the spending relates to express and enumerated responsibilities ascribed to the federal government under the U.S. Constitution. And that percentage is shrinking. With the exception of the Works Progress Administration (WPA) projects period during the Great Depression, from the beginning of the U.S. republic until the early 1970s, a majority of the federal budget was for defense and interest on the debt. That has, however, changed dramatically. Today, Social Security, health care, and interest on the debt far exceed defense spending, and the gap is projected to grow in future years.

Interest rates have fallen dramatically from their highs in the early 1980s. They are now at historically low levels even though we are adding debt at or near record rates. This is partially due to the Federal Reserve's unprecedented purchase of trillions in Treasury securities to help hold interest rates down. This can work for a while, but eventually interest rates will rise when normal market forces determine them. This is a very serious matter. For example, if interest rates return to pre-2007 levels, government spending on interest alone would rise by $800 billion a year!

The federal government's executive branch's major departments and agencies grew from three in 1789, to nine in 1912, to nineteen in 2019. These numbers do not include the many boards, commissions, task forces, and so on that comprise today's federal government.

What about the size of the total government workforce? This includes military, civilian, and contractor personnel. The following graphic, which is derived from federal Census data, shows that the first two categories have grown considerably over time. The blips every 10 years relate to the federal Census taking place.

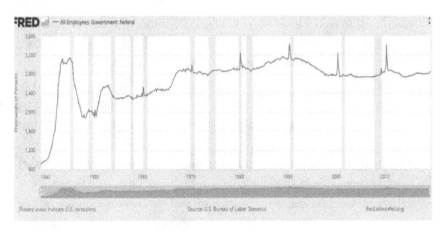

It has been extremely difficult to obtain reliable estimates of the number of federal contract workers over the years. In addition, many employees work on the many federal grants that are made to lower levels of government and nonprofits. As the below DBB graphic shows, while the number of recurring federal employees has been pretty flat since 1996, the number of contractor employees has grown significantly.

There are a number of reasons for the steady rise in contractors versus federal employees. First, the federal government manages based on appropriated funds and full-time equivalents (FTEs). The FTEs, in effect, represent the maximum authorized level of federal employees by department, agency, and so on. Various efforts have been made from time to time to reduce the number of FTEs in order to claim that government is

The U.S. government workforce

■ Contractors ■ Federal Employees ■ Grant employees

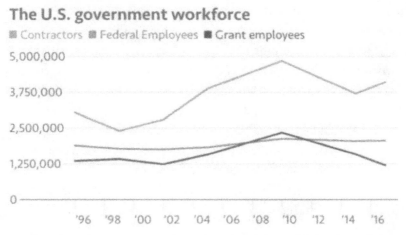

being reduced in size. However, the reduced number of federal employees could be more than offset by the number of federal contractors. As a result, the total workforce may not have shrunk. In addition, even if the total workforce size shrinks, the size of federal spending as compared to GDP could still be growing. As a result, having multiple metrics and being able to provide contextual sophistication in regard to any related claims is important.

There are times when it is fully appropriate to hire contractors rather the federal employees. For example, it is appropriate when the functions to be performed are not "inherently governmental" and the functions can be performed on a more economical basis with appropriate quality and security by contractor personnel. One of the biggest and long-standing debates between labor and management in government relates to what types of functions should be deemed to be "inherently governmental" and therefore ineligible for contracting out. Second, it can be appropriate when the skills and knowledge required are such that the government has to hire contractors because they cannot attract and retain an adequate number of federal employees due to federal compensation levels and/or employment rules. Third, it can be appropriate when there is a temporary need and it does not make sense to hire federal employees. One example is the Highly Qualified Expert (HQE) program, which allows for expedited hiring of persons with demonstrated expert skills in areas that the government needs for a limited period of time.

Clearly, the federal government has grown significantly over time, based on the amount of federal spending/GDP, the number of federal departments and agencies, and the size of the total workforce. It has also significantly increased its regulatory activity over the years, although both the Reagan and Trump administrations made concerted efforts to reduce regulatory burdens. The real questions should be: what should the federal government do, how should it do it, who should do it, and how should we measure success. This is a good transition to the topic of strategic planning.

While China has been engaged in strategic planning for many years, such planning is a relatively new activity for the U.S. federal government. The first requirement to perform strategic plans came as part of the Government Performance and Results Act of 1993 (GPRA). That Act required agencies to prepare five-year strategic plans and annual performance plans, and to issue annual performance reports. It was intended to improve planning, enhance transparency, and increase accountability. The GPRA Modernization Act was signed into law in 2010. It required agencies to identify key external factors that could affect achievement of mission and required all performance reports to be issued in machine-readable format.

While GPRA required planning and performance reporting at the agency level, it did not require it at the government-wide level. This is a huge void in effective strategic planning and performance management. Rather than having every agency do its own thing, there needs to be an overall strategic framework and performance plan that guides what agencies do. Such a government-wide plan is essential in order to effectively manage the overall size of government, ensure proper focus on top priorities, provide consistency between agencies, eliminate duplication and redundancies in government, and ensure proper accountability for results. This overall strategic framework and performance plan needs to come from the Office of Management and Budget (OMB) on behalf of the president.

Some argue that the annual budget is supposed to play this role. However, the budget document is merely a bid by the president for an annual appropriation request. It could include legislative proposals that may never become law. In addition, it does not include the type of outcome-based metrics that are essential to maximize performance and ensure accountability for the American people.

This is a good transition to my related activities as Comptroller General of the United States and head of the U.S. Government Accountability Office (GAO). After all, GAO is the agency in the federal government whose job is to help improve the performance, and ensure the accountability of, the federal government for the benefit of the American people. In addition, by better understanding my background, you will better understand my qualifications to make these comments.

President Clinton nominated me and I was confirmed unanimously by the U.S. Senate for the position of Comptroller General of the United States in 1998. The position is effectively the federal government's chief auditor and the de facto chief performance and accountability officer of the U.S. government. The Comptroller General also serves as CEO of GAO, which is a legislative branch agency. As a result, GAO works for Congress and the American people to help improve the performance and assure the accountability of the federal government for the benefit of the American people. To accomplish this, GAO performs various functions, including financial audits, performance evaluations, investigations, policy analyses, and best practices studies. It also issues auditing standards, legal opinions, and bid protest decisions.

As a leader, I have always believed in leading by example and practicing what you preach. I am also a big believer in the power of core values to help explain what an organization does, how it should do it, and how it wants to be perceived. As a result, when I became Comptroller General, I challenged GAO's personnel to embrace these principles and establish core values.

Because of the above, GAO developed and published its first comprehensive strategic plan in 2000. Since this plan spanned all federal government activities, and in the absence of a government-wide plan from OMB, it was the closest thing the government had to a comprehensive strategic planning framework. The plan focused on three types of key activities that would be performed by GAO on a prospective basis. They were: oversight, insight, and foresight. The plan was also built on three core values: Accountability, Integrity, and Reliability. Accountability represented what GAO did, Integrity represented how it did it, and Reliability represented how GAO wanted to be perceived. The plan also had specific goals and outcome-based objectives, including a targeted amount of financial benefits (savings) to be achieved for American taxpayers each year. This plan provided the basis for a major transformation of the GAO.

After preparing the plan, GAO engaged in many other transformational activities. These included reducing the number of field offices around the country from 16 to 11, eliminating a layer of management, reducing the number of organizational units from 35 to 13, and focusing much more attention outside of GAO and horizontally within GAO. It also included major changes to our internal knowledge sharing, external reporting, and congressional relations and public affairs activities. Of critical importance, it included a range of human capital reforms dealing with recruiting, training, performance management, personnel classification, and compensation practices. After all, the most valuable asset any organization has is its people, and such was definitely the case at GAO. Finally, it adopted a "balanced scorecard" approach to evaluating GAO's overall performance. The factors were outcome-based results, client feedback, employee feedback, and partner/stakeholder feedback.

The above reforms were challenging and at times very controversial, especially the reclassification effort that was designed to address a serious and long-standing pay equity issue. In the end, GAO was smaller, more efficient, more effective, more productive, more respected, and better positioned for the future. For example, in addition to reducing the size, streamlining the organization, and significantly increasing its productivity, GAO's return on investment (ROI) for taxpayers more than tripled to more than $100 in financial benefits for every dollar invested in GAO. The agency was also rated the second-best place to work in the federal government by its own employees.

And just why is the GAO experience so important? Because it proves that major transformational change can happen in government. Importantly, what we did at GAO is transferrable and scalable to other parts of government. I am also pleased to be able to say that according to my successor as Comptroller General, Gene Dodaro, whom I selected to be chief operating officer (COO) when I was Comptroller General, more than 95% of the changes that we made during my tenure were still in place. The real test of transformational change is whether it survives the test of time years after the leader who was the primary driver of the change leaves. I am also pleased that Gene Dodaro, who was my partner in making change happen, very deservedly became my successor. I know that he is committed to continuous improvement not just in principle but in reality, and his record confirms that.

What do I mean by transformation? My definition is: taking major steps to change the structure, policies, operational practices, and/or culture of an organization in order to improve performance, ensure sustainability, and promote continuous improvement for both today and tomorrow. What is the purpose of transformation? In my view it is to create a more positive future by taking steps to maximize value and mitigate risk within current and expected resource levels.

In order to achieve successful and sustainable transformation, it takes committed, consistent, capable and, at times, courageous leadership. The type of leaders who believe in getting things done with and through others. Leaders who look ahead in a broader and more integrated fashion to identify major challenges and opportunities. Leaders who take steps to capitalize on the opportunities before they expire and address the challenges before they reach crisis proportions. Leaders who do what is right for today and tomorrow even though it may not be popular. Leaders who recognize that the law is the floor of acceptable behavior, and who strive to do what is ethically and morally right as well. Unfortunately, we have way too few of these type of leaders in government today.

Transforming the federal government will be very tough and will take years. In doing so, it is important to have appropriate and reliable financial and performance metrics to set goals and assess progress. In this regard, I believe that it is appropriate to use enhanced federal financial statements, audit reports, and performance reporting as a primary basis for federal management and accountability. As discussed previously, current federal financial reporting needs to be improved (e.g., treatment of "trust fund" debt). Annual reports also need to include more outcome-based performance metrics based on strategic planning. The following represent three examples of how the current financial statements and annual audit reports can be used to focus management attention and assess performance.

- What type of opinion has been obtained on the annual financial statements? Most departments and agencies have an unmodified opinion on the financial statements, but the Department of Defense (DoD) and the U.S. government as a whole have received disclaimers of opinion on their financial statements for many years. DoD is making progress in this regard. In 2018 DoD conducted its first full-scale audit, which cost about $1 billion. That is a lot of money, but studies by the Marine Corps have demonstrated that changes resulting from an audit can result in savings of 1–1.5% of the budget. In DoD's case that is $7–$10+ billion dollars and a solid ROI. Audits also promote continuous improvement efforts.

- How much progress has been made in eliminating material internal control and other weaknesses, and significant deficiencies? The GAO noted 12 such items in its Fiscal 2019 Audit Report.

- How much progress has been made in reducing "improper payments?" These payments amounted to $175 billion on a government-wide basis in Fiscal 2019, of which 69% related to Medicare, Medicaid, and the Earned Income Tax Credit (EITC). At least $75 billion of the $175 billion was deemed to be unrecoverable by the federal government.

In addition to the above financial information, it is important to measure progress that is being made in connection with the GAO's High Risk List. There were 35 items on the GAO's High Risk List in Fiscal 2019. Assessing actual outcome-based performance results versus plan, trends over time, and comparisons to relevant competitor or comparator groups is also of critical importance. Governments tend to manage based on inputs and outputs rather than outcomes. This is outdated and unacceptable. Focusing on outcomes pertaining to related financial information can also help to assess "value for money" in connection with various government programs, policies, and activities. Clearly the federal government has a long way to go in employing modern cost accounting and ROI concepts that are widely used in the private sector.

Using audited financial statement information can also be important to help better assess fiscal responsibility and sustainability issues. For example, the following calculations were based on financial information that came directly from the Annual Consolidated Financial Report of the U.S. government for Fiscal Years 2000 and 2019. The additional demographic and economic data used to make the below calculations also came from official government sources.

Item Increase (Decrease) from FY 2000–2019
Net Financial Burden 332%
Net Financial Burden per Person 268%
Net Burden in Excess of GDP 565%
Ratio of Net Burden PP to Median HH Income 664%
Citizens' Wealth (253%)
Citizens' Wealth per Person (231%)

The net financial burden represents total liabilities, unfunded social insurance obligations, and commitments/contingencies minus total assets. The net financial burden in Fiscal 2000 and 2019 was $19.4 trillion and $83.9 trillion, respectively. The net financial burden per person figures in Fiscal 2000 and 2019 were $69,475 and $254,289, respectively. GDP figures in 2000 and 2019 were $10.25 trillion and $21.4 trillion, respectively. The ratio of net burden per person to median household income means that the net burden increased 6.64 times (or 664%) faster than median household income. As a result, the relative burden has increased dramatically and is continuing to increase. Median household income figures in 2000 and 2019 were $42,148 and $63,030, respectively. Citizens' Wealth is a novel metric created by Japonica Partners. It is determined by taking total GDP minus the net position on the federal government's balance sheet, and minus the debt held by the Social Security and Medicare Trust Funds. Citizens' Wealth declined from $3.09 trillion in 2000 to ($4.72) trillion in 2019. The Citizens' Wealth per person figures in 2000 and 2019 were $10,988 and ($14,308), respectively.

The below graphic by Kazarian Partners demonstrates just how dramatically Citizens' Wealth has declined between Fiscal 2000 and 2019. Importantly, the below does not include the significant decline that will occur in Fiscal 2020 due to COVID-19.

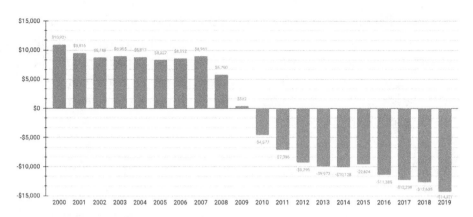

Notes: Net Worth numbers from Financial Reports of the United States Government; corrected for federal debt securities held by the Social Security and Medicare trust funds incorrectly claimed as intragovernmental debt holdings; 30 September fiscal year end. GDP and population data from IMF WEO October 2019 database.

The trends and ratios noted above serve to demonstrate the irresponsibility and unsustainability of the federal government's fiscal path. Importantly, all of the above numbers are prior to COVID-19, which has only made our situation worse.

Finally, as I have mentioned previously, accounting is how you keep score, and how you keep score matters. In my view the best metrics for measuring fiscal responsibility/sustainability and the impact of fiscal reform efforts are (1) the projected impact on debt held by the public/GDP over time, and (2) the immediate impact on net financial burden. Importantly, a major fiscal reform package would have zero immediate impact on debt held by the public/GDP, but it could reduce the net financial burden by many trillions of dollars depending on the reforms. Therefore, both metrics are appropriate in order to have a fuller and fairer view of the impact of fiscal reforms.

I feel pretty confident that I have built a case for major transformational change in government. That includes considering what the government does, who does it, how it is done, and how you measure success. When thinking about what the government does, it is important to consider which level of government should perform the function as well.

Importantly, as noted above, the purpose is to create a better future not just for us but for future generations of Americans. To do so, you need to believe in the concept of stewardship. And what is that? To me it means taking steps to improve performance today, leaving things better off when you leave than when you came, AND being better positioned for the future. In my view, this is what true leaders must do. It is also consistent with the language in the Preamble of the Constitution that refers to "the Blessings of Liberty to ourselves and our Posterity."

POSSIBLE REFORMS

The following package of reforms received more than 80% support from both representative groups of voters during the $10 Million a Minute Tour:

- **Develop a Consolidated Strategic Plan for the Federal Government:** The annual budget is not a strategic plan. If federal agencies are required to prepare periodic five-year plans and annual performance plans and performance reports, the consolidated federal government should too. The strategic plan should have specific goals and objectives, and the performance plans and reports should have specific outcome-based metrics. These government-wide documents should be prepared by the OMB on behalf of the president and in consultation with Congress, agencies, and other key stakeholders. The resulting documents should prove useful to the various agencies as they deal with their own planning and reporting.

- **Create a Government Transformation Task Force:** It is time to create an independent task force that would be comprised of citizens with proven track records of transforming large and complex organizations and who would recommend ways to streamline government and improve its economy, efficiency, and effectiveness. The task force would conduct its work over several years and would issue periodic reports with recommendations that would require consideration by Congress. Unlike President Reagan's Grace Commission or Vice President Gore's Reinventing Government Initiative, this task force should be formed through legislation with both the president and the congressional leadership having an appropriate number of appointments.

As I have said many times, if you do not have a plan all you have is prayer. Don't get me wrong; I am a person of faith and believe in the power of prayer. However, I want a plan *and* prayer.

The time has also come to recognize that in order to make major organizational changes and operational reforms, the table has to be set for Congress. The task force recommended above would be designed to do just that. At the same time, Congress would be the ultimate decider of whether or not to adopt the task force's recommendations via legislation, which will require the signature of the president to become law. While a veto override is theoretically possible, it is not realistic in this case nor would it be realistic in connection with a new fiscal responsibility commission.

In addition to the above reforms, there are two additional major reforms that need to be a top priority:

- **Presidential Reorganization Authority:** It is time to grant the president this authority. It has been granted 16 times to nine presidents in the past, most recently to President Reagan. Given the seriousness of the challenges we face and the need to address them sooner rather than later, this is a tool that should be in the president's toolbox for the good of the nation. It should be integrated with the strategic planning process noted above, and both that plan and this authority are long overdue.

- **Human Capital Reforms:** The federal government's human capital policies and practices are largely reflective of conditions that existed in the U.S. in the 1950s. It is critically important that these policies be modernized in order to attract, retain, and motivate top talent. This includes adopting more aggressive recruiting systems; streamlining the hiring process; providing limited temporary hire authority to all agency heads to meet critical needs; discarding the 15-level General Schedule (GS) system and adopting a properly designed broad banding system; increasing the emphasis on skills and knowledge in classification systems; improving training; moving to skills-, knowledge-, values-, and outcome-based performance management and reward systems; and streamlining the reassignment and removal process. We made great progress in these entire areas at GAO during my tenure, and they made a huge difference in our productivity and ROI. Importantly, what we did is transferrable and scalable to other government organizations.

- **Financial Statement and Audit Report Information:** As noted earlier in the chapter, financial, performance, and audit-related information needs to be used to a greater extent in ongoing management, assessing performance, and assuring accountability. It also can be helpful in assessing progress and putting our nation on a more prudent and sustainable fiscal path.

In summary, the federal government has grown dramatically, has become too siloed and hierarchical, lacks adequate intergovernmental and external coordinating mechanisms, employs outdated human capital policies and information systems, needs to modernize its metrics, and must become more future-focused and results-oriented. All of these issues need to be addressed as part of an overall effort to improve the attractiveness, economy, efficiency, effectiveness, credibility, and fiscal sustainability of the federal government.

CHAPTER 19

TAX POLICY

Taxes are the price we pay to maintain our government. Let me be clear at the start: The primary cause of our deficits and mounting debt burdens is the expanded roles being assumed by the federal government and the related increased spending. Stated differently, our primary fiscal problem is a spending problem. However, our current and projected deficits and debt burdens are so great, that we will not be able to restore fiscal sanity through additional economic growth and spending reductions alone. Therefore, it is appropriate to talk about taxes, or revenues.

Unfortunately, our fiscal situation is much worse than 2012 when the $10 Million a Minute Tour took place, and it has gotten even worse since COVID-19 hit. As a result, additional revenues will be needed to restore fiscal sanity than would have been the case had we taken action earlier. In addition, continued delays in making needed reforms are likely to further increase the need for additional revenues to close our fiscal gap and defuse our ticking debt bomb. And why do I say that? First, it is political reality given the types of changes needed and the groups that will be affected. Second, it's just MATH! That is the new four-letter word in fiscal policy just as JOBS is the four-letter word for defense restructuring.

BACKGROUND

There has been a huge increase in federal revenues as a percentage of the economy (GDP) since the founding of the republic. For example, revenues rose from about 2% of gross domestic product (GDP) in 1912 to 5% of GDP in 1934 to an all-time high of about 20.7% of GDP in 2000. In Fiscal 2019, total federal revenues were about 16.3% of GDP, which is below the average of 17.1% for the period 1984–2018. This compares to total federal spending in Fiscal 2019 of 20.8%, which is above the average of 20.5% for the period 1984–2018. As a result, revenues are below average and spending is above average, leading to well above-average deficits and mounting debt levels. And these numbers are before COVID-19.

The below graphic shows how federal revenues have increased dramatically as a percentage of GDP since 1934. At the same time, as the graphic shows, total federal revenues have generally stayed in a range of 15%–20% of GDP since 1950, and during that period spending continued to climb to more than 20% of GDP and rising before COVID-19.

Historical Federal Total Tax Revenues

Percentage Share of Gross Domestic Product (GDP), Fiscal Years 1934 - 2029

Source: Office of Management and Budget, Historical Tables, 2019.
Note: Data for 2019 through 2029 are from Congressional Budget Office (CBO)'s Budget and Economic Data projections (August 2019).

The increase in total revenues since WWII was driven by strong economic growth, which resulted in more revenues, an ability to keep tax rates at more reasonable levels, and an ability to add new programs. It also enabled the federal government to give tax cuts, or a "growth dividend," in good times. For example, this occurred in Fiscal 2001 when we had a large current budget surplus and projected increasing budget surpluses for more than 10 years. However, those days are over and the situation is very different today. Demographics and rising debt held by the public/GDP levels are working against growth. Why is this happening? Savings rates are down and the government debt resulting from deficits serves to crowd out more productive private-sector investments. At the same time, the U.S.

faces much tougher global competition in an increasingly interconnected world and global marketplace. Before COVID-19, Congressional Budget Office (CBO) was only projecting modest GDP growth of about 2% over time along with large deficits and mounting debt burdens. The long-term situation has been made worse by COVID-19. As a result, the growth dividend has reversed!

From 1789 to 1913, the primary source of revenues for the federal government was duties, tariffs, and excise taxes. That changed in 1914 after the 16th Amendment, which authorized a national income tax, was ratified by the states. The creation of Social Security in 1935 added payroll taxes beginning in 1937. The passage of Medicare in 1965 and the increases in payroll tax caps over time have served to increase the percentage in federal revenues from this source. Contrary to the belief of some, corporate income taxes have declined as a percentage of federal revenues and currently represent less than 10% of federal revenues.

The below Office of Management and Budget (OMB) graphic shows how the composition for federal revenues has changed significantly since 1940.

Income and Payroll Taxes Make Up a Growing Share of Federal Revenue

Composition of Federal Revenue Over Time, 1940-2023

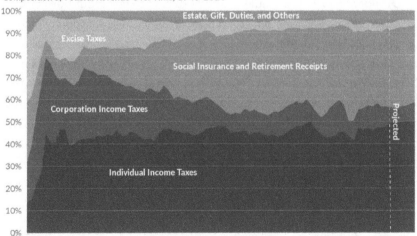

Source: Office of Management and Budget, "Percentage Composition of Receipts by Source: 1934-2021" and "Composition of 'Other Receipts': 1940-2021."

The following graphic shows the composition of federal revenues for Fiscal 2019.

The federal government collects revenues from a variety of sources

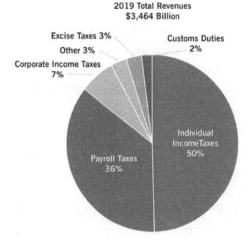

SOURCE: Office of Management and Budget, *Historical Tables, Budget of the United States Government: Fiscal Year 2021*, February 2020.
NOTE: Other includes estate and gift taxes, income from the Federal Reserve, and miscellaneous fees and fines.
© 2020 Peter G. Peterson Foundation   PGPF.ORG

As noted above, individual income taxes represent about 50% of total federal revenues, and payroll taxes represent about 36%. Corporate income tax revenues have fallen to about 7% of total federal revenues. Excise taxes and duties, which used to be the primary source of federal revenues until 1914, only represented about 5% of total federal revenues in Fiscal 2019.

The below graphic by the CBO makes it clear that federal tax revenues have not been adequate to cover federal spending since Fiscal 2002 and for most years prior to 1998. The gap has grown since then and is expected to continue to grow in the future. And the graphic below was made before the impact of COVID-19.

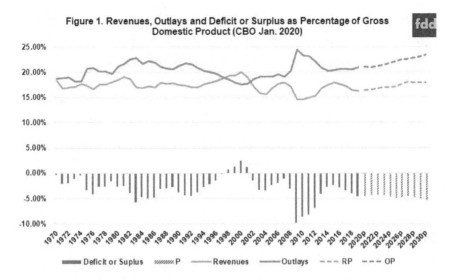

Figure 1. Revenues, Outlays and Deficit or Surplus as Percentage of Gross Domestic Product (CBO Jan. 2020)

While the total amount of federal revenues and the sources of those revenues are important, it is also important to explore the equity of the federal tax system. The following graphic shows that the federal tax system is progressive as a whole, since higher-income taxpayers pay higher effective tax rates. Reasonable people can and will differ on whether it is progressive enough.

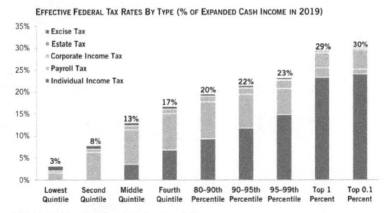

211

While the overall system is progressive, it is important to understand some underlying points. As noted in the graphic above, well over 50% of Americans pay more in federal payroll taxes than in federal income taxes each year, and payroll taxes are regressive. By that I mean, lower-income workers pay a higher percentage of their income in payroll taxes than higher-income workers do. In this regard, while the Medicare HI payroll tax is not subject to a tax cap, the much higher Social Security payroll tax had a wage-based tax cap of $137,700 in 2020. Therefore, any wages or self-employment income above this amount is not subject to the 6.2% payroll tax that is imposed on both employers and employees.

The graphic above also makes it clear that more than 40% of individuals do not pay any federal income tax. In addition, more than 20% actually receive a check from the federal government due to refundable tax credits, the largest of which is the Earned Income Tax Credit (EITC). The EITC has been used to help lower-income people in lieu of raising the minimum wage, which could result in some job losses and/or make it more difficult for minors and less skilled persons to obtain employment.

As the two Tax Policy Center (TPC) graphics below show, the top individual tax rates for individuals and corporations have varied widely over the years.

History of Tax Rates: 1913 – 2020

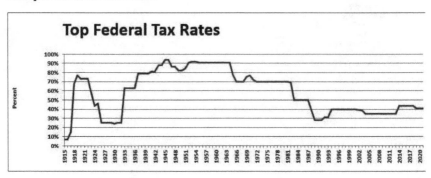

1   As adjusted by the Consumer Price Index Inflation Calculator from the U.S. Department of Labor, Bureau of Labor Statistics at http://www.bls.gov/data/inflation_calculator.htm.
2   For simplicity, unless otherwise noted, the historical federal income tax rates in this article refer to the highest tax rate.
3   http://data.bls.gov/cgi-bin/cpicalc.pl
4   http://www.irs.gov/pub/irs-soi/05inrate.pdf, p. 8.

Corporate income tax: History of top marginal tax rate for U.S. corporations

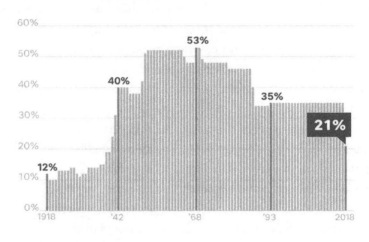

SOURCE Tax Policy Center
George Petras/USA TODAY

It is important to recognize that many major corporations operate around the world and can easily be headquartered in any number of countries. As a result, while most Americans have no desire to leave the country, companies can and will move their corporate headquarters if they believe it is in the best interests of their shareholders. In fact, corporate boards have a legal fiduciary responsibility to act in the interests of their shareholders. As a result, U.S. corporate tax policy needs to be competitive with other major countries.

While the top tax rate is important, the real metric that people need to focus on for all types of income taxes is the effective tax rate. By that I mean that actual percentage of total income that you pay in taxes. At the federal level, this can be affected by the type of income you have and how many deductions, exemptions, credits, and exclusions (i.e., tax preferences) that you have. For example, capital gains and dividends can be subject to a lower tax rate. In addition, interest income on municipal bonds is not taxed at all. There are also many tax preferences that need to be considered and that reduce taxable income. In general, higher-income people tend to benefit more from these special tax provisions. In addition, some very large corporations pay little or no taxes due to corporate tax preferences.

While raising revenue is the primary goal of tax policies, they can also be used to try and achieve other goals. For example, the Internal Revenue Code (IRC) is sometimes used to achieve a variety of economic and social goals (e.g., promote investment, retirement savings, research and development, health care coverage and home ownership, and help low-income/low-wage earners and households with children). Tariffs can also be used to protect certain industries from import competition (e.g., steel, autos).

The federal government foregoes about $1.4 trillion in revenue each year due to allowable deductions, exemptions, credits, and exclusions under the federal tax code. The largest tax preference in the IRC is the individual income and payroll tax exclusion for employer-provided and paid health care benefits. These tax preferences are sometimes referred to as tax expenditures. The largest tax expenditures are noted in the graphic below.

TABLE 1

Largest Tax Expenditures
Billions of dollars, fiscal year 2021

TPC

Rank	Tax expenditure	JCT	OMB
1	Tax exclusion for employer-sponsored health insurance	$190.3	$227.9
2	Reduced rates of tax on dividends and long-term capital gains	$167.5	$136.2
3	Tax benefits for employer defined contribution plans	$157.8	$90.7
4	Credit for children and other dependents	$118.8	$121.7
5	Tax benefits for defined benefit plans	$109.4	$75.8
6	Reduced tax rate on active income of controlled foreign corporations	$82.1	$43.0
7	Earned income credit	$73.1	$69.6
8	Depreciation of equipment in excess of alternative depreciation system	$56.6	$40.6
9	Subsidies for insurance purchased through health benefit exchanges	$52.8	$46.5
10	Deduction for charitable contributions	$49.6	$56.2
11	20-percent deduction for qualified business income	$47.4	$54.7
12	Exclusion of capital gains at death	$43.8	$53.6
13	Exclusion of untaxed Social Security and railroad retirement benefits	$41.5	$32.5

Source: Joint Committee on Taxation (JCT). "Estimates of Federal Tax Expenditures for Fiscal Years 2019-2023," December 2019; US Department of the Treasury. "Tax Expenditures: FY 2021," February 2020.

Notes: Estimates include both personal income and corporate income tax expenditure amounts. JCT regards the exclusion of net imputed rental income as an administrative necessity, and does not classify it as a tax expenditure. However, the Treasury does include it in its tax expenditure estimates ($130.4 billion for FY2021).

Now that we have an overview of the major elements of our tax system, it is important to address a frequently heard assertion. Namely, "Tax cuts pay for themselves." It is true that some tax cuts can stimulate additional economic activity, but very few, if any, actually pay for themselves. By that I mean that you generate more in total tax revenues after the cut than you would have before the cut. In general, the only tax cuts that would even have a chance of paying for themselves would involve dramatic reductions in tax rates such that the amount of work and economic activity subject to taxation would increase to such an extent that it would more than offset impact of lower tax rates. As shown in the prior graphics, there have been dramatic reductions in tax rates in the past. However, modest changes in tax rates are not likely to have significant behavioral implications, and therefore, will not "pay for themselves."

All too frequently in recent years we have heard the above-referenced mantra when there is a need to stimulate additional economic activity due to a recession or to increase the overall economic growth rate even when we are not in a recession. In fact, there have been a number of major tax reform efforts since 1980 designed to "simplify" the overly complex tax code and reduce rates in order to increase economic growth and improve the nation's competitive posture. There have also been some that increased taxes. The following are some of the more significant tax reform efforts during this period:

- **Economic Recovery Tax Act of 1981:** This legislation significantly cut individual income taxes by reducing marginal rates 23% over three years, decreasing the maximum capital gains tax rate from 50% to 20% along with other provisions.

- **Tax Reform Act of 1986:** This was a very comprehensive tax reform plan that reduced both individual and corporate taxes. It cut the top individual marginal tax rate to 28% and the top corporate tax rate to 34%. It also reduced or eliminated many tax preferences/expenditures and other provisions.

- **Omnibus Budget Reconciliation Act of 1990:** This legislation increased individual taxes by raising the top statutory tax rate to

31% while more than doubling the payroll tax cap for the Medicare HI program. It also limited tax deductions for certain high-income taxpayers, capped the top capital gains tax rate at 28%, and expanded the EITC for low-income workers along with other provisions.

- **Omnibus Budget Reconciliation Act of 1991:** The legislation increased both individual and corporate taxes. It imposed new individual tax rates of 36% and 39.6% and increased the top corporate tax rate to 35%. It repealed the Medicare HI payroll tax cap, expanded the amount of Social Security benefits subject to taxation, and further expanded the EITC, along with other provisions.

- **Economic Growth and Tax Relief Reconciliation Act of 2001:** This legislation reduced individual income taxes overall by cutting the tax rates for various income tax brackets and decreasing the top rate to 35%. It increased child and dependent care tax credits, increased education tax preferences, made major changes to estate and gift taxes, and raised retirement plan contribution limits, along with other provisions.

- **Jobs and Growth Tax Relief Reconciliation Act of 2003:** This legislation reduced taxes by expanding various tax brackets, reducing the capital gains tax rate to 15% and 5% for certain moderate-income taxpayers, reduced the tax rates applicable to dividends, modified the scheduled tax rates, significantly increased deductions for acquisition of business equipment, and provided $20 billion in relief to states along with other provisions.

- **Tax Cuts and Jobs Act of 2017:** This was comprehensive tax reform legislation that reduced taxes for both individuals and corporations. It lowered tax rates for individuals, increased the standard deduction, repealed personal and dependent exemptions, increased the child care tax credit, significantly increased the estate tax exemption, limited the deduction for state and local taxes, and repealed the individual mandate penalty under the Affordable Care Act (ACA), along with other provisions. All of the individual tax changes are scheduled to expire after 2025. The legislation also included a dramatic reduction in the corporate tax rate from 35% to 21%, and changed the basis of taxation for global businesses from a worldwide to territorial basis. It also modified the Alternative Minimum Tax (AMT) for individuals and eliminated it for corporations, along with other changes.

Did you notice a common denominator between the legislation noted above that cut taxes and the legislation that raised taxes? The ones that cut taxes were freestanding bills. The ones that raised taxes were done as part of the budget reconciliation process. Why? Because, among other things, you cannot filibuster a budget reconciliation bill, and it only requires a majority vote in the Senate. Therefore, any major fiscal reform legislation that involves tax increases, revisions to social insurance programs, and spending cuts is likely to be done as part of the annual budget reconciliation process.

POSSIBLE REFORMS

The following package of tax reforms received support from more than 80% of both representative groups of voters during the $10 Million a Minute Tour:

- **Broaden and Simplify the Tax System by Eliminating Loopholes:** The current tax system is way too complex. Most Americans should be able to complete their own one-page tax return (front and back). The number of tax brackets should be reduced, and the top individual tax rate should be set at 28%. Capital gains and dividends should be taxed at ordinary income tax rates. Most deductions, exemptions, credits, and exclusions should be eliminated, but some should be retained (e.g., interest on a primary home up to the maximum conforming loan amount, retirement contributions up to a stated level, charitable contributions, child care tax credits, EITC, significantly reduced exclusion for employer and provided health care).

- **Make the Income Tax More Inclusive and Progressive:** Require all individuals with income above a stated level (e.g., some function of the poverty level) to pay some income tax. More than 40% of taxpayers pay no income tax, and more than 20% actually receive a refund due to the EITC. It is important for all persons who make a stated level on income to pay something toward the basic and essential operations of government. At the same time, the current system should be made more progressive through the types of tax reforms noted above.

- **Make the Corporate Tax System More Competitive:** Achieve comprehensive corporate tax reform that would lower the rate to 25%, broaden the tax base, move to territorial versus worldwide taxation, and allow a deduction for dividends distributed. Most special tax preferences would be eliminated, but some would be retained (e.g., tax credits for basic research, special depreciation and depletion rules, catch-up retirement plan contributions).

Some of the above reforms have been adopted. For example, the top corporate tax rate has been reduced to 21%, and a territorial versus worldwide taxation basis has been adopted for global corporations. In addition, the individual standard deduction has been raised, and the state and local tax deduction has been limited at least through 2025. However, much remains to be done, and the gap between federal revenues and spending has grown and continues to grow.

There are at least three additional tax reforms that should be considered:

- **Wealth Tax:** As noted in Chapter 9, there are growing gaps between the "haves" and "have nots" in America, and wealth is being concentrated in a small percentage of the population. As a result, the time may have come to consider taxing wealth above a stated level (e.g., $50 million) at a relatively small percentage (e.g., 2–3%) as a means to raise revenue and make the tax system more progressive. Clearly the people who have accumulated a great deal of wealth have benefited from what America has to offer. However, if this tax is implemented, consideration should be given to eliminating the estate tax.

- **Consumption Tax:** From an economic and equity perspective, a consumption tax that provides a refundable tax credit based on income at a stated level (e.g., a function of the poverty level) might be the most economically efficient and equitable way to generate federal revenues. Proponents of the so-called "FAIR tax" advocated for this approach in lieu of the current payroll and income tax structure. However, the numbers did not work in their proposal, and it was a bridge too far politically. Another approach might be to increase consumption taxes on selected luxury and legal but unhealthy items (e.g., alcohol, tobacco, marijuana) as a supplement to other tax reforms.

- **Tax Dividends and Surcharges:** We must put our finances in order and defuse our ticking debt bomb. Consideration needs to be given to adding a new line on individual and corporate tax returns. That line would involve a temporary tax dividend (rebate) if the federal government does better than a stated target ratio of debt held by the public/gross domestic product (GDP) at the end of the prior fiscal year and a temporary tax surcharge if the federal government fails to meet the target ratio of debt held by the public/GDP. This approach would serve to increase the transparency of and accountability for Congress' fiscal actions or inactions. It would also serve to encourage Congress to take action sooner rather than later to put our financial house in order. As economic growth increased, the possibility of growth dividends in the future would also increase. Importantly, as discussed in Chapter 14, exceptions would be made in certain limited circumstances.

Clearly, additional revenues as a percentage of GDP will be needed to restore fiscal sustainability, but how we achieve those additional revenues matters. Importantly, policymakers need to decide how much total revenue is appropriate and then determine how best to raise it. Any tax reforms need to be consistent with the six principles and values agreed to by more than 85% of the representative groups of voters during the $10 Million a Minute Tour. The sooner we make the needed changes, the fewer the changes will need to be. It is just math and the principle of compounding.

CHAPTER 20

POLITICAL REFORMS

The U.S. is the longest-standing republic in the world and the second-largest democracy (India is the largest). As noted in Chapter 4, a republic is a representative democracy whereby voters elect representatives who then vote on their behalf. Direct democracies allow voters to decide issues directly (e.g., initiatives and referendums). While some states allow for initiatives and referendums, the federal government does not.

Despite the warnings of Washington, the U.S. political system is dominated by two political factions (parties): the Democrat Party and Republican Party. From time to time in the past, there have been attempts to form viable third parties, but none has stood the test of time. The larger third parties in the past tended to be associated with major personalities (e.g., Teddy Roosevelt for the Bull Moose Party and Ross Perot for the Reform Party).

For various reasons, politics has become more partisan and ideological in recent years. Democrat activists have become more liberal, and Republican activists have become more conservative. There has also been a decline in the number of swing districts in the House. These are the congressional districts that are up for grabs, and therefore draw the attention of both political parties.

The close margins in the House and Senate serve to raise the stakes in each election. Even though political independent/unaffiliated voters represent a growing plurality of registered voters, there are only three political independents in the House and Senate combined, and very few independents are appointed to Cabinet positions and major boards and commissions. Finally, many current federal elected officials are "career politicians" who want to keep their position for life. As a result, we now have a republic that is neither representative of nor responsive to the general public.

As the below graphic shows, between 1988 and 2018 both major political parties lost market share while independents (unaffiliated) voters increased their market share. In 2018, independent/unaffiliated voters represented a sizeable plurality of the voting population. These independent/unaffiliated voters determine the winner of most presidential elections and close congressional races. As a result, they can have a major impact on raising issues that need to be addressed and that both major parties are failing to address. One such key issue is fiscal responsibility.

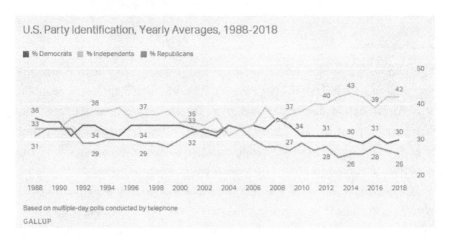

U.S. Party Identification, Yearly Averages, 1988-2018

■ % Democrats   ■ % Independents   ■ % Republicans

Based on multiple-day polls conducted by telephone

GALLUP

The battle for control of the U.S. Senate and House is an intense one that occurs every two years. About one-third of Senate seats are up for election every two years, given six-year terms in the Senate, and the entire House of Representatives stands for election every two years.

As the below graphic depicts, the margins between the two parties in both the House and the Senate has narrowed considerably in recent years. As a result, every election could result in a change of control. The party that controls each House appoints chairs for all the committees and controls the legislative agenda. As a result, elections have become even more partisan and heated since control is typically at stake. They have also become more negative, with too much focus on personalities rather than policy issues.

Because of the gerrymandering of congressional districts (i.e., a partisan process that results in maximizing the number of "safe" districts for the political party that controls the state legislature), the Cook Political Report estimates that at least 342 of the 435 seats in the House are "safe seats." This means the party that controls the seat is highly likely to retain control, and the real election contest is within the primary for the party that holds the seat. Primaries have lower turnouts than general elections, many primaries are closed party primaries where independent/unaffiliated voters cannot vote, and party activists tend to have a higher percentage

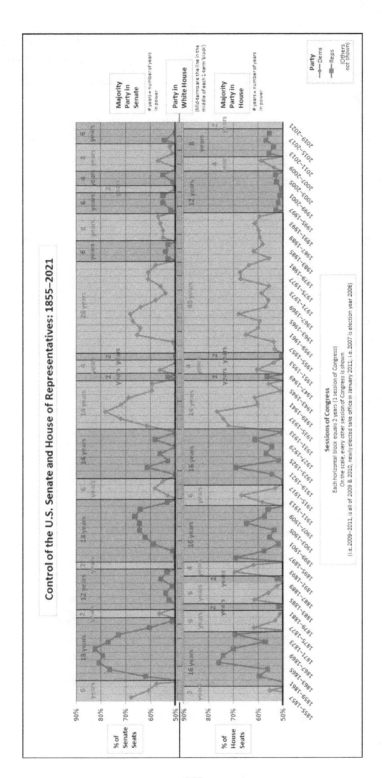

Control of the U.S. Senate and House of Representatives: 1855–2021

of turnouts in primaries. In addition, most Democrat Party activists are to the left of most voters, and most Republican Party activists are to the right of most voters. As a result, there is a greater ideological divide in Congress than in the past.

The gerrymandering of congressional districts can also help to explain the difference between public opinion regarding individual representatives versus Congress as a whole. While most individual members receive high ratings in their districts, Congress as a whole had a rating of 18% in late July 2020, down from 30% in late May 2020! The partisan and ideological stalemate over the next round of COVID-19-related legislation was resulting in significantly lower opinions of Congress.

While Congress has become polarized and gridlocked, there are rays of hope, one of which is the Problem Solvers Caucus in the House of Representatives. This caucus was created due to the efforts of, and with the continued support of, No Labels. The group includes an equal number of Democrats and Republicans who are committed to country over party and progress over polarization. It is the third-largest caucus in the House behind the Democrat and Republican caucuses. The Problem Solvers Caucus is making a difference, and the concept is now starting to take root in the Senate. I am one of the national cofounders of No Labels. I support their efforts and encourage you to do so as well.

Under the U.S. Constitution, presidents are elected based on which candidate wins a majority of the Electoral College rather than the popular vote. States select electors who, in most cases, vote for the candidate who wins a majority (or plurality) of the votes in the state. The number of electors each state receives is based on their number of House seats (which is determined by population) plus two for each state's Senate seats. Importantly, the Constitution does not dictate how the states allocate their electoral votes. In fact, two states (i.e., Maine and Nebraska) do not use a winner-take-all approach based on the statewide winner. Rather, they award one electoral vote for the candidate who wins each congressional district in their state and two (Senate votes) for the candidate who wins the statewide vote.

As the below graphic shows, in 2019 the Virginia Center for Politics projected that only 13 states would be deemed to be "swing states" in the 2020 presidential election. These states represented 164 electoral votes and would essentially determine who would win the presidential election in 2020. Common sense would say that a disproportionate amount of time and money would be allocated to these 13 states. As a result, the 37 other states were not likely to have as much activity since they are deemed to be "safe" for one party or the other. However, as Hillary Clinton and other candidates have found out in the past, sometimes states that you think are safe slip away. As result, if in doubt, the candidate should err on the side of spending time and money in a state that may make a difference in the final election result. Importantly, the type of redistricting reform noted below combined with using the electoral vote allocation employed by Maine and Nebraska could really shake up presidential campaigns and elections and significantly broaden the battlefield.

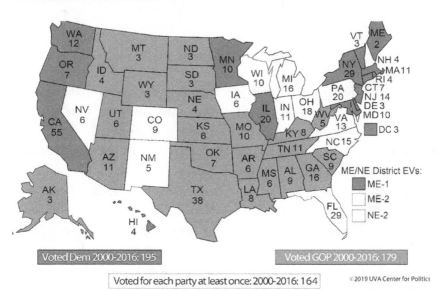

The polarization of politics is also spreading to the states. As shown in the below graphic, according to the National Conference of State Legislatures (NCSL), one party controls all but three state legislatures, and one of the three (i.e., Nebraska) is a nonpartisan unicameral legislature. This further proves that the political divide is not just at the federal level.

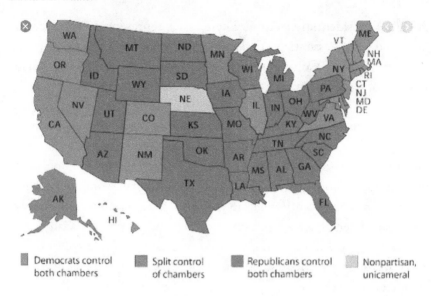

Democrats control both chambers | Split control of chambers | Republicans control both chambers | Nonpartisan, unicameral

THE 2020 ELECTIONS

It is clear that the 2020 elections, especially the presidential election, will be among the nastiest and most consequential in modern history. Both houses of Congress are in play. In addition, due to COVID-19, in-person campaigning has been significantly curtailed, and the televised debates will likely be more important than ever. Clearly, the personalities of the two major presidential candidates are very different. Let's face it, Trump is not really a Republican. He is a "Trumpster." In my view, the real focus in 2020 should be on the principles and priorities of the candidates rather than their personalities. As a result, the debates will likely significantly impact my decision regarding whom to vote for in the presidential race.

In the summer of 2020, my view was that the election should be about the future direction of the country and what the proper role of government should be since we are clearly at a crossroads in our country's history. Do we want a more expansive and intrusive government or a smaller and less intrusive government? Stated differently, do we want a Saul Alinsky principles-based future or a Founding Fathers principles-based future? Do not misunderstand what I am saying. I think slavery was immoral and should have been banned, that women should have been given the right to vote and own property at the outset, and I support the progress we have made and the need to do more in the way of civil rights and nondiscrimination. I also support maintaining a solvent, sustainable, and secure social safety net. However, I am opposed to abandoning the basic principles and values upon which our nation was founded and that made our nation exceptional and a beacon for the world. These founding principles and values were discussed in more detail in Chapter 4.

At the time of writing this book, COVID-19 was the number-one issue in the minds of voters followed by the economy and race relations/policing reforms. With regard to the economy, President Trump and the Republicans had the wind at their backs until COVID-19 hit. After COVID-19 arrived, the economy was still going to be a major issue but in a very different light. In addition, the handling of COVID-19 and the issues of health care were expected to be the major issues in the general election campaign. Given the tragic deaths of George Floyd and Rayshard Brooks, along with the related protests and disturbances in their aftermath, civil rights, policing policies, judicial reform, and law and order issues were also expected to be significant topics of interest in the general election campaign. As I was writing this book, I was not optimistic that the fiscal irresponsibility, national security, and other key challenges outlined in this book would be addressed in a much more meaningful manner than in the 2016 election cycle.

Regarding the congressional races, anyone who has spent any time in Washington knows that party control matters a lot, especially in the House of Representatives, where the minority party has very limited rights. As previously noted, the political party that controls a chamber selects the committee chairs and controls both the schedule and the legislative agenda.

As we approach the 2020 elections, the current lineup in Congress is as follows:

U.S. Senate:

- Republicans: 53
- Democrats: 45
- Independents: 2, who caucus with the Democrats

U.S. House of Representatives:

- Democrats: 235
- Republicans: 197
- Independents: 1
- Vacant: 2

All 435 seats in the House and 35 seats in the Senate are up this cycle. Of the 35 Senate seats that are up, 23 are held by Republicans and 12 are held by Democrats. As a result, given the relatively close margins in both houses of Congress, either or both houses could see a change of control. Most political experts in the early summer believed that the Senate had a better chance of flipping than the House.

Since this book is being published before the election, I cannot cover the outcome. However, one thing is pretty clear: No matter what the results of the 2020 presidential and congressional elections are, it is likely that the country will remain divided and the future will be uncertain. Only time will tell how things play out.

POSSIBLE REFORMS

The following package of reforms received more than 90% support from both representative groups of voters during the $10 Million a Minute Tour:

- **Reform the Redistricting Process:** The purpose of redistricting should be to maximize the number of competitive districts in a manner consistent with the Voting Rights Act of 1965 rather than to minimize the number of competitive districts, as it is today. Competition is one of the key principles that made America exceptional, and it needs to be more fully realized in our political system. As a result, the redistricting that is done every 10 years following the Census should be performed by independent and transpartisan bodies in a manner consistent with this competition objective. Some states have already moved to independent redistricting commissions (e.g., California).

- **Hold Integrated and Open Primary Elections:** The approximate 42% of voters who are independent/unaffiliated should not be disenfranchised from the primary process. As a result, primaries should include candidates of all political affiliations whereby all registered voters could participate and the top two vote getters would run off in the general election. The major political parties would still be able to endorse candidates in the primary races. Some states have already adopted this approach (e.g., California).
- **Institute Term Limits:** George Washington and our nation's other Founders were right. Federal elected officials should not be career politicians. They should come from the real world, serve for a limited period of time, and then return to the real world. Therefore, 12-year term limits should be imposed on both the House and the Senate. This is long enough to provide needed institutional memory. This change will require a constitutional amendment and would not be too big a price to pay for our future if the 12-year clock did not start to run until the amendment was ratified by the requisite number of states (38 at the present time).

In addition to the above reforms, there are at least two other political reforms that should be considered:

- **Campaign Finance Reform:** There is too much money in politics, and too much of the money is from special interests and "persons" who cannot vote. Political contributions should be limited to a reasonable amount, and only people who can vote should be able to make them. Therefore, corporations and unions would not be able to contribute to candidates. Given the Supreme Court's related "free speech" decision, this will likely require a constitutional amendment. Consideration should also be given to optional public financing approaches. Several states have adopted this for state elections (e.g., Connecticut).
- **Rank Choice Voting:** Ranked choice voting (RCV) describes voting systems that allow voters to rank candidates in order of preference, and then uses the results of those rankings to elect

candidates who best represent their constituents. Several states have adopted this reform for selected elections, and Maine has adopted it statewide.

All of the factors noted above have contributed to a lack of action on a number of important public policy issues, including fiscal, immigration, infrastructure, and environmental matters. More and more people are coming to believe that it will take meaningful political reforms to revitalize our republic and start making tough decisions that are in the interest of the public for both today and tomorrow. One such group is FixUS.

FixUS is a new project of the Committee for a Responsible Federal Budget (CRFB) based on the premise that we are unlikely to fix the debt until we address the underlying issues that are dividing the country and paralyzing our political system. It was launched in January 2020 with an understanding that the environment most conducive to enacting a debt deal—one that focuses on policy over politics, the long-term over the immediate, and a willingness to compromise and make hard choices— does not currently exist. FixUS is undertaking various initiatives and partnerships that seek to better understand the root causes of our national divisions and dysfunction, to bring attention and visibility to these problems, and to build support for necessary changes.

From a personal experience, while I have extensive public service experience in high-level appointed positions, including three presidential appointments with unanimous Senate confirmation each time, my only direct experience in running for elective office was in Connecticut. That experience confirmed my dad's belief that I cared too much about merit and had too much integrity to be in elective politics. He was right!

Let us hope that we can restore a republic that is representative of and responsive to the general public sooner versus later. Our collective future depends on it.

CHAPTER 21

OTHER FEDERAL POLICY ISSUES

This book has covered a number of major international and domestic issues of concern to the U.S. both at home and abroad. This final chapter will provide a few comments on several other major policy issues that need attention at the federal level.

IMMIGRATION

The U.S. is a country of immigrants. It is one of our greatest strengths and something that differentiates us from most every other nation on earth. We need immigrants, especially since the birth rate in America has fallen below 2:1 per female. Without immigration, our population as a whole will begin to not only age faster but also decline in number, as is already happening in Russia and many industrialized nations.

While we need immigrants, our current immigration policy needs to be modernized in a number of ways. First, we need to recognize and respect the difference between legal and illegal immigration. We are a country of laws, and we need to enforce them in a fair and equitable fashion. Second, we need to recognize that we are now competing in a global economic Olympics that will intensify in the years ahead. Third, we need to recognize that our nation's financial foundation has cracked, and we need to take steps to repair it. Fourth, we want to be a welcoming country but do not want nor can we afford to be the refuge nation for all persons in nations with dysfunctional governments and domestic security challenges that are not political or ideological in nature. Finally, we need to recognize that conditions have changed dramatically since the adoption of the U.S. Constitution in connection with immigration matters.

Given the above, several federal actions should be considered:

- Make Deferred Action for Childhood Arrivals (DACA) individuals legal immigrants with a pathway to citizenship. They came here as children with their parents, and they were not the people responsible for breaking the law.

- Provide a pathway to legal status (i.e., Green Card) for other illegal immigrants who have been in the U.S. for at least five years AND do not have criminal records either in the U.S. or elsewhere that would make them a threat to Americans. If they are a threat, they should be deported immediately.

- Revise the asylum rules to make it clear that it is for political asylum in situations where the person is threatened by their government for their beliefs rather than general domestic tranquility concerns in their country.

- Do not make illegal immigrants eligible for federal welfare programs. They would still be eligible for any state programs, as applicable.

- Require that at least one parent of a child born in the U.S. be a legal resident of the U.S. in order for the child to automatically become a citizen.

- Issue more temporary (e.g., seasonal) guest worker visas for the types of work where the demand for workers exceeds the supply (e.g., agriculture, lawn maintenance).

- Grant automatic legal status to persons graduating from U.S. institutions with highly desirable STEM degrees and provide a pathway to citizenship.

- Toughen border security and enforcement of laws that bar employers from hiring illegal immigrants.

- Tighten background checks and security screenings for individuals and countries that represent an increased national security threat to the U.S.

EDUCATION

The biggest gap that America has is an education gap. Education is the key to opportunity for self-sustainment and self-fulfillment. It is also the major factor in income and wealth disparities. At the same time, a college education is not the answer for all people.

Given the above, several federal actions should be considered:

- The Department of Education should be significantly reduced in size, and it should focus on a few key issues of national significance (e.g., identifying and sharing "best practices" and "lessons learned" in connection with selected key national challenges) and providing funding to challenged school systems to help in their adoption (e.g., education attainment disparities among minorities and the disabled). The balance of its responsibilities should be devolved to the states.

- The U.S. should learn from Germany and other countries in regard to assessing the interests and abilities of high school students and matching them to the needs of the country and its economy. However, we should not make such an assessment at too early an age.

- The U.S. should revise the current student loan programs to lessen the financial burden on existing borrowers but should significantly tighten the loan program in the future. These loans should be geared to providing financial assistance to individuals from low-income families and individuals who pursue degrees in fields where the country has a need and job opportunities are available. In addition, such loans should also be available from trade schools where the country has a need and the individual has an interest and ability. Such loans should be forgiven in whole or in part if the individual provides a stated amount of public service upon graduation.

ENVIRONMENT

Climate change is real, although reasonable people can and will differ on the reasons for it. In addition, air and water systems span geopolitical boundaries both domestically and internationally. It is also clear that, in addition to fiscal matters, the U.S. is not discharging its stewardship responsibility in the environmental area.

Given the above, the following federal policy actions should be considered:

- The U.S. needs to develop a new National Energy and Environmental Strategy. This strategy must recognize that any action in connection with environmental issues must balance economic, public health, environmental protection, and national security issues in a manner that does not cause undue harm or disruption. In this regard, North America is now self-sufficient in energy and we need to stay that way. This is a key national security issue.

- The U.S. should work together with other nations to achieve multilateral climate accords that involve all major nations, including China and India, and that are enforceable. If all major nations are not involved and/or the provisions are not enforceable, then these agreements are more form than substance.
- The U.S. should only provide taxpayer support, either directly through funding or indirectly through tax preferences, for energy activities that are consistent with the National Energy and Environmental Strategy and that are economically viable and environmental sustainable.

INFRASTRUCTURE

The U.S. has gone from a leading to lagging nation in regard to critical infrastructure. For example, our transportation system is inadequate, waterway systems have deteriorated, and the electrical grid is at risk. A number of other countries also have more advanced communications networks and artificial intelligence (AI) capabilities.

Given the above, the following federal policy actions should be considered:

- The federal government needs to take steps to ensure the financial integrity of the Transportation Trust Fund. This should include consideration of an increase in the gas tax that is integrated with an oil production fee.
- The federal government needs to invest at least an additional $1 trillion over the next 10 years in critical infrastructure projects. These projects should involve public/private partnerships to the maximum extent possible whereby user fees can be the primary source of financing rather than general taxes.

- The U.S. should consider implementing a federal infrastructure bank as a means to promoting and aiding in the financing of needed and economically viable infrastructure projects.
- The U.S. must take steps to better protect its electric grid from a cyber, electronic magnetic pulse (EMP), or other attack.

JUDICIAL/POLICING REFORMS

There is little question that minorities, especially Blacks, represent a disproportionate percentage of the population in prisons and are subject to more discrimination and abuse than Caucasians.

Given the above, the following types of federal policy actions should be considered:

- Possession of minor amounts of marijuana should be decriminalized on a nationwide basis, and any persons who are currently in prison solely for possession should be immediately released. However, illegal sale of marijuana should continue to be a federal crime.
- Sentencing guidelines should be revised and greater discretion provided to judges based on individual facts and circumstances.
- Additional transparency should be provided regarding the sentencing decisions of individual judges based on the type of case.
- Citizen oversight groups should be created to review allegations of police abuse.
- Body cameras and meaningful de-escalation training should be mandatory for all police departments.
- Chokeholds should be barred except in cases where the officer is faced with serious and imminent danger. There should be an automatic Grand Jury review for cases that result in the death of an individual.

INTERNATIONAL RELATIONS

The United States has been the global leader of the "liberal order" since the end of WWII. This includes being a leader in the creation and operation of all major international organizations during this period. The post-WWII era has, for the most part, been a period of peace and prosperity in various places around the world. World War III has been avoided, hundreds of millions have been pulled out of poverty, and trade and transportation have spread around the globe. At the same time, the U.S. is not nearly as well positioned as it was at the end of WWII from a variety of perspectives, and major challenges exist that must be addressed.

Given the above, the following federal policy actions should be considered:

- The U.S. should continue to provide leadership and support to major international institutions and, as necessary, support needed reforms of such institutions to make them more effective (e.g., UN, WHO, NATO). It should do so in a constructive and cooperative manner to the maximum extent possible. The truth is, the U.S. will need these types of relationships much more in the future than it ever did in the past.
- The U.S. should promote more multilateral and enforceable agreements in connection with a range of global issues (e.g., trade, nuclear non-proliferation, climate change, freedom of the seas, pandemics, intellectual property).
- The U.S. should seek to have a constructive relationship with China and other potential adversaries while taking the necessary steps to be able to fight and win an armed conflict should it occur.

While there are a number of other federal policies that are worthy of discussion, there is a limit to how long this book should be. So let's move on to the Conclusion.

CONCLUSION

This book has covered a lot of ground. Hopefully it has convinced you that the U.S. is an exceptional nation but that our nation's future is at risk. It has attempted to build a "burning platform" based on three key elements:

- A plausible but not predictive scenario of what things might look like in 2040 for the U.S. if we do not change course and start making some tough choices.
- Lessons learned from COVID-19 and how they should serve to increase our sense of urgency to make tough choices sooner versus later.
- Lessons from past great powers, other nations, and our own nation's history, including how we must learn from them if we want to remain a superpower and be the first great power to stand the test of time.

While the book has provided a wake-up call, it has also provided a range of sensible solutions to address our nation's challenges, most of which were supported by a supermajority of representative groups of voters in two swing states in 2012 as part of the $10 Million a Minute Tour. As a result, it does not just talk about problems; it offers sensible solutions. It also demonstrates that, as I have said for the past 15-plus years, the biggest deficit that America has at this time in our history is a leadership deficit, especially at the federal level. That deficit has existed for a number of years, includes all political affiliations, and crosses many geographic boundaries in the U.S.

After reading this book you may ask, "What does it mean to me?" The answer is fairly simple. The federal government has grown dramatically, promised too much, and must restructure. Some states and municipalities have as well. Therefore, when they ultimately take action, several things are inevitable:

- Taxes will go up!
- Social insurance programs will be restructured!
- Spending will be reprioritized and reduced!
- The resulting "bad news" will flow downhill to state and local governments!
- Ultimately individuals will pay the price for the irresponsibility of politicians, although the impact will vary among income groups.

The truth is, current federal income tax rates may now be the lowest they will ever be. Therefore, you need to review and reconsider your own retirement planning and investment strategies with this in mind. For example, Roth IRAs may make more sense than a traditional IRA. In addition, certain types of insurance products may make more sense (e.g., whole life insurance, indexed annuities).

The federal government is likely to increase the retirement eligibility age for Social Security and provide a lower replacement rate for middle- and upper-income individuals. The federal government is also likely to reduce health care tax preferences and subsidies while not expanding Medicare to include long-term care. At the same time, life expectancies are expected to increase further, health care costs continue to rise, and long-term care is likely to be a much bigger issue for most Americans.

Given the above, you need to review and reconsider your retirement planning and investment strategies. Will you have enough to last the entire life span for both you and your spouse, if any? Will you be able to leave what you want to charities, your children, grandchildren, and great-grandchildren, if you are fortunate to have them?

You also need to consider how much risk you want to take. There are three major types of risks that need to be considered over time:

- **Investment risk:** What is your tolerance for volatility, and who will bear the investment risk?
- **Health status risk:** Health care is the single largest cause of personal bankruptcies, and long-term care is very expensive. Can you deal with these costs?
- **Longevity risk:** How long are you and your spouse, if any, likely to live, and will you have enough assets and income to last your entire lifetime?

To answer the above questions you should consult a qualified and independent financial planning professional while conferring with your spouse and family. You will need to consider a range of issues, including savings vehicles (e.g., retirement plans), insurance products (e.g., life insurance, annuities, long-term care), getting out of debt before retirement, and your end-of-life wishes (e.g., traditional will, living will, burial plans).

You and I cannot directly control what our elected officials do to us, but we can control what we do for ourselves and our families. This needs to be Priority One. In this regard, since I believe in leading by example and practicing what I preach, I have already taken the above-referenced steps and more. I do not have any debt. I have a whole life insurance policy, several life annuities that are indexed to a flat annual rate or the rate of inflation, and several retirement plans (i.e., 401(k)s and IRAs), along with additional savings and investments. I have also taken steps to deal with end-of-life issues, whenever that may come. Hopefully, that will be a long time from now, God willing. As a result, I am confident that my wife and I are well set for retirement, and we hope it is a long and enjoyable one. I hope that for you and yours too.

What about our nation's challenges? If you love your country and family as I do, you will not be satisfied to just take care of yourself and say "to heck" with anything else. As a result, you should become informed and involved on key national, state, and local issues that are important. You should exercise your privilege to vote in every election. You should vote for people who are willing to tell the truth and make tough choices to create a better future irrespective of their party affiliation, if any. You should also do everything that you can to make sure our elected officials deal with large, known, and growing problems before a crisis hits, and hold them accountable if they fail to do so.

13 KEY POINTS

The following are 13 key points to remember regarding the contents of this book:

1. Based on past history and its current path, the U.S. is a declining global power and its future is at risk, but this can be changed by taking the types of actions noted in this book.
2. The most significant economic, national security, and domestic tranquility threat to the U.S. is fiscal irresponsibility.
3. The U.S. has made great progress in expanding civil rights for women and minorities and reducing discrimination since its founding, but more remains to be done. This includes addressing the major societal gap in the U.S., especially the education gap.

4. The U.S. needs to decide whether it will return to the basic principles and values on which it was founded and that made the country a superpower, or whether to move more toward socialist principles as advocated by Saul Alinsky.

5. The new Modern Monetary Theory is not only unproven, it is dangerous to the U.S. and the post-WWII international order.

6. Accrual-based financial statements and annual performance reports need to be used as a primary basis for management and accountability purposes.

7. Since past budget controls have failed to constrain the dramatic growth in public debt/GDP, the U.S. needs a constitutional fiscal responsibility amendment that focuses on getting debt held by the public/gross domestic product (GDP) down to a reasonable and sustainable level and keep it there.

8. The U.S. will need a new fiscal responsibility commission to engage the public and "set the table" for tough spending and tax choices to restore fiscal sanity. This commission needs to learn lessons from Simpson–Bowles, and its recommendations need to be acted on.

9. The U.S. needs to strengthen international alliances and agreements in light of a rising China and other changes in the global power structure.

10. The U.S. needs to engage in a major transformation of its defense strategy and structure in light of changing security threats and increasing fiscal pressures.

11. Constitutional amendments and other political reforms are needed to restore and revitalize the U.S. republic.

12. Individuals need to take steps to take care of themselves and their family in light of eventual tax and spending changes by the government.

13. Individuals need to become better informed and more deeply involved to help ensure the needed public policy reforms become a reality.

For those of you who want to take a shot at putting our nation's finances in order, there are at least three nonpartisan organizations that have created online fiscal games you can use. They are the Committee for a Responsible Federal Budget (CRFB), the Concord Coalition, and the Wilson Center. Their websites can be found in Appendix D.

In conclusion, our nation is at a critical crossroads in its history. It is time to wake up, America! In the final analysis, we must all remember that it is "We the People" who are responsible and accountable for whom we elect and what they do or fail to do while they are in office. We must do our best to help eliminate the nation's leadership deficit. I can assure you that I will do my part to help create a better future; all that I ask is that you do yours. If we all do our part, America will stay a respected and effective superpower, and stand the test of time. Let's make it happen!

APPENDIX A
INFLATION

Inflation occurs when you have a general increase in prices and a drop in the purchasing power of money. In order to understand the threat of inflation, it is helpful to understand an economic equation. I promise that this is the only equation in the book!

$$MV=PT$$

Under the above formula, M is the money supply defined as total bank deposits and total cash in circulation. V is the speed at which money flows (i.e., circulation and use) around the economy from producer to consumer and so on. P is the general level of prices in the economy, and T is the total number of transactions (i.e., products and services) in a year. PT would then be a measure of gross domestic product (GDP) for the year since it would represent the total amount of goods and services produced that year times the average price level at which the goods and services are traded during the year.

Given the above, if V (circulation) and T (number of transactions) are stable, by reducing M (money supply) through the sale of Treasury securities the Fed will help to control inflation. Quantitative easing occurs when the Fed purchases Treasury securities or other assets to raise M (money supply) and, so if V (circulation and use) is fixed, it will push up P (prices) and have an inflationary effect if the economy is near full employment where T (transactions) cannot expand. If there is additional economic capacity because the economy is not at full employment, then T (transactions) will grow. The more likely outcome is a mix of both.

Quantitative tightening reduces M (money supply), so if V (circulation and use) is fixed, it will push down P (prices) or T (transactions) or both. This occurs when the Fed sells Treasury securities and assets that it holds.

In today's recessionary and deflationary world, the quantitative easing route would be a welcome result. But if banks, companies, or households sit on the extra cash, sending V (circulation and use) plummeting, M (money supply) may go up while P (prices) and T (transactions) still tumble. History tells us that changes in V (circulation and use) have never been a reliable basis for determining policy. However, looking at this equation helps to explain during a serious recession policymakers' efforts to use monetary policy only to bring an economy out of recession as being ineffective. However, using additional fiscal stimulus (e.g., tax cuts and/or spending increases) when fiscal policy is already irresponsible and unsustainable only serves to exacerbate our debt held by the public/GDP challenge and contribute to an "economic decline loop."

APPENDIX B
IMPORTANCE OF PUBLIC DEBT/GDP

A number of studies have been conducted over the years that demonstrate how too much public debt/gross domestic product (GDP) can result in a significant drag on GDP growth. For example, a North Carolina State University study in 2010 noted that adverse economic consequences occur when public debt/GDP exceeds 77%. That study did acknowledge that the actual level of public debt/GDP would vary by country. Another 2010 study by Rogoff and Reinhart reached a similar conclusion at a level of 90% of public debt/GDP. That study was later criticized for having a computational error. In addition, a 2011 study by an international group of master's-level students at Stanford University from around the world, including China, addressed the issue. The students worked under my direction and used International Monetary Fund (IMF) data to project that the U.S. would experience significant adverse GDP effects when debt held by the public/GDP exceeded about 124%. That study noted significant variances by country. It also ranked the U.S. number 28 in its novel Sovereign Fiscal Responsibility Index (SFRI) based on three criteria (i.e., fiscal space, fiscal path, and fiscal governance). Importantly, it also noted that the U.S. ranking would rise to number eight if the recommendations of the National Fiscal Responsibility and Reform Commission (i.e., Simpson–Bowles Commission) were adopted. See https://blog-pfm.imf. org/files/sovereign-fiscal-responsibility-index.pdf for the full study.

Academic studies are not conclusive regarding the exact public debt/ GDP ratio at which economic growth is negatively impacted. However, a nonpolitically or ideologically motivated observer will note that since the early 2000s a growing public debt/GDP ratio over an economic cycle has been associated with falling rates of economic growth. In addition, the correlation has grown with a higher public debt/GDP ratio over time.

The truth is, no one really knows what level of public debt/GDP will result in a significant drag on economic growth. Nor does anyone know in advance what level of public debt/GDP will result in a crisis of confidence in the government and the value of the dollar. However, four things are clear. First, additional public debt increases interest costs, which buy nothing and increase pressure for higher taxes absent other spending reductions. Second, additional government debt crowds out more productive private-sector investment. Third, too much public debt/ GDP can have a significant negative effect on the economy (GDP) and can eventually result in an economic decline loop and ultimately a crisis of confidence. Fourth, the U.S. has already exceeded the first two public debt/GDP levels and, based on a July 2, 2010 Congressional Budget Office (CBO) study, is on track to exceed the third within no more than 10 to 12 years. As noted in Chapter 2, total debt held by the public/GDP levels was 106% of GDP as of June 30, 2020 due to the significant economic contraction and additional debt attributable to COVID-19. While this percentage may decline somewhat during a post-COVID-19 economic recovery, the structural fiscal imbalance will result in increased debt held by the public/GDP levels over time.

DEBT BRAKES

Various European Union countries, all part of the Organisation for Economic Co-operation and Development (OECD), have adopted policies to control growth in their public debt/GDP ratios. The most recent documented examples are Sweden and Switzerland. These countries have adopted sets of budgetary rules called "debt brakes" based on fiscal amendments to their constitutions (Swiss) or Parliamentary Agreement (Sweden), or both. Following their adoption and implementation, these countries experienced significant recoveries in economic growth rates because, among other things, confidence returned to their capital markets. (See *Can the Debt Growth Be Stopped?* by Professors John D. Merrifield and Barry W. Poulson, Lexington Books, 2016).

This "debt brake" strategy is in direct contrast to the American "neo-Keynesian" strategy that has been followed informally since 2000. Under that strategy, several administrations have attempted to stimulate economic growth through a combination of tax cuts and increased spending initiatives. The tax cut proposals typically used unrealistic post-tax cut economic growth rate assumptions that mathematically resulted in lower debt held by the public/GDP ratio projections over time. This approach was used on several occasions to help convince the political establishment that tax cuts will "pay for themselves" and even reduce the public debt/GDP ratio. The problem is, they have not. In fact, this "tax cut and spending increase stimulation strategy" has served to exacerbate our growing debt challenge.

Evidence shows that any economic stimulation resulting from this strategy tends to wear off within a year or two, and a new and lower economic growth rate becomes a reality along with higher public debt/GDP ratios. Therefore, the strategy is not only ineffective at addressing our structural debt challenge, it is counterproductive. For example, to cite the most recent example of the tax cut in 2017, the CBO projected that, if adopted, economic growth would be about 2.5% in 2018 and 2019 and would drop to less than 2% in 2020, whereas the administration projected a 3.5% recurring growth rate when presenting the proposal. In reality, economic growth rates in 2018 and 2019 were 2.9% and 2.3%, respectively, and the economic growth rate will likely be negative in 2020 due to COVID-19.

The sovereign debt studies referred to above, combined with recent U.S. experience and the "debt brake" concept used by other countries, serve to illustrate three key points. First, focusing on public debt/GDP is the right approach to achieving fiscal sustainability. Second, our recent strategy of combining tax cuts and spending increases has not only been ineffective, but it has also served to compound our structural debt challenge. Finally, it is possible to control public debt/GDP and stimulate additional growth, but it may take a constitutional fiscal responsibility amendment that focuses on controlling debt held by the public/GDP to achieve sustainable success.

APPENDIX C
GLOSSARY OF SELECTED TERMS

Appropriations: The annual sum of money allocated by Congress for specific discretionary spending purposes. Spending in excess of the allocated amounts is a violation of law that can result in both civil and criminal penalties.

Citizens' Wealth: This is a new and insightful metric created by Japonica Partners to better measure the financial position and progress of a sovereign state. With regard to the U.S., it is calculated by taking gross domestic product (GDP) and subtracting the net position of the federal government per the audited balance sheet, and any debt held by the Social Security and Medicare Trust Funds. Citizens' Wealth has gone from a positive $3.1 trillion in Fiscal 2000 to a negative $4.7 trillion in Fiscal 2019, and it is continuing to decline. Japonica focuses on Citizens' Wealth per person and changes over time in assessing the financial integrity of sovereign nations.

Discretionary Spending: Federal spending that is implemented through the annual appropriations process. At the federal level, this includes, but is not limited to, all express and enumerated responsibilities of the federal government outlined in the Constitution. Discretionary spending was about 30% of total federal spending in Fiscal 2019, down from about 40% in Fiscal 2010 and 97% in Fiscal 1913, and the percentage is projected to decline over time. Defense was about half of discretionary spending in Fiscal 2019, and the percentage of defense spending is projected to decline over time.

Economic Decline Loop: Occurs when public debt/GDP ratios and interest costs as a percentage of the budget increase to unreasonable levels. The result is reduced financial capital available for private-sector investment and additional downward pressure on federal discretionary spending. The International Monetary Fund (IMF) and other organizations have shown that reduced recurring economic growth and job creation rates will occur over time when public debt/GDP levels rise above reasonable levels. The United States in currently in an economic decline loop.

Federal Debt Held by the Public: The total federal public debt (see Federal Public Debt definition) minus debt held by federal trust funds (e.g., Social Security, Medicare, and other federal government trust funds). This amounted to 106% of GDP as of June 30, 2020.

Federal Deficit: The amount of annual federal spending in excess of annual federal revenues calculated on a cash basis.

Federal Financial Burden: The total of all federal public debt, other liabilities (e.g., traditional payables, civilian and military retirement plan liabilities, and environmental cleanup costs), unfunded obligations (e.g., Social Security and Medicare), and various federal commitments and contingencies as of a particular point in time. At the end of Fiscal 2019, this amounted to almost $90 trillion (using a 75-year time horizon for social insurance programs), and the number is growing faster than the economy.

Federal Fiscal Year: The annual accounting, budgeting, and appropriations period that begins on October 1 and ends on September 30 each year.

Federal Government Trust Funds: These are accounting devices that are used to monitor the financial condition of various federal government programs (e.g., Social Security, Medicare, transportation, federal pension plans). These "trust funds" hold U.S. Treasury debt that is not readily marketable but is guaranteed as to both principal and interest by the federal government. The debt held by the trust funds resulted from years when revenues exceeded expenditures. However, expenditures now exceed revenues, and the trust funds are being depleted and are projected to become exhausted at various dates in the future. Importantly, these trust finds are not subject to the same fiduciary standards as private-sector trust funds.

Federal Public Debt: The total amount of U.S. Treasury-issued debt that is held by all parties (e.g., individuals, private pension plans and trusts, federal government trust funds, central banks, and other entities).This amounted to 136% of GDP as of June 30, 2020.

Gross Domestic Product (GDP): The total amount of goods and services produced each year in a country. This measure is used to represent the size of a country's economy.

Mandatory Spending: Annual federal spending that is determined by statutory eligibility requirements and benefit formulas (e.g., Social Security, Medicare, Medicaid, income security programs, agricultural subsidies, and interest on the federal debt). These spending amounts are not part of the annual appropriations process and are in essence "on autopilot" absent a change in the applicable statutes. Mandatory spending was about 70% of total federal spending in Fiscal 2019, up from about 60% in Fiscal 2010 and 3% in Fiscal 1913, and the percentage is projected to increase over time. The primary reasons for the projected future increases are a reduction in the worker-to-retiree ratio, increased health care costs, and additional interest expense.

Modern Monetary Theory (MMT): A new and unproven macroeconomic theory that asserts the U.S. can borrow without limit as long as it borrows in dollars and inflation is under control. While inflation is not a problem today, current fiscal and monetary policies are unsustainable. As a result, absent structural reforms, inflation is likely to be a problem over time, and this will drive up interest rates and compound the federal fiscal problem. For example, if long-term Treasury rates were to return to about 6%, the level they were before 2006, about 20% would be added to the federal budget each year due to expanded interest costs alone. And what do you get for interest? Nothing!

Net Federal Financial Burden: The total federal financial burden less federal assets per the consolidated financial statement of the U.S. government.

Present Value: The amount of money that, if invested now at a given rate of compound interest, will accumulate to a specified amount at a specified future date. In the case of social insurance programs (e.g., Social Security and Medicare), it relates to the amount that needs to be invested today to close the gap between projected spending and projected revenues over 75 years. In the case of federal employee pension and retiree health care programs, it is the amount needed to be invested today to pay for all benefits accrued to date.

Purchasing Power Parity (PPP): It is a popular metric used by macroeconomic analysts that compares different countries' currencies through a "basket of goods" approach. PPP allows economists to compare domestic economic productivity, standards of living, and relative purchasing power between countries.

Structural Budget Deficit: This exists when there is a recurring imbalance between revenues and expenses at the federal, state, and/or local level even when there is full employment. Such is the case today at the federal level, and the gap between projected spending and revenue levels is growing over time due primarily to known demographic trends, rising health care costs, and increasing interest burdens.

Tax Expenditures: These represent revenue losses attributable to provisions of federal tax laws that allow a special exclusion, exemption, or deduction from gross income or that provide a special credit, a preferential rate of tax, or a deferral of tax liability. Total tax expenditures amount to about $1.4 trillion in Fiscal 2019 and rising.

Unfunded Obligations: The difference between the projected total payments and expenses and the amount of projected dedicated revenues (e.g., payroll taxes) attributable to a program (e.g., Social Security, Medicare) over a stated period of time (i.e., typically 75 years for Social Security and Medicare) presented in "present value" dollar terms. At the end of Fiscal 2019, the total unfunded obligations for Social Security and Medicare amounted to about $59 trillion, and that amount is growing faster than the economy.

APPENDIX D
LIST OF SELECTED DEFENSE, FISCAL, AND POLITICAL REFORM ORGANIZATIONS

AARP: www.aarp.org
American Enterprise Institute: www.aei.org
Americans for Tax reform: www.americansfortaxreformfoundation.org
Atlantic Council: www.atlanticcouncil.org
Business Executives for National Security: www.bens.org
Bipartisan Policy Center: www.bipartisanpolicy.org
Brookings Institution: www.brookings.edu
CATO Institute: www.cato.org
Center for American Progress: www.americanprogress.org
Center for Budget and Policy Priorities: www.cbpp.org
Center for Naval Analysis: www.cna.org
Center for New American Security: www.cnas.org
Center for State Led National Debt Solutions: www.csnds.org
Center for Strategic and Budgetary Assessments: www.csbaonline.org
Center for Strategic and International Studies: www.csis.org
Center for the Study of the Presidency and the Congress: www.the
    presidency.org
Committee for a Responsible Federal Budget: www.crfb.org
Committee for Economic Development: www.ced.org
Concord Coalition: www.concordcoalition.org
Congressional Budget Office: www.cbo.gov
Council on Foreign Relations: www.cfr.org
Defense Business Board: www.dbb.defense.gov
East-West Institute of Advanced Studies: www.ewias.org
Foreign Policy Institute: www.fpri.org
Foundation for Defense of Democracies: www.fdd.org
Government Accountability Office: www.gao.gov
Heritage Foundation: www.heritage.org

Hoover Institution: www.hoover.org
Institute for Defense Analysis: www.ida.org
Japonica Partners: www.japonica.com
Joint Committee on Taxation: www.jct.gov
Lexington Institute: www.lexingtoninstitute.org
Manhattan Institute: www.manhattan-institute.org
Mercatus Center: www.mercatus.org
National Academy of Public Administration: www.napawash.org
National Academy of Social Insurance: www.nasi.org
New America Foundation: www.newamerica.org
No Labels: www.nolabels.org
Office of Management and Budget: www.whitehouse.gov/omb
Peter G. Peterson Foundation: www.pgpf.org
Peterson Institute for International Economics: www.piie.com
Pew Charitable Trust: www.pewtrusts.org
Project on Government Oversight: www.pogo.org
RAND: www.rand.org
Stimson Center: www.stimson.org
Stockholm International Peace Research Institute: www.sipri.org
Tax Foundation: www.taxfoundation.org
Third Way: www.thirdway.org
Truth in Accounting: www.truthinaccounting.org
Urban-Brookings Tax Policy Center: www.taxpolicycenter.org
Volcker Alliance: www.volckeralliance.org
The Wilson Center: www.wilsoncenter.org